I0007213

THE INTELLIGENT HOME

Embracing AI Technology

By
Michael Lawson

THE INTELLIGENT HOME

Embracing AI Technology

CONTENTS

INTRODUCTION

Our homes have long been a reflection of both our needs and our aspirations. As we transition into an era defined by rapid technological advancements, the integration of artificial intelligence (AI) into our living spaces represents one of the most significant transformations in modern life. This book embarks on a journey to explore how AI technologies can elevate the concept of a home, turning it into a dynamic environment that anticipates your needs, maximizes convenience, boosts efficiency, and enhances security.

The idea of a "smart home" can be traced back to speculative fiction, where automated homes served as a symbol of a futuristic utopia. Today, this once-distant dream is becoming an accessible reality, made possible by the convergence of AI, Internet of Things (IoT), and advanced connectivity solutions. But, with a plethora of devices, systems, and platforms available, the path to building an intelligent home can appear overwhelming. This book aims to demystify the process, offering practical guidance and actionable insights to help you navigate the complexities of this transformative journey.

Artificial intelligence in the home isn't just about convenience; it's about creating living spaces that actively improve our quality of life. Imagine a home where lighting, climate control, and security systems intuitively adjust based on your preferences and routines. Envision a kitchen where smart appliances streamline meal preparation, while health and wellness devices monitor your well-being and offer personalized recommendations. Picture an entertainment system that adapts to your tastes, intelligently curating content to suit your mood. All these scenarios are within reach thanks to AI's ever-expanding capabilities.

At its core, a smart home is built upon the principles of connectivity and integration. Devices and systems that were once disparate now work in concert, creating a cohesive environment tailored to your lifestyle. Whether you're a technology enthusiast eager to experiment with the latest gadgets, a busy professional seeking to simplify daily chores, or someone concerned about home security, there's an AI solution designed to meet your needs.

The foundation of a smart home lies in understanding the technology that underpins it. You don't have to be an expert to start; a basic comprehension of AI and smart home ecosystems can go a long way. As we delve into the chapters ahead, you'll gain clarity on essential topics such as selecting the right smart home hub, integrating devices seamlessly, and setting up robust networking solutions. This foundational knowledge will empower you to make informed decisions that align with your unique requirements and goals.

One of the fascinating aspects of AI in the home is its adaptability. These systems continually learn from your interactions, refining their responses and improving their performance over time. This adaptive learning process means that your smart home grows with you, evolving to better suit your habits and preferences. It's akin to having a responsive, intelligent companion that enhances your daily life through continual innovation and personalization.

Voice assistants epitomize the convenience of AI-driven living. These digital helpers, capable of controlling a multitude of smart devices through simple voice commands, have become ubiquitous in modern homes. From managing your schedule to controlling lighting and entertainment systems, voice assistants bridge the gap between advanced technology and everyday usability. As you progress through this book, you'll discover the potential of voice assistants and learn how to harness their capabilities to effortlessly manage your home's various functions.

But the benefits of AI extend beyond convenience. Safety and security are paramount concerns for any household, and AI technologies offer unprecedented solutions. Smart cameras, motion sensors, and intelligent locks provide real-time monitoring and alerts, ensuring peace of mind whether you're at home or away. Moreover, these systems can be integrated with emergency response protocols, offering a proactive approach to home safety.

Energy efficiency is another key advantage of a smart home. With AI-driven energy management systems, you can optimize power usage, reduce waste, and lower your utility bills. Smart thermostats, plugs, and switches allow for precise control over your home's energy consumption, making sustainability an attainable goal. This book will guide you through the myriad ways in which AI can contribute to a more eco-friendly household, benefiting both your wallet and the environment.

The scope of AI in the home extends to personalized experiences and entertainment. From smart lighting scenes that adapt to your activities, to AI-powered televisions that recommend content based on your preferences, the potential for customization is virtually limitless. This book will explore how these technologies can create a home environment that feels uniquely yours, providing joy and relaxation amidst the demands of everyday life.

Healthcare and wellness are increasingly becoming focal points in smart home innovation. AI-infused wearables and health devices help monitor vital signs, track fitness goals, and maintain overall well-being. By integrating health data within the smart home ecosystem, these technologies provide valuable insights and recommendations that support a healthier lifestyle. In this book, you'll learn how to leverage these advancements to create a home that actively contributes to your health and well-being.

Of course, the journey to a smart home is not without its challenges. Issues such as connectivity problems, device malfunctions, and ensuring data privacy require careful consideration and troubleshooting. This book dedicates sections to addressing these potential pitfalls, offering solutions and best practices to help you overcome them. Armed with this knowledge, you'll be well-equipped to maintain a smooth and secure smart home operation.

Looking ahead, the future of AI in homes is brimming with possibilities. Emerging technologies and predictive trends point towards even greater integration and functionality. As AI continues to evolve, ethical considerations and privacy concerns will also come to the forefront. This book provides a forward-looking perspective on these topics, helping you stay informed and prepared for advancements on the horizon.

The pages that follow offer a comprehensive roadmap for integrating AI into your home, blending technical information with practical advice. Whether you're embarking on this journey for the first time or seeking to expand an existing smart home setup, this book will serve as a valuable resource. With clear explanations, step-by-step guidelines, and inspirational insights, you'll be empowered to create a home that harnesses the full potential of artificial intelligence.

Welcome to a new chapter in home living, where AI transforms your space into a smart, connected, and efficient haven. As you navigate through the chapters, you'll uncover the myriad ways in which AI can redefine your home, making it a place of comfort, safety, and personalized experiences. The journey to a smarter home begins here, and the possibilities are as limitless as your imagination.

Chapter 1:
Understanding AI in the Home

Artificial Intelligence (AI) has swiftly transitioned from a futuristic concept to an integral part of daily living, particularly in the realm of smart homes. Understanding AI's role in the home means recognizing how it can seamlessly integrate into our living spaces to enhance convenience, efficiency, and security. Whether through smart thermostats learning your preferred temperature settings or AI-powered security cameras detecting and alerting you to unusual activity, AI technologies work tirelessly and intelligently to make your home more responsive and adaptive to your needs. As we delve into the fundamental aspects of AI in the home, you'll gain valuable insights into how these systems function and how they can be effectively implemented and managed to transform ordinary living spaces into intuitive, connected havens. Through this foundational knowledge, you'll be well-equipped to navigate the evolving landscape of AI-driven home automation.

Defining Artificial Intelligence

Artificial Intelligence, often simply referred to as AI, is a broad and transformative field underpinned by computer science. At its core, AI aims to create machines and software capable of performing tasks normally requiring human intelligence. These tasks include but aren't limited to learning, reasoning, problem-solving, perception, and language understanding.

The term "Artificial Intelligence" itself is an umbrella encompassing a variety of different subfields and technologies, each contributing to the bigger picture of machine intelligence. These subfields include machine learning, neural networks, natural language processing, and robotics. On a practical level, AI can be simple, like a spam filter in your email inbox, or exceedingly sophisticated, like autonomous vehicles navigating complex urban environments.

AI isn't something emerging from a vacuum; it's the culmination of decades of research, technological advances, and societal shifts. Astonishingly, the concept of AI has origins dating back to ancient mythology and early mechanical devices designed to simulate simple human actions. Today, however, AI is more science than fiction, deeply embedded into the fabric of modern technology.

What makes AI particularly interesting in the context of home automation is its ability to process vast amounts of data and learn from it. This means that AI can adapt and provide more personalized, efficient, and secure experiences in our homes. Through various algorithms and models, AI systems are designed to understand and interpret complex datasets, mimicking human decision-making to some extent.

Central to modern AI is machine learning, a branch that focuses on developing algorithms that enable computers to learn from and make decisions based on data. In a smart home, machine learning algorithms allow devices to "understand" user behavior patterns and preferences over time, leading to a more customized and seamless interaction with the environment.

Consider smart thermostats as a prime example. These devices utilize machine learning to recognize when you are most likely to be home and determine your preferred temperatures for various times of the day. The AI continually analyzes data points such as ambient temperature, time of day, and even your GPS location to optimize energy usage without requiring manual input.

While machine learning equips devices with the ability to learn from data, natural language processing (NLP) empowers them to interpret and respond to human language. Voice assistants like Amazon's Alexa, Google Home, and Apple's Siri use NLP to interact with users, allowing for hands-free control over many aspects of a smart home. Yet, these voice assistants do more than just follow commands; they can engage in contextual conversations, manage tasks, and even provide personalized recommendations.

Neural networks, another piece of the AI puzzle, attempt to mimic the human brain's structure and function. In a home setting, neural networks can be engaged in facial recognition systems for security, identifying known residents, and even differentiating between family members and potential intruders. This capacity makes AI a potent ally in bolstering home security measures.

One fundamental aspect that often goes unmentioned is the role of data in the functioning of AI systems. AI relies on vast troves of data to train and improve itself continually. In a smart home, data is generated through various sensors, devices, and user interactions. The data gets analyzed, patterns are recognized, and subsequently, actions are taken to improve the overall living experience.

However, with great power comes great responsibility. As AI systems are integrated more into our daily lives, there is an ever-growing need to address concerns around privacy and data security. It's imperative to understand that AI systems collect and process personal information, which, if not secured properly, can be subject to misuse. Ethical considerations and robust data protection measures are essential in ensuring that the benefits of AI technology do not come at the expense of personal privacy.

Now that we have a foundational understanding of artificial intelligence, let's talk about its transformative power. The value proposition of AI in the context of a smart home lies in its capacity to automate and optimize daily tasks, making life more convenient, efficient, and secure. This isn't just a temporary technological phase; it's a progressive step towards a more connected future.

Imagine walking into a home that anticipates your needs. Lights turn on as you enter a room, the thermostat adjusts to your preferred temperature, and your favorite music starts playing automatically. This level of automation isn't futuristic; it's achievable now through the effective deployment of AI technologies within the home.

Periods of human history are often defined by technological advancements—think the Industrial Revolution or the digital age. We're currently on the brink of another monumental shift, driven by intelligent technologies seamlessly blending into our everyday lives. By effectively harnessing AI, we can radically rethink what our homes can do, moving beyond mere functionality to an enriched living experience.

As we proceed further into this book, we'll detail how to integrate, configure, and optimize various AI-driven devices and systems within your home. These insights aim to provide a comprehensive guide for anyone aiming to create a smarter living environment. The chapters ahead will delve into specific applications of AI in different parts of the home, from smart lighting solutions to advanced home security systems and automated kitchen appliances.

Artificial Intelligence in the home isn't just about the "smart" factor; it's about enhancing the quality of life. It's about systems that cater to your unique preferences and behaviors, creating a living space that is not only smart but also intuitive and responsive. As we continue to advance technologically, the dream of a fully automated, intelligent home becomes not just possible but probable.

In conclusion, defining artificial intelligence involves understanding its various technologies, capabilities, and roles in our lives. AI's implementation in the home environment is not just a luxury but a pathway to achieving greater convenience, efficiency, and security. As we move forward, we will delve deeper into each facet of smart home technology, providing you with the tools and knowledge needed to build your intelligent living space.

Evolution of Smart Homes

The concept of smart homes has come a long way since its early days. Initially, the idea of a connected home was little more than science fiction, a vision of the future depicted in movies and TV shows. But as technology advanced, so did the reality of smart homes. The journey began with basic automation systems in the early 20th century, including mechanical timers and switches that controlled appliances like lights and heaters.

By the 1970s, home automation took its first significant leap with the advent of X10 technology. X10 allowed devices to communicate via existing electrical wiring. Though primitive compared to today's standards, it gave homeowners the first taste of electronic control over their household devices through remote controls and basic scheduling. Despite its limitations, X10 was a ground-breaking technology, setting the stage for more advanced systems to come.

Fast forward to the 2000s, and the explosion of the internet revolutionized home automation. Wi-Fi and broadband connections made it possible for home devices to be connected and controlled from anywhere in the world. The internet enabled a new level of convenience and control. Homeowners could now manage their homes remotely, adjusting thermostats, monitoring security cameras, and even receiving alerts for potential issues. The integration of the internet into home systems marked a pivotal moment in the evolution of smart homes.

The introduction of the smartphone added yet another layer of sophistication. With powerful processors and intuitive interfaces, smartphones became the central control hub for many smart home systems. Apps provided seamless interaction with home devices, allowing users to manage everything from lighting to security settings with a few taps. This convergence of mobile technology with home automation significantly accelerated the adoption of smart home solutions.

In recent years, artificial intelligence (AI) has become the linchpin in the evolution of smart homes. AI brings unprecedented capabilities to home automation, offering personalized experiences and more intelligent responses. With AI, devices can learn from users' habits and preferences, optimizing operations for increased comfort and energy efficiency. For example, AI-driven thermostats can learn a household's routine and adjust heating and cooling systems accordingly to save energy without compromising comfort.

Voice assistants like Amazon Alexa, Google Assistant, and Apple's Siri have revolutionized user interaction with their homes. These AI-powered assistants can execute complex commands using natural language processing, making it easier than ever to manage a smart home. Want to dim the lights while watching a movie or lock the doors as you're heading to bed? A simple voice command does the trick. The incorporation of voice assistants has not only enhanced convenience but also broadened the user base to include individuals with varying levels of technological proficiency.

The AI in today's smart homes goes beyond mere control. It provides predictive maintenance capabilities, identifying potential issues before they become significant problems. This proactive approach extends the life of appliances and systems, reducing downtime and repair costs. Moreover, AI adds a layer of safety by monitoring environmental conditions and alerting homeowners to potential hazards like smoke, carbon monoxide, and water leaks.

Interconnectivity is another hallmark of modern smart homes. Different devices and systems can now communicate with each other, creating a more cohesive and efficient environment. For instance, smart security systems can work in tandem with lighting and entertainment systems to give the appearance of occupancy when no one is home, deterring potential intruders. The synergy between various home systems through AI and IoT (Internet of Things) technologies enhances the overall smart home experience.

Security remains a critical aspect in the evolution of smart homes. As connectivity increases, so do the challenges related to data privacy and cybersecurity. Manufacturers and software developers have begun prioritizing secure interfaces and encrypted communications to protect personal information. Multifactor authentication and regular firmware updates are becoming standard practices to mitigate potential vulnerabilities. This focus on security ensures that the convenience and efficiency gained through smart home technology do not come at the cost of privacy.

Energy management has also seen significant advancements with the rise of smart homes. AI-enabled devices can monitor energy consumption patterns and suggest ways to reduce waste, contributing to both lower utility bills and a smaller carbon footprint. Smart plugs, switches, and energy-efficient appliances work in harmony, creating a greener and more sustainable living environment. This aspect of smart home technology aligns well with growing environmental consciousness and the push for sustainable living practices.

The affordability and accessibility of smart home technologies have also improved dramatically. Early adopters might recall the high costs and complexity of initial smart home setups. Today, the landscape is dramatically different. A multitude of smart devices are available at various price points, catering to a broad spectrum of consumers. DIY smart home solutions have democratized the technology, allowing even those with limited technical expertise to enhance their living spaces with AI.

As technology continues to evolve, the future of smart homes looks increasingly promising. Ongoing advancements in AI, machine learning, and IoT will drive further innovations, creating homes that are even more intuitive, efficient, and secure. Future smart homes are expected to leverage edge computing, reducing latency and improving real-time decision-making. The integration of 5G technology will further enhance connectivity and support the growing number of smart devices within homes.

Moreover, we can anticipate more personalized and adaptive environments. AI systems will become more adept at understanding individual preferences and routines, offering tailored experiences that enhance daily life. For instance, smart kitchens could suggest recipes based on dietary needs and available ingredients, while smart health devices could provide personalized wellness recommendations.

In conclusion, the evolution of smart homes is a testament to the transformative power of technology. From basic automation to sophisticated AI-driven systems, smart homes have become an integral part of modern living. They offer unparalleled convenience, efficiency, and security, making our lives not only easier but also more enjoyable. As we continue to embrace these innovations, our homes will evolve alongside technology, promising a future where the line between mere living spaces and intelligent environments continues to blur.

CHAPTER 2:
SETTING UP YOUR SMART HOME

Setting up a smart home can transform the way you live, making everyday tasks easier, enhancing security, and increasing energy efficiency. To begin, you'll need an effective central hub, which acts as the brain of your smart home by connecting and controlling various devices seamlessly. It's vital to pick a hub that supports a wide array of devices and standards, ensuring future expandability. Once you've selected the right hub, the next step is to integrate devices such as smart lights, thermostats, and security systems. Each device's setup might slightly differ, but most modern smart home products are designed for easy installation and user-friendly operation. By unifying all these elements, you lay the foundation for a connected home where you can control everything with simple voice commands or through a single app, paving the way for a more convenient, secure, and efficient lifestyle.

Choosing the Right Hub

Selecting the right hub is a foundational step in creating a cohesive and efficient smart home environment. The hub acts as the central command center, orchestrating various devices to communicate seamlessly with one another. When choosing a hub, consider compatibility with the devices you already own or plan to purchase, as well as the ease of integration with voice assistants and other AI-driven technologies. Look for a hub that supports a wide array of communication protocols like Wi-Fi, Zigbee, and Z-Wave, ensuring future-proof versatility. Ease of use, support for automation routines, and reliable customer service are also crucial factors. Making an informed choice will empower you to build a smart home that is both efficient and capable of evolving with technological advancements.

Popular Smart Home Hubs serve as the backbone of any intelligent living space, offering a cohesive platform where various devices interconnect, communicate, and perform harmoniously. Choosing the right hub sets the stage for an efficient, seamless smart home experience. Below are some of the most popular smart home hubs that have gained traction among users seeking to integrate a variety of smart devices into their homes.

First on the list is the **Amazon Echo**. Well-known for its voice assistant, Alexa, the Amazon Echo doubles as a versatile smart home hub. This device is compatible with thousands of smart home products from lights and thermostats to security systems and appliances. Its ability to execute voice commands gives it an edge, offering hands-free control that's particularly useful in a busy household. Additionally, Amazon continues to expand its ecosystem, providing regular updates and new integrations, which ensures that your smart home hub stays advanced and relevant over time.

Google Nest Hub is another strong contender. Leveraging the prowess of Google Assistant, this hub offers high-quality voice recognition and response capabilities. Its compatibility with Google's extensive range of services makes it a choice hub for those already embedded in the Google ecosystem. From displaying your calendar to controlling smart lights and even streaming your favorite shows, Google Nest Hub brings all your home devices under one roof. One of its standout features is its capability to display visual responses, giving you an added layer of interaction with your smart home environment.

Moving on to the **Samsung SmartThings Hub**, this hub distinguishes itself with its robust range of connectivity. Supporting both Zigbee and Z-Wave protocols, it opens the door to a wider spectrum of compatible devices. Whether you're looking to integrate sensors, cameras, lights, or other smart appliances, SmartThings has you covered. Additionally, the SmartThings mobile app is praised for its user-friendly interface, making the initial setup and subsequent management straightforward and intuitive. Samsung's consistent updates ensure that the hub remains compatible with the latest smart home technologies, giving you peace of mind that your system will stay current.

The **Apple HomeKit** solution is ideal for those deeply entrenched in the Apple ecosystem. Managed through an Apple TV, HomePod, or iPad, HomeKit provides seamless integration with other Apple devices, offering a unified user experience. Siri, Apple's voice assistant, serves as the control interface, allowing for hands-free operation. HomeKit's focus on security is a strong selling point, employing end-to-end encryption to ensure that your data remains protected. Its secure and user-friendly platform makes it an attractive choice for users who prioritize privacy alongside functionality.

Hubitat Elevation stands out for its local processing ability. Unlike many hubs that rely on cloud-based processing, Hubitat Elevation performs all automation locally, reducing latency and dependency on an internet connection. This makes it a reliable hub for users concerned about internet outages affecting their smart home functionalities. It's particularly popular among tech enthusiasts who take pride in customizing and refining their smart home setups. Hubitat's community is active and supportive, often providing user-generated solutions to expand the capabilities of the hub.

A notable mention is the **Wink Hub 2**, which offers a broad array of compatibility options. Supporting Wi-Fi, Bluetooth, Zigbee, and Z-Wave, it's one of the most versatile hubs available. Wink's user interface is straightforward, designed to make device pairing and smart home management as effortless as possible. It's an excellent choice for users looking for a hub that provides simplicity without sacrificing the diversity of devices it can manage.

The **Amazon Echo Plus** takes the benefits of the Amazon Echo and adds built-in Zigbee support. This additional functionality eliminates the need for a separate bridge or hub for Zigbee devices, simplifying your smart home setup. Amazon Echo Plus brings enhanced versatility, making it easier to integrate a broader range of devices. Furthermore, its high-quality speaker system ensures you get excellent audio performance for all your media and communication needs.

For those who seek a touch of luxury, the **Savant Smart Home Hub** is a high-end solution offering a highly customizable smart home experience. Known for its sleek interface and comprehensive control options, Savant excels in creating a tailor-made environment. Whether it's lighting, climate control, or entertainment, Savant provides integrated solutions designed to enhance life's comfort and convenience. This hub is particularly favored by users willing to invest in a premium smart home experience.

Support and Updates: Regular updates are crucial for maintaining compatibility with new devices and security standards. Hubs like Amazon Echo and Google Nest Hub are known for their continual enhancements.

Connectivity: Protocols like Zigbee and Z-Wave are essential for integrating a wide range of smart devices. Hubs that support multiple protocols offer more versatility.

User Interface: A user-friendly interface can significantly simplify the management of your smart home system. Consider the ease of setup and daily operation when choosing a hub.

Voice Control: Voice assistants such as Alexa, Google Assistant, and Siri provide hands-free operation, which enhances convenience and user experience.

Local vs. Cloud Processing: Local processing, as seen in Hubitat Elevation, offers faster response times and reduced reliance on internet connectivity.

Security: Hubs with robust security features, like Apple HomeKit, ensure that your smart home ecosystem remains protected against potential threats.

In conclusion, selecting the right smart home hub is pivotal for achieving a connected, efficient, and secure living environment. Whether you're drawn to the wide-ranging compatibility of Samsung SmartThings, the elegant interface of Savant, or the local processing power of Hubitat Elevation, the right choice will depend on your specific needs and preferences. By investing in a robust and compatible hub, you're laying the foundation for a smart home that truly enhances your everyday life.

Integrating Devices

Once you've chosen the right hub for your smart home, the next step is integrating various devices. The beauty of a smart home lies in its interconnectedness. Your devices should communicate seamlessly to provide a coherent and efficient user experience. This process may seem daunting, but breaking it down into manageable steps will simplify everything. Let's delve into how you can integrate devices effectively and turn your home into a smart home ecosystem.

First, identify the range of devices you want to integrate. Start with the basics such as smart thermostats, lights, and security systems. These are foundational elements in any smart home setup. Ensure these devices are compatible with your chosen hub. Most hubs support a variety of protocols like Zigbee, Z-Wave, and Wi-Fi, but it's wise to double-check compatibility before purchasing or integrating new devices. Compatibility is key to avoiding the frustration of malfunctioning hardware.

One of the pivotal steps in integrating devices is setting them up in the hub's accompanying app. Each device typically comes with a unique setup process. For instance, a smart thermostat will require you to link it to your Wi-Fi network, and then add it to the hub's app using a specific code or scanning a QR code. Follow the manufacturer's instructions meticulously. A systematic approach pays off here—going through each step methodically ensures that the devices are correctly registered and ready for interaction with other smart devices in your system.

Once you've successfully connected your primary devices, the next step is to start configuring them to interact with each other. This process is often referred to as 'creating routines' or 'automation scenarios'. For example, you can program your smart lighting to turn on when your smart door lock is disengaged, signaling someone has arrived home. Similarly, your smart thermostat can adjust the temperature based on the time of day or the energy usage patterns you've set. These routines are what bring the 'smart' into a smart home, and they can be as simple or as complex as you desire.

To achieve seamless integration, make use of IFTTT (If This Then That) platforms. These platforms allow diverse devices to communicate even if they operate on different protocols. IFTTT can bridge gaps between devices, creating more comprehensive and intricate automation scenarios. For example, you might want your smart lights to flash when your smart doorbell rings, even if they are made by different manufacturers. IFTTT can make this possible, expanding the scope of what your smart home system can accomplish.

Voice assistants like Alexa, Google Assistant, or Siri also play a significant role in integrating devices. They serve as the interface through which you can control and monitor your smart devices using voice commands. By linking your devices to a voice assistant, you make the interaction more natural and effortless. Imagine saying, "Good night," and having your home respond by locking doors, turning off lights, and adjusting the thermostat— all automatically. This convenience significantly enhances your smart home experience.

Security is another aspect you don't want to overlook. As you integrate various devices, ensure that your network is secure. Use strong, unique passwords for your hub and devices. Regularly update firmware to protect against vulnerabilities. A secure network ensures that your smart home remains a safe haven and not a target for cyber threats. Secure integration involves creating guest networks, thereby isolating your smart home devices from other personal devices like laptops and smartphones.

Once the primary devices are connected and routines are set, consider expanding your ecosystem. Add secondary devices like smart plugs, sensors, or cameras to further enhance your smart home. Smart plugs are particularly versatile, turning any standard appliance into an automated component of your home. Motion sensors can trigger actions based on movement, like turning on lights or sending alerts when unusual activity is detected. Cameras offer an additional layer of security and can be integrated with other devices for a comprehensive surveillance system.

Don't forget about integrating AI-powered devices that offer adaptive learning capabilities. These devices analyze your habits and preferences over time, making your home even smarter. For instance, an AI-powered lighting system can learn your daily schedule and adjust lighting accordingly. Similarly, an intelligent thermostat can optimize energy use based on your routines and preferences, contributing not only to convenience but also to energy efficiency.

Additionally, home entertainment can be elevated through device integration. Smart TVs, streaming devices, and audio systems can be interconnected to provide a seamless entertainment experience. Linking your entertainment system to a voice assistant allows for voice-controlled searches, adjusting volume, or changing channels, adding another layer of convenience. Picture this: you're cooking dinner and simply ask your voice assistant to play your favorite show or adjust the music—no more fumbling with remotes or knobs.

A holistic approach to integrating devices will yield the best results. Think about how each device can complement another. For instance, integrating your smart fridge with your shopping list app ensures that you're always aware of what's running low. Connect your lawn's sprinkler system to weather forecasts so that it skips watering on rainy days. There is virtually no end to the creative and functional uses for a well-integrated smart home.

Lastly, it's essential to stay updated with the latest advancements. The smart home industry is evolving rapidly, with new devices and capabilities being introduced continuously. Keep an eye out for software updates and new device releases that could further simplify your home's operations. Joining forums or online communities focused on smart homes can also be beneficial. You'll gain insights and tips from other users, and stay ahead with best practices for integrating devices efficiently.

In conclusion, integrating devices into your smart home setup is a journey that combines planning, executing, and continuously optimizing. By ensuring compatibility, setting up effectively, implementing security measures, and expanding thoughtfully, you can achieve a smart home that offers unparalleled convenience, efficiency, and security. Embracing this approach will transform your living space into a futuristic haven that adapts to your lifestyle and needs, ushering in an era where your home doesn't just serve you, but anticipates and caters to your every requirement.

CHAPTER 3:
SMART HOME NETWORKING

As smart homes become more interconnected, setting up a robust networking system is essential for seamless device communication and efficient home management. In this chapter, we'll explore the foundational elements that ensure your smart home runs smoothly without hiccups. From understanding the critical role of Wi-Fi in supporting numerous devices simultaneously to the benefits of mesh networks in extending coverage throughout your home, it's necessary to choose the right network structure tailored to your home's specific needs. Additionally, we'll delve into Zigbee and Z-Wave, two popular wireless protocols that enhance device reliability and power efficiency. These networking solutions not only help in reducing latency but also in improving the overall smart home experience by ensuring every gadget, sensor, and controller works harmoniously. By mastering smart home networking, you can unlock the potential of your AI-integrated environment, making life more convenient, secure, and efficient.

Wi-Fi Essentials

Wi-Fi is the backbone of any smart home. It's more than just an internet connection; it's the lifeline that ties all your smart devices together. Wi-Fi reliability and strength are crucial because if your network falters, your entire smart home setup could crumble into a pile of unresponsive gadgets. Before diving into advanced aspects of AI-driven homes, it's essential to understand the role of Wi-Fi and how to optimize it.

First and foremost, your choice of router can make or break your smart home experience. A powerful router equipped with the latest 802.11ax (Wi-Fi 6) standard can dramatically improve network performance. Wi-Fi 6 offers faster speeds, higher capacity, and better performance in crowded areas. If you have many smart devices, this is a game changer. With its increased data throughput and efficiency, Wi-Fi 6 is designed to keep multiple devices connected without sacrificing speed.

Placement of your router is also a crucial factor. Walls, metal objects, and even appliances can obstruct Wi-Fi signals. Ideally, your router should be positioned centrally in your home, away from obstructions, and at a higher elevation like a shelf or wall mount. This ensures a more uniform distribution of the Wi-Fi signal. Minimizing interference from other electronic devices, like microwaves or cordless phones, is also important for maintaining a strong signal.

Security should never be an afterthought when setting up your Wi-Fi network. A secure network prevents unauthorized access and keeps your data safe. Use strong, unique passwords for both your Wi-Fi network and router admin settings. WPA3 encryption is recommended as it provides better security than older WPA2. It's also a good idea to regularly update your router's firmware to patch any vulnerabilities.

Moreover, understanding and managing your network's bandwidth is vital, especially when you have multiple devices streaming videos, downloading content, or running software updates. Quality of Service (QoS) settings on your router can help prioritize traffic to ensure that your most important activities, like video calls or streaming, receive the necessary bandwidth. Smart homes often run numerous background processes, and setting up QoS can minimize interruptions and lags.

Signal strength is another significant factor. Investing in Wi-Fi extenders or mesh networks can help eliminate dead zones and ensure consistent coverage throughout your home. Wi-Fi extenders boost the signal of your existing router, while mesh systems use multiple nodes to provide seamless coverage across a larger area. Mesh networks are particularly useful for large homes or those with challenging layouts where a single router might struggle to cover the entire space.

Compatibility between your Wi-Fi network and smart home devices is an important consideration. Some older or more budget-friendly smart devices may only support the 2.4 GHz band, which offers a longer range but slower speeds compared to the 5 GHz band. A dual-band router allows these devices to connect easily while enabling newer devices to take advantage of faster 5 GHz speeds. Tri-band routers, which include two 5 GHz bands and one 2.4 GHz band, can handle even more devices efficiently.

Setting up a guest network can be an excellent strategy for enhancing security without inconveniencing your guests. A guest network allows visitors to connect to the internet without accessing your primary network. This isolates them from your main network's devices and data, adding an extra layer of security. It's also useful when hosting gatherings where many people might need internet access.

Latency and jitter are additional aspects to consider for a smooth smart home experience. Latency refers to the delay before a transfer of data begins following an instruction, while jitter refers to the variation in packet arrival times. High latency and jitter can cause lag and disruptions in your smart home devices. Opting for a high-quality router that specifically advertises low-latency performance can mitigate these issues.

Furthermore, some routers come with built-in AI capabilities for network optimization. These AI-driven routers can learn your network's usage patterns and automatically adjust settings to enhance performance. They might prioritize bandwidth for streaming services in the evening or reduce interference when they detect multiple devices are using the network heavily.

Proactively monitoring your Wi-Fi network can prevent many common issues. Various apps and tools allow you to keep an eye on network performance in real-time. Some router manufacturers offer proprietary apps that provide insights into connected devices, data usage, and potential security threats. Understanding these metrics can help you identify problems before they affect your smart home's functionality.

Utilizing advanced network features such as MU-MIMO (Multi-User, Multiple Input, Multiple Output) technology can also boost performance. MU-MIMO allows a router to communicate with multiple devices simultaneously, rather than sequentially. This is particularly beneficial in a smart home with several devices constantly demanding network resources. It improves overall network efficiency and reduces wait times for data transmission.

Lastly, while Wi-Fi is indispensable, considering networking alternatives like Ethernet can be beneficial for specific devices. High-bandwidth devices like smart TVs or gaming consoles may perform better with a wired connection. Ethernet provides a stable and high-speed connection, free from wireless interference. Integrating wired connections with your Wi-Fi network can ensure that critical devices always have the best possible performance.

By mastering these Wi-Fi essentials, you're laying a solid foundation for a smart home that's not just connected but seamlessly integrated and highly efficient. Your smart home journey hinges on the reliability and strength of your Wi-Fi network, making it the linchpin of everything that follows. Investing time and resources into optimizing your Wi-Fi will pay dividends in the form of a flawlessly functioning smart ecosystem.

Mesh Networks

As we develop smarter homes, we encounter the need for robust, reliable networks that can handle an increasing number of connected devices seamlessly. This is where mesh networks come into play. They fundamentally transform the concept of home networking by offering a more sophisticated, adaptive solution compared to traditional Wi-Fi setups.

Traditional Wi-Fi networks often struggle with coverage issues, dead zones, and fluctuating speeds, especially in larger homes or spaces with many rooms. Mesh networks address these problems by using multiple nodes (or units) placed strategically throughout the home. Each node communicates with the others, creating a single, cohesive network that blankets the entire space with a strong, consistent signal.

One of the primary benefits of mesh networks is their scalability. As your network needs evolve, adding more nodes is straightforward and effective. This means whether you're expanding your home, adding a new room for an office, or simply looking to boost performance in an area with poor signal, a mesh network can adapt to your requirements.

Another advantage is the seamless handoff between nodes. In a traditional setup, moving from one part of the house to another often involves a noticeable drop in connection as your device switches from one Wi-Fi router to another. Mesh networks eliminate this issue by ensuring that your device maintains an optimal connection to the nearest node, providing a smooth, uninterrupted experience regardless of your movement within the space.

Mesh networks also excel in terms of installation and management. Modern mesh systems come with user-friendly apps that simplify the initial setup process. These apps guide users through each step, from placing nodes in optimal locations to configuring network settings.

Once set up, the mesh network continuously optimizes itself, adjusting to interference and traffic patterns to ensure peak performance.

Security is another area where mesh networks shine. Given our focus on integrating AI and increasing the number of connected devices, ensuring a secure network is paramount. Mesh systems often include advanced security features such as automatic firmware updates, which protect against vulnerabilities without requiring user intervention. Additionally, features like guest networks, parental controls, and device prioritization grant homeowners greater control over their network environment.

One noteworthy aspect of mesh networks is their compatibility with smart home devices. As you integrate AI-driven gadgets and systems into your home, a stable and reliable network becomes crucial. Mesh networks provide the bandwidth and consistency needed to run multiple smart devices simultaneously, whether they are smart speakers, security cameras, or automated lighting systems.

The importance of a robust mesh network can't be overstated when considering the growing trend of remote work. With more people setting up home offices, a dependable internet connection is vital for productivity. Mesh networks mitigate the risks of dropped video calls and slow download speeds, ensuring a smoother remote work experience.

For those concerned about environmental impact, newer mesh network systems are designed with energy efficiency in mind, aligning with sustainable smart home practices. These systems consume less power while providing superior networking capabilities, making them a responsible choice for eco-conscious homeowners.

Cost is often a consideration when upgrading to a mesh network. While the initial investment may be higher than traditional routers, the long-term benefits often justify the expense. The enhanced coverage, ease of use, and improved reliability ensure that homeowners get the most out of their network, supporting a wide range of smart home applications without frequent upgrades or troubleshooting.

Mesh networks are also future-proof. As technology advances and the number of connected devices in homes increases, mesh systems can adapt and scale. This future-readiness is crucial for maintaining a stable, high-performance network as new AI-driven technologies emerge.

In summary, mesh networks represent a significant advancement in home networking technology. They address the limitations of traditional Wi-Fi networks by offering scalable, easy-to-manage, and secure solutions. For anyone looking to enhance their smart home with AI-powered innovations, investing in a mesh network is not just a wise decision—it's an essential one. The reliability, performance, and adaptability of mesh systems ensure they are perfectly suited to meet the demands of modern, connected homes, ultimately contributing to a more efficient, seamless, and enjoyable living experience.

Zigbee and Z-Wave

In the vast landscape of smart home networking, Zigbee and Z-Wave stand out as two of the most prominent wireless communication protocols. These protocols are integral to connecting a myriad of smart devices, ensuring seamless interoperability and functionality within your smart home ecosystem. Understanding how Zigbee and Z-Wave operate, their advantages, and potential limitations can fundamentally enhance your smart home experience, leading to a more responsive, secure, and efficient living environment.

Zigbee is known for its low power consumption and robustness. One of its primary advantages is its ability to support numerous devices simultaneously, capable of handling a mesh network that includes up to 65,000 nodes. This capability makes Zigbee an ideal choice for larger networks where multiple devices need to communicate effectively. Zigbee's network can self-heal, which means if one device fails or gets disconnected, the network finds alternative paths for data transmission, ensuring uninterrupted operation.

In contrast, Z-Wave, while supporting fewer nodes (around 232 devices), excels in its straightforward setup and compatibility. Z-Wave uses a standard frequency (908.42 MHz in the U.S.) that is less crowded than the 2.4 GHz frequency used by many Wi-Fi and Zigbee devices. This distinction minimizes interference, providing a more stable and often faster connection. Z-Wave's range between devices also tends to be longer, around 100 meters in open space, enhancing its reliability for larger homes or properties with multiple floors.

When considering which protocol to integrate into your home, it's also essential to note the interoperability of devices. Zigbee devices from different manufacturers can, in theory, connect seamlessly; however, due to varying implementations of the protocol, this isn't always flawless. Z-Wave has stricter interoperability standards, leading to a higher likelihood that devices will work together right out of the box. This could be a deciding factor if you're looking for a hassle-free integration experience.

Both Zigbee and Z-Wave offer significant advantages in terms of security. Zigbee uses Advanced Encryption Standard (AES) 128-bit encryption to safeguard data transmitted over the network. Similarly, Z-Wave utilizes AES-128 encryption and mandates Security 2 (S2) framework for an added layer of security. These protocols ensure that your smart devices exchange information securely, mitigating risks associated with unauthorized access and cyber threats.

Another notable aspect of Zigbee and Z-Wave is their influence on the market of smart home products. Devices compatible with these protocols range from smart bulbs, thermostats, locks, sensors, home entertainment systems, and much more. For example, products that operate on Zigbee often include those from major players like Philips Hue and Samsung SmartThings, while Z-Wave's ecosystem includes offerings from companies such as GE and Honeywell.

Furthermore, the mesh nature of these networks means every connected device also acts as a signal repeater, strengthening the network's capability. This is particularly crucial in larger homes or setups where walls and other physical obstructions might impede signal propagation. With each additional device, the network grows more resilient and capable of covering larger areas without degradation in performance.

The interplay between these protocols and smart home hubs is another layer of consideration. Many smart home hubs, such as the Samsung SmartThings Hub, incorporate both Zigbee and Z-Wave radios, offering the flexibility to choose and intermingle devices from both ecosystems. This dual-compatibility enriches the user's ability to customize and expand their smart home setup without being confined to a single protocol.

In practical terms, application scenarios demonstrate the strengths of each protocol. For instance, deploying Zigbee in environments with a high density of devices, such as smart lighting systems, leverages its capability to handle numerous, rapidly communicating nodes. On the other hand, Z-Wave's longer range and more stable frequency make it particularly suitable for security-oriented devices like door locks and motion sensors, which benefit from extended and reliable connectivity.

Despite their strengths, understanding the coexistence with other network technologies is vital. Zigbee's 2.4 GHz band is shared with Wi-Fi, Bluetooth, and many other wireless communications, which can lead to potential interference. Strategies such as channel selection and network planning become instrumental in mitigating such conflicts. Z-Wave, due to its sub-1GHz frequency, generally avoids this interference but isn't entirely immune to electronic noise and obstructions. Proper placement and environmental assessment remain key for optimal performance.

Moreover, the evolution of these protocols shouldn't be overlooked. Both Zigbee and Z-Wave have undergone significant updates and improvements over the years. Zigbee 3.0 unified various Zigbee standards into a single protocol, enhancing compatibility, ease of use, and security. Z-Wave has similarly stepped forward with Z-Wave Plus and Z-Wave Plus V2, which offer extended range, better battery life, and upgraded firmware capabilities.

Interoperability also extends to cloud integration. Both Zigbee and Z-Wave networks can interface with cloud services, allowing remote control and monitoring of your devices through apps and web portals. This connectivity adds another dimension to smart living, enabling users to interact with their homes from virtually anywhere in the world. It's this continuous connectivity that underscores the transformative potential of smart home tech.

Ultimately, your choice between Zigbee and Z-Wave should align with your specific needs, preferences, and the existing technology ecosystem. Both have robust developer communities and widespread adoption, ensuring that whichever path you choose, there will be support and continuous innovation. By understanding the nuances of these protocols, you can better harness their power to create a truly intelligent, responsive, and future-proof home environment.

Each protocol's ecosystem continues to grow, driven by user demand for seamless, intuitive, and reliable smart home experiences. Whether it is through the streamlined device integration of Zigbee or the strong and stable connections of Z-Wave, both protocols are instrumental in ushering in an era of smart living where technology works unobtrusively to enhance daily life. The path forward is marked by continual improvement, ensuring that smart homes of today will evolve effortlessly into the even smarter homes of tomorrow.

CHAPTER 4:
VOICE ASSISTANTS

Voice assistants have rapidly become a cornerstone in transforming a regular home into a smart home, bringing unprecedented convenience and efficiency to our daily routines. With the ability to carry out an array of tasks through simple vocal commands, these voice-activated helpers can control smart devices, answer questions, play music, set reminders, and even manage shopping lists. Their integration facilitates a hands-free lifestyle that fosters a more streamlined household operation. Whether you're asking your assistant to dim the lights, adjust the thermostat, or lock the doors, voice assistants are designed to seamlessly interconnect with various smart home devices, promoting an interconnected ecosystem. Moreover, they offer customizable commands that can cater specifically to your household's unique needs, making both mundane and intricate tasks much more manageable. Embracing the use of voice assistants is not merely about technological advancement; it's about enhancing your overall quality of life through simple, yet powerful, voice interactions.

Popular Voice Assistants

Voice assistants have become a cornerstone in the evolution of smart homes, offering unprecedented convenience and efficiency. The main players in this realm include Amazon's Alexa, Google Assistant, Apple's Siri, and Microsoft's Cortana. Each comes with its unique set of capabilities, integrations, and ecosystems, compelling users to choose the one that best fits their needs. Understanding their characteristics is crucial for anyone embarking on their journey to create a smart, interconnected home.

Amazon Alexa is arguably the most widely recognized voice assistant. Since its introduction in 2014, Alexa has evolved significantly, boasting over a hundred thousand skills. Amazon's Echo devices, powered by Alexa, are at the heart of many smart homes. Alexa can control thousands of smart devices from various manufacturers, making it a highly versatile choice. What sets Alexa apart is its ability to comprehend natural language, making interactions smoother and more intuitive. Additionally, its compatibility with Amazon services like Amazon Prime, Kindle, and Fire TV creates a seamless user experience.

One of Alexa's standout features is its *routine management*. With routines, users can group various commands to execute simultaneously with a single voice command. For example, saying "Alexa, good morning" could turn on the lights, read the weather report, and start the coffee maker. This level of automation enhances the efficiency and convenience of daily life.

Google Assistant offers robust search capabilities powered by Google's immense data pool. Released in 2016, Google Assistant runs on various devices, including Google Nest products and many Android smartphones. What makes Google Assistant particularly compelling is its contextual understanding and ability to handle follow-up questions naturally. This rich conversational capability can make interactions feel more fluid and less scripted.

A powerful feature of Google Assistant is its deep integration with Google services such as Gmail, Google Calendar, and Google Maps. This integration allows for complex functionalities like checking your schedule, sending emails, or navigating to your next appointment. Furthermore, Google Assistant's compatibility with numerous smart home devices solidifies its position as a strong contender in the voice assistant arena.

Apple's Siri is another major player in the market, geared heavily towards users entrenched in Apple's ecosystem. Introduced in 2011 as the first mainstream voice assistant, Siri has the advantage of being deeply embedded in Apple's extensive array of products, from iPhones to HomePods and even CarPlay. Its seamless integration with Apple services like iMessage, Apple Music, and HomeKit makes it an appealing option for Apple enthusiasts.

Siri excels in executing tasks within the Apple ecosystem, such as sending texts, playing music, or setting reminders. However, its compatibility with non-Apple devices and services is relatively limited compared to Alexa and Google Assistant. Despite this limitation, Siri offers impressive voice recognition and is continually evolving with new updates to improve its functionality and user experience.

Microsoft Cortana, while less prevalent in the consumer market, holds a strong position in enterprise settings. Since its release in 2014, Cortana has aimed to bridge productivity and smart home management, benefiting users who rely heavily on Microsoft services such as Office 365 and Outlook. Cortana's integration with these services allows for sophisticated task management, enhancing productivity for business professionals.

Although Microsoft has scaled back on Cortana's consumer-facing capabilities, it continues to refine the assistant for business applications. Cortana can still control smart home devices through partnerships with Alexa and other platforms. For users invested in the Windows ecosystem, especially in a professional context, Cortana remains a valuable tool.

Bixby, Samsung's voice assistant launched in 2017, aims to offer a differentiated experience through device-centric controls. Bixby is integrated into Samsung's range of products, from smartphones and tablets to smart TVs and appliances, providing a unified user experience within the Samsung ecosystem. Bixby's approach focuses on understanding and executing complex, multi-step commands within Samsung devices, enhancing their operational efficiency.

A standout aspect of Bixby is its *Bixby Vision* feature, which uses the camera to provide contextual information about the environment, such as identifying objects or translating text. This visual recognition capability offers a unique layer of interactivity that can be highly beneficial in a smart home setup.

Sonos Voice Control, introduced by the renowned audio company Sonos, is designed with a specific focus on managing audio experiences within smart homes. Unlike other general-purpose voice assistants, Sonos Voice Control aims to deliver high-quality, hands-free music and audio management. Leveraging advanced voice recognition, it offers users the ability to control multi-room audio systems, customize playlists, and seamlessly switch between different music services.

Each of these voice assistants brings unique strengths and particular specializations, catering to diverse user preferences and needs. While some excel in device compatibility, others shine in seamless integrations with existing services. When selecting a voice assistant for your smart home, it's essential to consider the ecosystem you're already invested in and the types of functionalities you prioritize.

Integrating these voice assistants typically involves straightforward setup processes, although some may require additional steps depending on compatibility and device specifics. Many smart home devices are now designed to work with multiple voice assistants, offering flexibility and allowing users to switch between different ecosystems should they choose to. As technology continues to advance, the capabilities and integrations of these popular voice assistants are only expected to grow, offering even more opportunities to enhance home automation and connectivity.

Custom Commands

Voice assistants have become integral parts of our smart homes, acting as the central hub for controlling various connected devices. While most voice assistants come pre-loaded with numerous capabilities out of the box, the real power and versatility come when we delve into custom commands. Custom commands enable you to tailor your voice assistant to perform specific tasks designed to meet your unique needs, providing a level of personalization that enhances efficiency and convenience.

Creating custom commands can revolutionize how you interact with your smart home. Imagine walking through your front door and saying a single phrase that triggers a series of actions: the lights turn on, the thermostat adjusts, your favorite playlist starts, and the coffee machine begins brewing. Such multi-step routines, also referred to as scenes or macros in some platforms, can be seamlessly executed using custom commands. This level of automation minimizes the effort required to manage multiple tasks, freeing up more time for you to enjoy the things that matter most.

To start, it's crucial to understand that custom commands vary across different voice assistant platforms. Whether you're using Amazon's Alexa, Google Assistant, or Apple's Siri, each system has its own set of tools and frameworks for creating and managing custom commands. While the underlying principles are often similar, the implementation process does differ.

Let's begin with Amazon Alexa. With the Alexa app, you can create custom commands through the Routines feature. Routines are like programmable actions; you can set up a trigger phrase and link it to multiple responses. For example, by saying, "Alexa, start my morning," you could have Alexa turn on the bedroom lights, read out your calendar events, update you on traffic conditions, and start playing a news podcast. The application offers a user-friendly interface allowing even those with limited technical know-how to set up sophisticated routines.

Google Assistant offers a comparable functionality through its routines. Google's platform integrates deeply with its suite of services—from Calendar to Maps—making it especially powerful for users embedded within the Google ecosystem. Customizing commands in Google Assistant generally involves specifying a trigger phrase and a sequence of actions directly through the Google Home app. Additionally, you can configure routines to activate based on time or location, adding layers of context-based automation that make your smart home even more intelligent.

Apple's Siri, part of the HomeKit environment, takes a similar approach with its Shortcuts app. Siri Shortcuts allow you to bundle a range of actions that can be triggered by custom phrases or even through automation based on time of day or sensor readings. The Shortcuts app provides incredible flexibility, letting users string together actions from a wide variety of apps and services. This is particularly powerful for iPhone or iPad users who want a cohesive experience across their Apple devices.

Of course, the potential of custom commands goes far beyond simple automation. Advanced users can exploit these platforms to create commands that interact with web services, retrieve online information, or control third-party applications. For example, you could set up a custom command to inform you of stock prices, control IoT devices that may not be directly supported by popular voice assistants, or even initiate complex multi-platform workflows using services like IFTTT (If This Then That) or Zapier.

The possibilities become virtually limitless when you integrate voice assistants with other smart home systems and platforms. Systems like SmartThings and Home Assistant offer even more fine-grained control, allowing for a deeper level of customization. These platforms often provide APIs and scripting capabilities, enabling tech-savvy homeowners to create bespoke interactions that would be impossible with standard methods. You can script a series of actions to respond to environmental changes detected by sensors. For example, if the indoor temperature rises above a certain threshold, a command could instruct your voice assistant to activate the air conditioning, close the blinds, and notify you.

Another exciting aspect of custom commands is their ability to enhance accessibility. For individuals with disabilities, custom commands can simplify daily tasks and provide a higher degree of independence. By tailoring commands to suit specific needs, people with mobility challenges can control their home environment without needing to interact with physical devices. Voice commands can be crafted to perform essential tasks, from opening doors to adjusting appliance settings, ensuring a more inclusive living space.

Moreover, custom commands can be used to safeguard your home and family. Integrating voice assistants with security systems allows you to set up commands that provide real-time updates on your home's status. Imagine saying, "Goodnight," and your voice assistant not only locks all the doors and activates the alarm system but also gives you a summary of the day's activities, such as any motion detected by outdoor cameras. In emergency situations, custom commands can be designed to quickly relay critical information or summon assistance, contributing to a safer living environment.

For families, custom commands can help manage household routines and chores. By setting up reminders and task lists accessible through voice commands, you can foster a more organized and harmonious home. For instance, children can have custom commands like "Homework time," which could dim the lights, limit access to entertainment devices, and play focus music. These small adjustments can create an environment conducive to productivity and reduced distractions.

Custom commands also extend to smart entertainment systems. A simple phrase like, "Movie night," could trigger your voice assistant to lower the lights, close the blinds, turn on the home theater system, and start playing your selected movie or TV show. Integrating these commands with streaming services adds another layer of convenience, as you can navigate content libraries, control playback, and adjust volume all through voice interactions.

As we look to the future, the scope and power of custom commands are only set to expand. Machine learning and AI advancements are making voice assistants smarter, more intuitive, and capable of understanding more complex tasks. Future iterations may include natural language processing advancements, allowing voice assistants to better comprehend context and even predict your needs based on learned behavior patterns. Essentially, your smart home will not only respond to your commands but anticipate them, creating an environment that continuously adapts to your lifestyle.

In conclusion, custom commands are a cornerstone of making voice assistants work more effectively within your smart home. By understanding the tools available on your chosen platform and how to leverage them, you can transform a functional smart home into an intelligent, responsive environment. Whether you're optimizing routines, enhancing accessibility, boosting security, or simply making daily tasks more manageable, custom commands offer unparalleled opportunities for personalization and efficiency. As technology continues to evolve, the role of custom commands will only become more vital in crafting the smart homes of tomorrow.

Integrating Voice Assistants with Smart Devices

Voice assistants have rapidly evolved from simple tools for setting reminders and playing music to central hubs managing a myriad of smart devices in your home. They have become the heart of smart home systems, making it simpler and more intuitive to interact with technology. But how do you get started with this integration? It isn't as complex as it seems, and a little guidance can go a long way in helping you harness their full potential.

Let's start with the essentials. First, ensure that the smart devices you plan to integrate are compatible with your chosen voice assistant. Popular voice assistants like Amazon Alexa, Google Assistant, and Apple Siri have a wide array of supported smart devices, but it's critical to confirm compatibility to avoid any hiccups down the line. You can usually find a list of compatible devices on the voice assistant's website or app.

Once you've confirmed compatibility, the next step is setting up the voice assistant itself. This typically involves unboxing the device, plugging it in, and following the setup instructions provided via an app. For example, with Amazon Alexa, you'll use the Alexa app to connect the device to your Wi-Fi network and personalize your settings. This process is similar across different voice assistants. The app will guide you through each step, ensuring you're ready to move on to the more exciting part: integration.

With your voice assistant up and running, it's time to connect your smart devices. This usually involves linking your smart devices to the voice assistant's ecosystem. For instance, if you have smart lights, you'll use the manufacturer's app to link these lights to your voice assistant. Then, open the voice assistant's app to discover new devices. The app will scan for compatible smart devices and add them to your control network.

Once linked, voice commands become the bridge between you and your devices. Imagine entering your living room and saying, "Alexa, turn on the lights," or "Hey Google, set the thermostat to 72 degrees." These commands simplify daily routines and can significantly increase overall home efficiency. It's the small tasks, often repeated, that add up to substantial time savings.

For a more seamless experience, consider setting up custom commands, often referred to as "routines" or "scenes" depending on your voice assistant. These commands allow multiple actions to be triggered by a single phrase. For instance, saying "Goodnight" could turn off your lights, lock your doors, and adjust your thermostat to an energy-saving mode—all in one go. Customizing these routines ensures that your smart home operates in a way that aligns perfectly with your lifestyle.

But integration isn't just about convenience; it's also about increasing the security and efficiency of your home. Smart locks integrated with voice assistants can provide an additional layer of security. You can check if your doors are locked or even lock them remotely with a simple voice command. Similarly, integrating smart thermostats can lead to energy savings through more efficient home heating and cooling. Voice assistants can learn your preferences and adjust settings automatically, ensuring your home is always at the perfect temperature.

This is where things get truly exciting. Integrating voice assistants with smart devices isn't just about controlling individual components; it's about creating an interconnected ecosystem where the whole is greater than the sum of its parts. For instance, linking your security system with your voice assistant can lead to better response times in emergencies. If your smart smoke detector goes off, you could have your voice assistant turn on all the lights, unlock the doors, and call the fire department with a single command. It's about creating an environment where technology works together to enhance your quality of life.

For those concerned about privacy, it's worth noting that most voice assistants offer robust privacy controls. You can manage your data, delete voice recordings, and control what information is shared with the voice assistant. Taking the time to understand and configure these settings is crucial for ensuring your smart home is not only convenient but also secure.

Voice assistants also enhance accessibility, making smart homes more inclusive. For seniors or individuals with disabilities, the ability to control home devices using voice commands can increase independence and improve quality of life. Smart home technology can be particularly valuable for those with mobility issues, making it easier to perform daily tasks that might otherwise require assistance.

As technology continues to advance, the integration between voice assistants and smart devices will only become more seamless. New protocols and standards are being developed to make cross-device communication more reliable and faster. This ongoing evolution means that the investment you make in integrating your voice assistant with smart devices today will pay off even more in the future.

It's also important to stay updated with software and firmware updates for both your voice assistant and your smart devices. These updates often include new features, improved security measures, and enhanced compatibility, ensuring that your smart home system remains cutting-edge and secure.

Moreover, manufacturers frequently introduce innovations that expand the capabilities of voice assistants and smart devices. For example, advancements in natural language processing (NLP) are making voice assistants more intuitive, understanding not just the words but the intent behind them. This means more accurate responses and a smoother interaction experience overall.

Finally, consider future-proofing your smart home by investing in systems that support open standards and protocols. This ensures that your devices can integrate with new technologies as they emerge, keeping your home smart and adaptable. Voice assistants themselves are continuously evolving, with new skills and functionalities being added regularly by developers worldwide.

In summary, integrating voice assistants with smart devices transforms how we interact with our homes, making them more convenient, efficient, and secure. By setting up compatible devices, creating custom commands, and staying updated, you can fully leverage the power of voice-assisted smart living. The potential for a more connected home is vast, and with each new development, it only gets better.

CHAPTER 5:
SMART LIGHTING SOLUTIONS

As we delve into smart lighting solutions, envision a world where the mere touch of a smartphone or the sound of your voice can transform your home's ambiance. Smart lighting is not just a futuristic gimmick but a practical innovation that brings unprecedented convenience, efficiency, and adaptability to our living spaces. Imagine walking into a room and having your lights adjust to your preferred brightness and color, or scheduling them to turn on and off to save energy while you're away. These intelligent systems integrate seamlessly with other devices, creating a cohesive and responsive home environment that adapts to your daily needs and routines. By incorporating smart bulbs, automated schedules, and voice control, you can craft an ecosystem that harmonizes with your lifestyle while also contributing to energy conservation and cost savings. Whether you're looking to set the perfect mood for a gathering, enhance security by simulating occupancy, or simply reduce your carbon footprint, smart lighting solutions offer a versatile and enriching enhancement to any modern home.

Types of Smart Bulbs

As we delve deeper into smart lighting solutions, it's essential to understand the different types of smart bulbs available. These innovative lighting solutions not only illuminate our homes but also pave the way for a more connected and efficient living space. With the rapid advancements in AI technologies, smart bulbs have evolved to offer more than just on and off functions, transforming the way we interact with our home environments.

Firstly, let's talk about **Wi-Fi-enabled smart bulbs**. These bulbs connect directly to your home Wi-Fi network, eliminating the need for a central hub. This makes them an accessible option for those just starting with smart home technology. Most Wi-Fi smart bulbs can be controlled via smartphone apps, allowing you to adjust brightness, color, and even set schedules from anywhere. The ability to integrate with voice assistants like Amazon Alexa, Google Assistant, or Siri adds an extra layer of convenience, enabling hands-free control.

Next, we have **Zigbee smart bulbs**. Zigbee is a communication protocol that creates a mesh network around your home. This means each bulb connects to another, ensuring a robust and reliable network, even if one bulb fails. Zigbee bulbs typically require a compatible hub, such as the Philips Hue Bridge or Samsung SmartThings Hub. Despite the need for a hub, Zigbee bulbs are known for their low power consumption and longer battery life, making them a cost-effective solution in the long run.

Z-Wave smart bulbs are another popular choice. Like Zigbee, Z-Wave operates on a mesh network, offering excellent reliability and range. Z-Wave technology is known for its lower interference from other wireless devices, ensuring a stable connection. These bulbs generally require a compatible Z-Wave hub but can be integrated into broader smart home ecosystems, providing seamless control over multiple devices.

For those inclined towards simplicity and ease of installation, **Bluetooth smart bulbs** might be the ideal choice. These bulbs connect directly to your smartphone through Bluetooth, without the need for an internet connection or a hub. While Bluetooth smart bulbs offer quick and straightforward setup, their range is relatively limited compared to Wi-Fi or Zigbee alternatives. This means they are most effective in smaller spaces or single rooms.

Let's not overlook **color-changing smart bulbs**. These bulbs allow you to choose from millions of colors, adding an element of fun and personalization to your home. With the ability to adjust color temperature and brightness, you can create the perfect ambiance for any occasion. Whether you're hosting a party or winding down for the evening, color-changing bulbs can enhance your environment in innovative ways. Commonly associated with brands like Philips Hue and LIFX, these bulbs are perfect for creating dynamic and adaptable lighting scenes.

On the other hand, **white-tunable smart bulbs** focus on varying shades of white light. From warm whites that mimic sunset hues to cooler whites that resemble daylight, these bulbs can adjust according to the time of day and your personal preference. This feature can be particularly beneficial in maintaining your natural circadian rhythm, promoting better sleep and overall well-being. By tweaking the color temperature, you can ensure your home lighting is attuned to your daily needs.

Some smart bulbs come with **integrated sensors**. These bulbs can detect motion, ambient light, and even temperature, adjusting their functionality accordingly. For instance, motion-sensor smart bulbs can turn on when you enter a room and switch off when you leave, adding an extra layer of convenience and energy efficiency. These advanced features are particularly useful in areas like hallways, bathrooms, or entryways, where lights are often left on unintentionally.

Adopting smart bulbs with **built-in dimming capabilities** can also be a game-changer. Unlike traditional dimmer switches, these bulbs allow you to adjust brightness levels through apps or voice commands without any additional hardware. This makes it easier to find the perfect lighting intensity, creating a comfortable atmosphere for various activities, whether you're reading, watching a movie, or having a family dinner.

Now, onto the **smarter energy-efficient bulbs**. These bulbs are designed to consume less energy while providing the same or better light output compared to traditional incandescent or CFL bulbs. Equipping your home with energy-efficient smart bulbs not only reduces your carbon footprint but also lowers your electricity bills. Many of these bulbs come with Energy Star certification, ensuring they meet strict efficiency guidelines.

Another interesting category is **voice-controlled smart bulbs**. These bulbs integrate seamlessly with voice assistants, allowing you to control your lighting through spoken commands. Imagine walking into a room and simply saying, "Turn on the lights" – the convenience can't be overstated. For those looking to enhance accessibility, especially for the elderly or people with disabilities, voice-controlled smart bulbs offer significant benefits.

Lastly, there are specialized **smart outdoor bulbs**. Designed to withstand the elements, these bulbs are perfect for illuminating gardens, patios, and driveways. Many outdoor smart bulbs come with weather-resistant features and robust construction, making them durable and reliable. With smart control capabilities, you can automate outdoor lighting to enhance security, provide visibility, and create an inviting ambiance for your outdoor spaces.

In summary, the types of smart bulbs available today cater to a wide range of needs and preferences. Whether you prioritize ease of installation, energy efficiency, advanced features, or aesthetic versatility, there's likely a smart bulb that fits your requirements. As we embrace these innovations, our homes become more intuitive and responsive to our everyday needs. Imagine a world where your lighting adjusts itself based on the time of day, your mood, or even your daily schedule – the possibilities are truly inspiring.

The next sections will explore how to automate and schedule these smart bulbs to maximize their potential and integrate them seamlessly with other smart home devices. But for now, understanding the different types of smart bulbs is the first step in transforming your home into a more intelligent, energy-efficient, and personalized space.

With the variety of options available, taking the time to choose the right smart bulbs can significantly enhance your smart home setup. Not only will you enjoy the convenience and efficiency offered by these advanced lighting solutions, but you'll also take a step towards creating a more harmonious and responsive living environment.

Continue to explore the world of smart lighting and let these innovations light up your life in new and exciting ways.

Automation and Scheduling

When it comes to smart lighting solutions, automation and scheduling are at the heart of transforming your living space into an efficient, responsive environment. Imagine a home that anticipates your needs and adjusts the ambiance before you even realize a change is necessary. With advancements in artificial intelligence, this dream is a reality that's well within reach.

Automation in smart lighting isn't just about convenience—it's about creating an ecosystem that works in harmony with your lifestyle. By using sensors and adaptive algorithms, your home can learn your routines and adjust lighting settings accordingly. For instance, your living room lights could gradually dim as the evening progresses, setting the stage for a relaxed atmosphere without any manual intervention. This sort of dynamic interaction not only enhances comfort but can also contribute to energy savings by ensuring lights are only on when needed.

Furthermore, scheduling options allow for precision control over your lighting systems. You can tailor schedules to fit various parts of your day: morning routines, work hours, or bedtime rituals. Imagine waking up to a gentle increase in brightness, mimicking a natural sunrise, designed to wake you naturally and more peacefully. Conversely, you can schedule lights to dim gradually in the evening, helping to signal to your body that it's time to wind down and prepare for sleep.

Let's dive deeper into the nuts and bolts of how this works. Many smart lighting systems are compatible with various platforms and can be controlled via mobile apps, enabling you to set up complex schedules with ease. These applications often feature user-friendly interfaces that make creating, modifying, and deleting schedules a simple task. Some even offer templates to get you started quickly.

Another crucial aspect of automation is the integration with other smart home devices. For example, your lights can be programmed to interact with your smart thermostat, so when you leave the house and adjust the temperature accordingly, the lights will switch off automatically. Likewise, motion sensors can be strategically placed around your home to detect movement, ensuring that lights come on when someone enters a room and turn off when they exit. These interactions create a seamless, intelligent environment that requires minimal manual input.

The possibilities don't end there. Voice control, which we'll discuss in another section, can also play a significant role in enhancing automation. Commands like "Goodnight" can trigger a sequence of events—dimming or turning off the lights, locking doors, and adjusting the thermostat. But beyond voice controls, AI-driven systems have the potential to learn from your habits over time, optimizing both comfort and efficiency.

Consider also the role of external factors in your automated lighting schedules. Weather conditions, time of year, and even astrological events can all be accounted for. For instance, your lighting system can be programmed to adjust based on the amount of natural light streaming into your home. During brighter summer months, your lights can dim automatically to save energy. Conversely, during the darker days of winter, they can provide extra illumination to mimic the longer daylight hours.

Setting up these systems may seem daunting, but many smart lighting providers offer robust customer support and detailed tutorials to guide you through the process. Additionally, automation and scheduling are often enhanced through regular software updates from manufacturers, ensuring that your system evolves and improves over time.

One often overlooked aspect of smart lighting automation is the peace of mind it offers when you're away from home. Scheduling lights to turn on and off at specific times can give the illusion that someone is home, deterring potential intruders. Further integration with home security systems can make this even more effective, as lights can be set to flash or turn on brightly if an alarm is triggered, drawing attention to your property.

For those concerned about energy consumption, most smart lighting systems include features that monitor and report on energy usage. This data can be invaluable for fine-tuning your schedules to be more energy-efficient, contributing to both lower bills and a reduced carbon footprint. In this way, smart lighting automation goes beyond convenience to offer tangible environmental benefits.

Additionally, smart lighting isn't confined to the inside of your home. Many systems offer solutions for outdoor lighting, which can be automated for security and aesthetic purposes. Imagine a garden where the lights gradually shift colors to showcase your landscape during the evening or a driveway that lights up when you return home late at night, all without lifting a finger.

As we look to the future, the integration of machine learning and AI will only deepen. Imagine a home that constantly learns from your daily patterns and preferences, adapting in real-time to create an ever-more personalized environment. This is the future of smart homes, and smart lighting is leading the charge.

Ultimately, the key to unlocking the full potential of smart lighting lies in thoughtful planning and strategic implementation of automation and scheduling. Embrace these technologies, and you'll find that your home not only meets your needs but anticipates and adapts to them, creating a space that's both brilliantly functional and effortlessly elegant.

Voice Control

Voice control is one of the most transformative features in the realm of smart lighting solutions, bringing a level of convenience and accessibility that was only imagined in science fiction not too long ago. With robust voice control functionalities, you no longer have to fumble for the light switch or interrupt what you're doing to adjust your home's lighting. Simply using your voice, you can orchestrate the ambiance of your space effortlessly.

Imagine walking into your home with your hands full of groceries, and a simple command like "turn on the kitchen lights" illuminates everything you need. Voice control isn't just a convenient gimmick; it can make everyday tasks smoother and more intuitive. It can trigger specific lighting scenes, adjust brightness levels, and even change light colors—all without lifting a finger.

Voice-controlled smart lighting typically relies on popular voice assistants such as Amazon Alexa, Google Assistant, and Apple's Siri.

These platforms are designed to integrate seamlessly with various smart lighting brands. However, it's crucial to ensure that the voice assistant you're using is compatible with the smart lighting system you have. Most modern smart bulbs and hubs are designed to work across multiple ecosystems, but double-checking compatibility can save you headaches later on.

Customization is one of the key benefits of integrating voice control with your smart lighting. By creating custom commands, you can program a variety of lighting scenes suited to different activities and moods. Want to set the perfect ambiance for a dinner party? You might set a command like "dinner party mode" to dim the lights and bring up some warm, cozy hues. Or perhaps you're winding down for the night—"bedtime mode" can soften the lights to a gentle glow, aiding in a smooth transition to sleep.

Integrating voice control with smart lighting also brings significant advantages for accessibility. It can be a game-changer for individuals with mobility issues, allowing them to manage their home's lighting without needing to physically interact with switches or devices. For elderly residents or individuals with disabilities, voice control can significantly enhance their quality of life, offering them ease and independence.

Another impactful benefit of voice-controlled smart lighting is the ability to integrate it with other smart home systems for a more cohesive and comprehensive experience. For example, you can link your lighting settings with your home security system. Commands like "goodnight" can not only turn off the lights but also activate security cameras and lock the doors. This integration streamlines multiple processes into a single command, enhancing both convenience and security.

While voice control is remarkable, it does have limitations and potential pitfalls to be aware of. One of the primary issues can be the accuracy and recognition capabilities of your chosen voice assistant. Sometimes background noise or unclear speech can lead to misinterpretations. Home environments are dynamic, and there will be instances where the voice assistant struggles to recognize your commands correctly. Regular updates and calibrations can help minimize these issues, providing more accurate voice recognition over time.

Furthermore, privacy concerns are a legitimate consideration when introducing any form of voice-activated technology into your living space. Since voice assistants continually listen for their wake words, there's an ongoing debate about data security and the potential for unauthorized listening. It's essential to review the privacy policies of your voice assistant provider and to configure settings that enhance your security, such as muting the microphone when not in use or setting complex wake words that are less likely to be triggered accidentally.

Incorporating voice control in smart lighting also opens up avenues for fun and creative exploration. You can experiment with different scenes and moods personalized to your lifestyle. Whether it's a calming meditation session, a dynamic workout routine, or an immersive movie night, the right lighting can make all the difference. Voice control allows you to experiment effortlessly, enabling you to find the perfect settings that suit your mood and activities.

For those inclined towards technology, creating custom voice commands and automation rules can be an engaging project. Platforms like IFTTT (If This Then That) offer additional customization layers, allowing you to connect voice commands with other smart home functions and services. For example, you could set a command that not only adjusts the lighting but also starts playing your favorite playlist or reads out the latest weather report. The possibilities are nearly endless, limited only by your creativity and the compatibility of your devices.

Voice control in smart lighting solutions is far from a novelty; it is an essential component of modern smart home ecosystems. As artificial intelligence continues to evolve, we can expect even more advanced capabilities, smoother integrations, and enhanced user experiences. The future of smart lighting is not just bright; it's intelligent, responsive, and increasingly attuned to our needs and preferences.

As we look ahead, it's clear that voice control will continue to pave the way for more innovative smart home solutions. As this technology matures, it will undoubtedly integrate more deeply with our daily habits and routines, making our homes not just more comfortable and convenient but also smarter in the truest sense. Incorporating voice control into your smart lighting setup is an investment in both the present and future of home automation, ensuring you remain at the cutting edge of convenience and efficiency.

CHAPTER 6:
SMART CLIMATE CONTROL

Imagine walking into your home after a long day to find the temperature just right without having to lift a finger. Smart Climate Control is about more than just convenience; it's about creating a living environment that learns and adapts to your needs. Whether it's the seamless integration of smart thermostats that adjust based on your routine or the ability to set up automated climate zones personalized for different rooms, the impact on both comfort and energy efficiency is profound. Moreover, linking climate control with voice assistants allows for effortless command over your home's atmosphere, providing a blend of luxury and practicality. Embracing these technologies turns your home into a sanctuary where the climate is always perfectly tuned to your preferences, enhancing both your quality of life and your home's efficiency.

Smart Thermostats

Smart thermostats have revolutionized how we manage our home's climate, offering unprecedented control, convenience, and efficiency. These devices are not just about setting the temperature; they fundamentally alter the way we interact with our living spaces, making it possible to create environments that are not only comfortable but also eco-friendly and cost-effective. With the right smart thermostat, managing your home's heating and cooling system becomes a seamless, intuitive experience.

The most immediate benefit of smart thermostats lies in their ability to learn and adapt. Modern devices come equipped with AI algorithms that analyze your daily routines and adjust the climate settings accordingly. Whether it's turning down the heat when you leave for work or warming up the house just before you return, these devices aim to provide the optimal climate without requiring manual adjustments. This capability not only ensures comfort but also leads to significant energy savings.

Energy efficiency is a primary concern for many homeowners, and smart thermostats address this directly. Traditional thermostats operate on a fixed schedule that often doesn't account for real-life variations. Smart thermostats, however, use sensors and data analytics to dynamically adjust settings. By learning when rooms are occupied and incorporating weather forecasts, they optimize heating and cooling cycles to minimize energy consumption. Many models provide reports and insights via connected apps, giving you a clear picture of your usage patterns and potential areas for improvement.

Integration is another key aspect. Smart thermostats can connect with other smart home devices to create a seamless ecosystem. For instance, they can work with motion sensors to detect when a room is unoccupied and adjust the temperature to save energy. They can also integrate with smart blinds and windows, optimizing natural light and heat to maintain a balanced indoor climate. This interconnected approach not only enhances comfort but also contributes to lower utility bills.

One of the standout features of smart thermostats is their compatibility with voice assistants. Whether you use Amazon Alexa, Google Assistant, or Apple Siri, you can control your thermostat with simple voice commands. This adds an extra layer of convenience, allowing you to make adjustments hands-free. Imagine lying in bed and feeling a bit too warm; a simple voice command can bring immediate relief without the need to get up.

Modern smart thermostats also incorporate advanced features like geofencing. This technology uses your smartphone's location to determine whether you're home or away. When you leave, the thermostat can automatically switch to an energy-saving mode, and when you're on your way back, it can adjust the settings to ensure a comfortable environment upon your arrival. This smart feature ensures that your home is always at the perfect temperature without you having to lift a finger.

The user interface of smart thermostats is designed for simplicity and ease of use. Most devices come with intuitive, touch-screen controls, and their companion apps offer a range of functionalities that can be accessed from anywhere. These apps allow you to create schedules, receive performance alerts, and even manage multiple properties if you have more than one home. This level of control makes it easier than ever to maintain a comfortable living environment while staying on top of energy usage.

For those concerned about environmental impact, smart thermostats offer a sustainable solution. By optimizing energy usage, they contribute to a reduction in carbon emissions. Many utility companies also recognize the value of smart thermostats and offer rebates or incentives for installing them, making it financially attractive as well as environmentally responsible.

Security and data privacy are critical in the era of connected homes. Reputable smart thermostat manufacturers prioritize these aspects, ensuring that your data is encrypted and that the devices are regularly updated with the latest security patches. This safeguards your personal information and prevents unauthorized access, allowing you to enjoy the benefits of a smart thermostat without compromising your privacy.

The installation of smart thermostats has become increasingly user-friendly. While professional installation is always an option, many devices come with comprehensive guides and tutorials that enable a straightforward DIY setup. With features like step-by-step instructions within the app and compatibility checks for your existing HVAC system, getting started has never been easier.

Smart thermostats are not just for high-end homes. While early models were sometimes costly, the market has expanded, offering a range of options to suit different budgets. From basic models that provide essential functionalities to advanced versions with all the bells and whistles, there's a smart thermostat for everyone. The long-term savings on energy bills often offset the initial investment, making it a financially sound decision for most households.

Accessibility is another important factor. Features like remote control through apps and voice activation make smart thermostats incredibly user-friendly for people of all ages and abilities. This inclusive design ensures that everyone in the household can benefit from the technology, enhancing overall quality of life.

In summary, smart thermostats are a game-changer in home climate control. They provide a perfect blend of comfort, convenience, and efficiency, making them a must-have for any smart home enthusiast. By learning your habits, optimizing energy usage, and integrating seamlessly with other smart devices, they offer a futuristic solution to modern living. Embracing this technology is a step towards a smarter, more sustainable, and ultimately more enjoyable home environment.

Automated Climate Zones

In the quest for a truly connected and efficient home, smart climate control stands out as one of the most transformative applications of artificial intelligence. Among the spectrum of possibilities, automated climate zones bring a new level of sophistication and personalization to home comfort. These systems are more than just adjustable thermostats; they are an intelligent mesh of sensors and algorithms designed to tailor the indoor climate to the specific needs of each part of your home, adapting in real-time to the ever-changing dynamics within.

Imagine waking up on a chilly morning to find your bedroom warm and inviting, yet as you move to the kitchen, it's a bit cooler, preparing your senses for the day ahead. Automated climate zones make this scenario possible by allowing different parts of your home to maintain distinct climate settings. This level of control isn't just about luxury; it's about optimizing energy use and cutting down on waste. For instance, there's no need to heat or cool the guest bedroom if it's unoccupied, and this localized approach translates to substantial energy savings over time.

To set up automated climate zones, smart thermostats are a crucial component, but they are not the whole story. you'll also need temperature sensors placed strategically around your home. These sensors feed real-time data to a central system, which then makes intelligent decisions based on the gathered information. The granularity of control these systems offer means you can program or even let the AI learn your preferences over time, making automated adjustments seamlessly. It's a dance between your home and the technology, always tuning to your presence and habits.

Integration with other smart home devices further elevates the capabilities of automated climate zones. For example, when your smart home system detects that you have arrived home, not only does it unlock the front door and turn on the lights, but it also adjusts the climate according to the time of day and your personal preferences. And it's not just about heating and cooling. Humidity levels, air quality, and even the airflow can be fine-tuned to create the ideal environment.

Consider the advantages of zoning in a multi-story house. Typically, the upper floors are warmer due to rising heat, while the basement might remain cooler. Automated climate zones can address these discrepancies by independently controlling each floor. During the summer, the system can keep the upper floors cooler while ensuring the basement stays at a comfortable temperature, balancing overall energy consumption more effectively. In the winter, the smart system does the reverse, ensuring even warmth throughout the home without overworking the heating system.

But how does this technology work in practice? It starts with a user-friendly interface where you can set your preferences. Most systems offer mobile apps, giving you remote control no matter where you are. Forgot to adjust the settings before leaving for a week-long trip? No problem. Just open the app and set the whole house to an energy-saving mode. As technology advances, voice commands via popular assistants like Alexa or Google Assistant are becoming commonplace, making adjustments as simple as saying, "Set the living room to 72 degrees."

Advanced systems even incorporate machine learning to predict and learn from your behaviors. Over time, they anticipate your needs before you even have to make a manual change. For instance, if you consistently lower the temperature before bed, the system notes this pattern and begins to do it automatically. This predictive feature is a hallmark of how AI is transforming smart climate control—a proactive rather than reactive approach to managing your home's environment.

The real magic, however, lies in the ability of these systems to communicate with each other. Devices from different manufacturers can integrate under a unified smart home hub. For instance, if the weather forecast predicts a sudden drop in temperature, your smart system can proactively begin warming the house before you arrive home. This interoperability is crucial for creating a cohesive and responsive climate control system that fits seamlessly into the smart home ecosystem.

Setting up automated climate zones requires consideration and careful planning. Placement of sensors and choosing the right hardware are vital steps. It can be a DIY project if you're tech-savvy, but many opt for professional installation to ensure everything is configured correctly. Hiring a professional can also save you time and ensure that your system is optimized for maximum efficiency from the start.

One of the primary benefits of automated climate zones is energy efficiency. By only heating or cooling occupied areas, you reduce unnecessary energy expenditure, which is both good for the environment and your utility bill. According to several studies, homeowners can save up to 30% on energy costs through proper zoning and smart climate control practices.

Notably, automated climate zones contribute to the overall health and well-being of the household. Proper temperature and humidity control can mitigate the risks associated with mold and allergens. For families with specific health needs, precise climate control ensures a comfortable and safe environment tailored to individual requirements. It's a holistic approach to home care, combining comfort, health, and efficiency.

In terms of future advancements, the integration of AI promises to bring even more enhancements to automated climate zones. Next-generation algorithms could offer predictive maintenance, alerting homeowners to potential issues before they become problems. There's also increasing potential for systems to integrate with renewable energy sources, dynamically adjusting climate controls based on the availability of solar or wind power, further aligning with sustainable living practices.

As we continue to move toward smarter and more interconnected homes, the role of automated climate zones becomes even more pronounced. This technology not only enhances living conditions but also supports a more sustainable and efficient future. By embracing these intelligent systems, homeowners are investing in a significant upgrade that promises both immediate and long-term benefits.

Integration with Voice Assistants

Voice assistants have rapidly become a fundamental element of the smart home ecosystem, transforming the way we interact with our living spaces. Imagine coming home after a long day, and with just a simple voice command, your thermostat adjusts to the perfect temperature, your lights dim, and your favorite music starts playing. This seamless interaction is at the heart of smart climate control, where voice assistants like Amazon's Alexa, Google Assistant, and Apple's Siri enable a hands-free experience.

Integrating voice assistants with smart climate control devices, such as thermostats, air conditioners, and even fans, allows homeowners to manage their environment effortlessly. To start, it is crucial to choose compatible devices. Most modern smart thermostats, like the Nest Thermostat or Ecobee SmartThermostat, are designed to work with multiple voice assistant platforms. This compatibility ensures that users are not restricted to a single brand or system, giving them the flexibility to tailor their smart home setup to their specific needs.

The process of integrating these devices typically begins with adding the thermostat or climate control device to the corresponding voice assistant's ecosystem. For instance, integrating a smart thermostat with Alexa involves enabling the thermostat's specific skill within the

Alexa app and linking the device through a user account. Similarly, Google Assistant and Siri have comparable processes involving their respective apps and system integrations.

Once set up, users can issue commands like "Hey Google, set the living room temperature to 72 degrees" or "Alexa, turn off the bedroom fan." These commands can be as specific or as general as the device capabilities allow, providing unparalleled convenience and precision.

Beyond basic commands, the true power of voice assistants lies in their ability to automate routines and scenarios. For example, during the summer, a homeowner might create a "good morning" routine that gradually increases the temperature to a comfortable level before they wake up. Similarly, a "good night" routine can ensure the house cools down and the ceiling fans are set to low as everyone settles in for the night.

Integration with smart climate control extends beyond just comfort; it also contributes significantly to energy efficiency. Voice assistants can be programmed to optimize heating and cooling schedules based on daily routines and presence detection. By integrating smart sensors that monitor room occupancy, the system can ensure energy is not wasted on unoccupied spaces. Commands like "turn off the AC when I leave" or "reduce heating when no one is home" can make a significant impact on energy consumption and utility bills.

Integrating smart climate control with voice assistants also provides valuable data insights. Modern thermostats connected through voice assistants can track usage patterns and energy consumption, offering homeowners detailed reports via their respective apps. These insights enable users to make informed decisions about their energy usage, promoting sustainable living.

Moreover, the accessibility features of voice assistants cannot be overlooked. For individuals with mobility impairments or aging homeowners, controlling the climate through voice commands can be a game-changer. The ease of issuing verbal instructions eliminates the need to physically interact with devices, enhancing the overall quality of life. With simple phrases like "Siri, make it cooler" or "Alexa, turn on the heater," these individuals can manage their environment independently and comfortably.

While the integration process is generally user-friendly, there are considerations to keep in mind. Ensuring a stable and secure Wi-Fi connection is paramount since many smart devices and voice assistants rely on internet connectivity. Security is another critical aspect. Homeowners must ensure that their smart devices and voice interfaces are protected against unauthorized access, which might involve employing strong passwords, two-factor authentication, and regularly updating firmware.

Privacy concerns are also at the forefront of smart home technologies. Voice assistants are always listening for their wake word, which raises potential privacy issues. Homeowners should be aware of how their data is collected, stored, and used. It is advisable to review privacy settings within the voice assistant apps and be cautious about the permissions granted to third-party services integrated with voice-controlled devices.

Overall, the integration of voice assistants with smart climate control represents a significant leap toward the vision of a fully automated and intelligent home. By leveraging the strengths of voice recognition and AI, homeowners gain a new level of control over their living environment, blending comfort, efficiency, and innovation in everyday life.

In conclusion, as we look towards the future, the synergy between voice assistants and smart climate control will only become more sophisticated and streamlined. Home automation is poised to reach new heights, making our living spaces more intuitive and responsive. The convenience and practical benefits offered by these integrations make them not just a luxury but a valuable addition to any modern home. The continuous advancements in AI and smart home technology promise an exciting journey toward truly intelligent living. Embrace the change, and let your voice be the key to a smarter home environment.

CHAPTER 7:
HOME SECURITY SYSTEMS

Home security systems have evolved significantly with the integration of artificial intelligence, transforming the traditional means of safeguarding our homes into highly sophisticated and interactive networks. By leveraging smart cameras, motion sensors, and smart locks, we can now create a holistic security environment that not only alerts us to potential threats but also learns and adapts to our routines. This chapter dives into how AI-driven devices can offer real-time surveillance, precise threat detection, and seamless control via mobile applications, making it easier than ever to monitor and secure our living spaces from virtually anywhere. Whether it's detecting unusual activity through pattern recognition or locking doors with a voice command, the intelligent systems discussed here aim to provide peace of mind and a stronger sense of security for you and your family.

Smart Cameras

Smart cameras have revolutionized home security. They seamlessly blend advanced artificial intelligence features with everyday practicality, providing homeowners with an unprecedented level of security and peace of mind. These devices are more than just cameras; they are sophisticated systems designed to monitor, alert, and even deter potential intruders. By integrating AI with high-definition video, smart cameras can analyze and interpret data in real-time, offering functionalities that go far beyond simple video recording.

One of the standout features of modern smart cameras is their ability to differentiate between different types of motion. Traditional security cameras would alert you to any motion detected, whether it was a stray cat, a weather event, or an actual intruder. Smart cameras, however, use AI algorithms to analyze motion and specifically recognize human shapes. This reduces false alarms and ensures that you are alerted only when there's a potential security threat.

Moreover, these cameras often come equipped with facial recognition technology. This capability allows the camera to learn the faces of friends and family, differentiating them from strangers. Over time, the system becomes more adept at identifying familiar faces and can notify you when someone it doesn't recognize appears on your property. This feature not only enhances security but also adds an element of personalization by welcoming identified individuals with custom greetings or messages.

Integration with other smart home devices is another significant advantage of smart cameras. For instance, you can configure your smart camera to work in tandem with smart lighting systems. If the camera detects motion outside your home after dark, it can trigger the outdoor lights to turn on. This sudden illumination can deter potential intruders and immediately alert you to any unusual activity. Similarly, smart cameras can be connected to voice assistants, allowing you to view live footage or recorded clips via simple voice commands.

Audio features in smart cameras have also come a long way. Many of the latest models offer two-way audio, enabling you to listen to what's happening in the vicinity of the camera and speak to anyone on your property through an integrated speaker. This can be particularly useful for communicating with delivery personnel, instructing service providers, or even scaring off trespassers.

Beyond security, smart cameras also serve various convenience and utility functions. For pet owners, these cameras can keep an eye on pets while you're away. Some models even incorporate pet-specific features, like alerts for unusual behavior or integrated treat dispensers that can be controlled remotely. For parents, nursery cameras provide peace of mind by monitoring babies and toddlers, offering features such as temperature and humidity sensors to ensure the environment is comfortable and safe for little ones.

One cannot overlook the importance of image and video quality in smart cameras. From 1080p full HD to 4K ultra HD, the clarity of footage has seen dramatic improvements. Superior image quality ensures that every detail is captured, making it easier to identify faces, read license plates, or observe minute movements. Night vision is another critical feature, with infrared and low-light technology enabling clear footage even in complete darkness.

Cloud storage is often an important consideration when selecting a smart camera. Many manufacturers offer subscription-based cloud storage, where footage is saved and accessible for a specific period. While convenient, this does raise concerns about data privacy and security. However, some smart cameras also offer local storage options, such as SD cards or network-attached storage (NAS) devices, providing users with the flexibility to choose based on their privacy preferences and budget.

Let's not forget the user experience. The best smart cameras come with companion apps that are both intuitive and feature-rich. These apps allow homeowners to view live footage, review alert history, set up motion zones, and customize alerts. User-friendly apps make it easy to get the most out of your smart camera, ensuring that you remain connected and informed at all times.

Installation has also become relatively straightforward. Most smart cameras are designed for DIY setup, with step-by-step guidance provided through the app. Some include mounting kits and tools, making physical installation a breeze. Wireless models eliminate the need for complicated wiring, relying instead on Wi-Fi connectivity. However, wired options are still available for those who prefer a more permanent and reliable solution.

While there's no doubt that smart cameras offer numerous benefits, they do come with their set of challenges. Network reliability is paramount; a weak Wi-Fi signal can result in lag or poor video quality. It's advisable to invest in a robust mesh network or Wi-Fi extender to ensure consistent connectivity. Moreover, given the increasing sophistication of cyber threats, ensuring that the camera's firmware is regularly updated and that robust passwords are used is essential for maintaining security.

Smart cameras are not just for the tech-savvy. They are accessible and beneficial for everyone, from young professionals keen on integrating the latest technology into their homes, to elderly homeowners seeking an added layer of security and peace of mind. They offer a blend of innovation, convenience, and safety, making them a cornerstone in modern home security systems.

In conclusion, smart cameras have redefined what home security means. With capabilities like motion detection, facial recognition, two-way audio, and integration with various smart home devices, they provide a comprehensive security solution that is both intelligent and user-friendly. As technology continues to evolve, we can only expect these cameras to become even more sophisticated, bringing new features and enhanced security to our homes.

Motion Sensors

Integrating motion sensors into a home security system can profoundly elevate the sophistication and effectiveness of your security measures. At the core, motion sensors are devices that detect movement within a specified range. They act as vigilant sentinels, constantly scanning spaces for any unauthorized activity and triggering responses to secure the premises. But, how do these small devices make such a big impact in the ever-evolving landscape of smart homes?

The functionality of motion sensors primarily hinges on different technologies—infrared, ultrasonic, microwave, and tomography. Each type has its unique mechanism for detecting motion. Passive Infrared Sensors (PIR), for instance, detect body heat, registering changes in infrared radiation within their monitoring zone. These sensors are widely used due to their reliability and cost-effectiveness. On the other side, you have ultrasonic sensors that emit ultrasonic waves and measure the reflection off a moving object. This variety tends to be more sensitive and can cover larger areas.

Motion sensors are vital for a range of security applications. One of the most straightforward uses is for triggering alarms. If a sensor detects unexpected motion, it can send an alert to your mobile device or immediately alert a professional monitoring service. Whether it's a text message, a phone call, or a notification through a dedicated app, real-time alerts ensure that homeowners can quickly respond to potential threats.

Beyond sounding alarms, motion sensors can also be integrated with other smart home devices to create a layered security system. For example, when linked with smart lighting, motion sensors can activate exterior lights, floodlights, or even indoor lights if they detect activity in certain zones. This not only helps to deter intruders but also provides a clearer view for security cameras.

Speaking of cameras, motion sensors work seamlessly with smart cameras. Advanced security systems use motion detection to trigger camera recordings, ensuring that you have visual documentation of any event that triggered an alert. Some systems even offer customizable motion detection areas, allowing users to define specific zones where any detected movement will prompt recording while ignoring other zones. This can eliminate false alarms caused by everyday activities that don't pose risks.

Imagine coming home late at night; as you step onto your driveway, motion sensors can trigger pathway lights to guide you safely to your door. These sensors can also activate your indoor lights and adjust the climate control systems automatically, providing a comfortable environment as soon as you enter. The synergy between motion sensors and other elements of your smart home ecosystem can significantly enhance not just security, but convenience and energy efficiency as well.

Consider the scenario of family members arriving at different times. Motion sensors in conjunction with user profiles can identify and customize settings for each individual. For example, one family member may prefer the living room lights to turn on and the thermostat set to a specific temperature upon entering. All these personalized experiences can be pre-configured and adjusted through connected applications, making the home environment uniquely tailored for each resident.

One transformative application of motion sensors lies in monitoring vulnerable areas like windows and doors. With advanced AI and machine learning algorithms, motion sensors can distinguish between normal and suspicious activities, reducing false positives that can be triggered by pets or falling objects. These sensors are clever enough to differentiate between a human and an animal or identify the difference between a moving tree branch and a potential intruder.

It's also crucial to highlight the benefits of integrating motion sensors with other smart safety devices like smart locks. Imagine a security breach at your front door; a motion sensor could trigger the smart lock to engage, preventing unauthorized entry. Complemented by a real-time security camera feed, such a setup provides robust security measures.

In addition to home security, motion sensors can serve an essential role in emergency response systems. They can detect falls or unusual movement patterns, which can be critical for families with elderly members. For instance, a sudden trip or fall in a monitored area triggers alerts to caregivers or emergency services, ensuring timely assistance.

To maximize the effectiveness of motion sensors in your home security network, it's important to place them strategically. Key locations include entry points like doors and windows, hallways, and secluded areas which might otherwise be blind spots in your security coverage. Installing motion sensors at multiple heights can also account for different perspectives, ensuring comprehensive coverage.

Battery life and power sources also play a pivotal role in the uninterrupted functionality of motion sensors. Most modern motion sensors come with long-lasting batteries that can last several months to a few years. However, integrating them into your home's power supply could be a more permanent and reliable solution. Regularly checking battery status—many systems offer automatic alerts—ensures that your motion sensors stay operational without unexpected downtimes.

Finally, don't forget the importance of integrating motion sensors with your home's central AI system. Artificial Intelligence can provide predictive analysis based on regular movement patterns, identifying anomalies that warrant attention. Imagine your home recognizing that no one should be in the backyard at midnight and instantly alerting you to that presence—this kind of smart analysis is where the future of home security is headed.

Motion sensors exemplify the convergence of technology and practicality. They provide a layer of intelligence and responsiveness, transforming how we secure our homes. Whether used alone or as part of an integrated smart home ecosystem, these devices are instrumental in creating a secure, efficient, and ultimately more convenient living environment. As AI continues to evolve, expect motion sensors to become even more refined and capable, continually pushing the boundaries of what's possible in home security.

Smart Locks

With the advent of smart home technology, securing your home has never been more efficient or intuitive. One of the most transformative elements in modern home security systems is the smart lock. These devices don't just secure doors; they offer a whole new level of control, accessibility, and convenience. But what exactly makes a smart lock "smart," and how do they integrate with the rest of your AI-powered home?

At its core, a smart lock is a keyless entry system that leverages various technologies to provide remote access, control, and monitoring capabilities. Unlike traditional locks, which require a physical key, smart locks operate via smartphone apps, voice commands, biometrics, or specialized key fobs. This means you can lock or unlock your door from anywhere in the world, provided you have an internet connection.

The installation of smart locks brings multiple advantages. For starters, they offer enhanced security features. Many models come with tamper alerts, which notify you if someone is attempting to break in. Some even have built-in sirens that trigger in the event of a forced entry. These features, combined with the ability to monitor the status of your locks in real-time, provide peace of mind that your home is secure.

Another significant benefit is the convenience factor. Have you ever left home and wondered if you locked the door? With a smart lock, you can check and lock it from your phone. Moreover, the days of hiding spare keys under the doormat are gone. You can grant temporary access to guests, family members, or service providers via digital keys, which can be revoked at any time.

Integration is a vital aspect of smart locks. Most modern smart locks are compatible with various smart home ecosystems like Amazon Alexa, Google Home, and Apple HomeKit. This means you can create routines that lock your doors as part of a "Goodnight" automation, which could include turning off the lights and adjusting the thermostat. It's about making your life simpler and more connected.

Let's delve into the types of smart locks available. There are mainly three types: Wi-Fi-enabled locks, Bluetooth-enabled locks, and Z-Wave/Zigbee locks. Each has its strengths and ideal use-case scenarios. Wi-Fi locks offer remote access but are often more power-hungry. Bluetooth locks provide excellent battery life but require you to be within a certain range. Z-Wave and Zigbee locks offer a balanced approach and work seamlessly with other smart home devices.

Battery life is a crucial consideration for smart locks. Depending on the type and usage, batteries can last anywhere from a few months to over a year. Most smart locks will alert you when the battery is running low, ensuring that you're never caught off guard. Some even offer power-saving modes or alternative power options like solar panels.

Security protocols and encryption are central to the effective operation of smart locks. These devices often utilize advanced encryption standards to protect against unauthorized access. However, it's essential to keep your software updated to mitigate potential vulnerabilities. Regular firmware updates from the manufacturer frequently address security flaws and improve efficiency.

While the benefits are abundant, there are challenges as well. One of the primary concerns is hacking. Although smart locks are designed to be secure, any internet-connected device is potentially vulnerable.

Therefore, it's crucial to follow best practices for securing your network, such as using strong, unique passwords and enabling two-factor authentication where possible.

Another challenge pertains to power failure. Since these locks rely on battery power, a dead battery could potentially lock you out. Most smart locks come with a backup method, such as a physical key or an external battery terminal. It's always wise to familiarize yourself with these backup options.

How do you choose the right smart lock for your home? The answer depends on your needs and existing smart home setup. If remote access is a priority, a Wi-Fi-enabled lock might be the best choice. If you're deeply embedded in an ecosystem that uses Z-Wave, a lock compatible with that protocol will be more appropriate. Some models even offer unique features like built-in cameras or video doorbells, adding an additional layer of utility.

Installation is generally straightforward and can be done by most DIY enthusiasts. However, it's always a good practice to follow the manufacturer's instructions meticulously. Proper installation ensures that the smart lock integrates perfectly with your door, functioning as intended.

The future of smart locks is incredibly promising, with emerging technologies poised to make them even more integrated and secure. Innovations such as geofencing can lock or unlock your door automatically when you arrive or leave your home, and advancements in biometric authentication could replace the need for any key or code entirely, identifying you through facial recognition or fingerprint scanning.

In summary, smart locks offer impressive versatility and security, transforming how we perceive and manage entry to our homes. Embracing this technology means taking a significant step toward a fully integrated, AI-powered living environment where convenience and security go hand in hand. By selecting the right smart lock for your needs, you're not just adding a device to your home; you're investing in a smarter, safer future.

CHAPTER 8:
SMART HOME ENTERTAINMENT

Smart Home Entertainment is revolutionizing how we experience leisure and media in our living spaces. With AI-powered televisions, viewers can enjoy personalized content recommendations and even voice-controlled navigation. These TVs come equipped with high-quality displays, seamless streaming capabilities, and intelligent assistants that understand user preferences, making binge-watching sessions more tailored and interactive. Smart speakers, another crucial element, not only play your favorite tunes with impressive audio quality but also integrate with other smart devices for hands-free control across your home. Streaming devices are the crown jewel of modern entertainment setups, offering access to a wide range of services and content with just a simple command or touch of a button. They make the most out of high-speed internet connections, ensuring smooth, uninterrupted playback. As AI continues to evolve, the boundaries of home entertainment will only expand, offering more immersive and convenient experiences that bring the future of entertainment into the present.

AI-Powered Televisions

Navigating the realm of *AI-powered televisions* can feel like stepping into the future of home entertainment. These aren't just devices for watching your favorite shows or movies; they're the epitome of interactive, intelligent systems designed to provide a personalized viewing experience. With the infusion of artificial intelligence, televisions have evolved far beyond their traditional roles. Imagine a TV that learns your preferences, synchronizes with other smart devices, and adapts to your needs in real time. Welcome to the world of AI-powered televisions.

The first thing that stands out about AI-enhanced TVs is their recommendation algorithms. Much like streaming services that suggest content based on your viewing history, modern AI TVs come with sophisticated algorithms capable of discerning your likes and dislikes. Over time, your television can offer suggestions so accurate that you might wonder if it can read your mind. This feature saves you the hassle of endlessly scrolling through options, making your downtime more enjoyable and efficient.

But it doesn't stop there. Voice control has become a standard feature in the new generation of smart TVs. Through integrations with popular voice assistants like Amazon Alexa, Google Assistant, or Apple Siri, you can control your TV without lifting a finger. Want to switch channels, adjust the volume, or find a specific movie? Just say the word. For those who value convenience and accessibility, this hands-free operation is a game-changer.

Another aspect of AI-powered televisions worth noting is their image and sound optimization capabilities. Using AI algorithms, these televisions can automatically adjust picture settings based on the ambient light in the room and the type of content you are watching. Whether you are indulging in a dark, atmospheric movie or a brightly lit sports game, your AI TV ensures you get the best possible viewing experience. Similarly, audio enhancements can adapt to minimize background noise, highlight speech, and offer a sound experience akin to being in a theater.

Let's delve into the concept of *integration*. AI-powered TVs can seamlessly connect with other smart home devices, rendering a unified ecosystem. Imagine your television dimming the lights when you start a movie or pausing your show when the doorbell rings. This level of interconnectedness adds layers of convenience and complements your overall smart home environment. The benefits of such integrations are manifold, simplifying daily tasks and creating a more enjoyable and efficient living space.

Security is another dimension where AI-powered televisions are making strides. These TVs can serve as additional nodes in your home's security system. For instance, when linked with security cameras, your TV can display live feeds, alert you to unusual activities, or even work as a command center for your entire home security setup.

Customization is a prime feature too. These TVs can learn different user profiles and adapt the content and settings preferences accordingly. If your household has diverse tastes, the AI can recognize who's watching and tailor the recommendations and settings specific to that user. Over time, this leads to a highly personalized viewing experience for every family member, making a single TV versatile enough for everyone.

AI-driven advancements extend into gaming as well. Modern televisions come with low latency modes and AI-enhanced graphics that provide an unparalleled experience for gamers. The TV can dynamically adjust settings to ensure smoother gameplay and enhanced visuals. With the rise of cloud gaming, these AI features become indispensable, making the transition between watching a show and gaming almost seamless.

Let's not forget the aspect of energy efficiency. AI-powered televisions often come with features like automatic shut-off and energy-saving modes. They can detect inactivity and power down to save energy, which is a small step but an important one in creating an eco-friendly home.

In terms of software updates, the AI aspect ensures that your television improves over time. Updates can be rolled out to enhance performance, fix bugs, and introduce new features. This means that purchasing an AI-powered TV is not just a one-time improvement; the device continually evolves, ensuring you always have the latest functionalities.

While the technology sounds futuristic, it's surprisingly user-friendly. Manufacturers have invested heavily in making sure these smart TVs are intuitive to set up and use. Features like easy connection guides, user-friendly interfaces, and customer support all contribute to a smoother user experience, ensuring that integrating an AI-powered television into your home is as hassle-free as possible.

Looking ahead, the future of AI-powered televisions promises even more exciting advancements. Enhanced augmented reality (AR) and virtual reality (VR) features are on the horizon, as are improved integration capabilities with even more smart home devices. It's clear that the smart TV is no longer just a device for passive entertainment. It's a hub of interaction, learning, and adaptation that will continue to elevate your home entertainment experience to new heights.

In summary, AI-powered televisions are a pivotal component in the landscape of smart home entertainment. They bring together the elements of personalization, convenience, interconnectivity, and efficiency. As technology continues to evolve, these smart devices will only get better, making them an indispensable addition to any modern home. So, as you venture further into your smart home journey, consider the immense potential AI-powered televisions can bring to your living space.

Smart Speakers

As the heartbeat of modern smart home entertainment systems, smart speakers have carved out an essential niche in our living spaces. These compact yet powerful devices not only stream music and podcasts but also serve as versatile hubs for home automation. With their built-in voice assistants, smart speakers facilitate hands-free control of a variety of smart home devices, ranging from lighting to security systems.

The sheer convenience offered by smart speakers cannot be overstated. Imagine walking into your home with arms full of groceries and being able to turn on the lights or play your favorite playlist using just your voice. Whether you're looking to control your thermostat, check the weather, or even get the latest news updates, smart speakers make everyday tasks more seamless and accessible. It's no wonder they have become a cornerstone of smart home setups.

Smart speakers have evolved significantly since their inception. The earliest models were often limited to basic voice commands and music playback. Today's smart speakers, however, boast advanced features like high-fidelity audio, multi-room playback, and even artificial intelligence-powered recommendations. These enhancements transform them from mere gadgets into essential components of the connected home.

One of the standout features of modern smart speakers is their ability to integrate with various streaming services. Whether you prefer Spotify, Apple Music, Amazon Music, or another service, smart speakers can effortlessly stream music from your preferred platform. They can even learn your musical tastes over time, offering personalized recommendations that enhance your listening experience. By syncing with other smart devices, smart speakers can adjust the lighting or thermostat to match the mood of your current playlist, providing an immersive experience.

Beyond entertainment, smart speakers play a pivotal role in home automation. With voice assistants like Alexa, Google Assistant, and Siri at their core, these devices act as central hubs for controlling a myriad of smart devices. For instance, you can create routines that combine multiple actions into a single command. Saying "Good Morning" could trigger a series of events, such as turning on the lights, starting the coffee maker, and reading out your daily schedule. This level of integration simplifies daily tasks, making your home feel more responsive and personalized.

It's not just about convenience and entertainment. Smart speakers also contribute to home security. They can be integrated with smart cameras, doorbells, and security systems to monitor your home more effectively. If an unusual sound or motion is detected, your smart speaker can alert you in real-time, allowing you to take immediate action. Some models even include features like intercom systems, enabling communication between different rooms in the house.

In terms of design, smart speakers have come a long way. They are now available in various shapes, sizes, and finishes to blend seamlessly with your home décor. From sleek, minimalist designs to more elaborate options that double as decorative pieces, there's a smart speaker to suit every aesthetic preference. This ensures that they can be placed in any room without disrupting the visual harmony of your home.

Moreover, smart speakers are becoming more inclusive and adaptive. They can be crucial for individuals with mobility impairments or those who benefit from voice-controlled interfaces. By enabling hands-free operation of various household functions, smart speakers can significantly enhance the quality of life for people with disabilities. This aspect of smart technology showcases its potential to contribute positively to an inclusive and accessible living environment.

Technological advancements in natural language processing and artificial intelligence have also improved the responsiveness and accuracy of voice assistants within smart speakers. The ability to understand context, follow multi-step commands, and even recognize individual voices makes these devices incredibly user-friendly. For instance, a smart speaker can distinguish between family members and provide personalized responses, ensuring that each user gets a tailored experience.

When it comes to connectivity, the best smart speakers support multiple communication protocols, including Wi-Fi, Bluetooth, and even Zigbee. This versatility allows them to connect effortlessly with a wide array of smart devices, from smart plugs and switches to home entertainment systems. The integration capabilities of smart speakers are continuously expanding, driven by ongoing updates and improvements from manufacturers.

However, it's crucial to consider privacy and security when incorporating smart speakers into your home. Since these devices are always listening for their wake word, it's important to manage your privacy settings and be aware of how your data is being used. Leading manufacturers provide clear options for reviewing and deleting voice recordings, giving you control over your personal information. Securing your home network with strong passwords and regular updates further ensures that your smart speaker remains a safe and reliable companion in your smart home ecosystem.

Looking ahead, the future of smart speakers promises even more exciting developments. Advances in machine learning and AI will likely lead to even smarter, more intuitive devices that can anticipate your needs based on your habits and preferences. Seamless integration with emerging technologies like augmented reality and enhanced home automation platforms will further solidify their role as indispensable components of smart home entertainment systems.

In summary, smart speakers are not just gadgets; they are integral to the modern smart home. Their ability to provide rich entertainment experiences, facilitate home automation, enhance security, and offer customization makes them invaluable tools for creating a connected, efficient, and secure living space. As technology progresses, the capabilities and applications of smart speakers will continue to expand, offering even greater value and utility to smart home enthusiasts.

As you've seen, integrating smart speakers into your home can dramatically transform how you interact with your living space. They epitomize the blend of convenience, functionality, and innovation that lies at the heart of smart home technology. With the right setup, smart speakers can make your home not just smarter but truly intelligent, responsive, and uniquely tailored to your lifestyle.

Streaming Devices

When it comes to elevating your smart home entertainment experience, streaming devices are indispensable. These compact yet powerful gadgets have redefined how we consume media, offering unprecedented convenience and customization. At their core, streaming devices allow you to access a plethora of content from various online platforms, directly on your smart TV or monitor.

One of the biggest advantages of integrating streaming devices into your smart home setup is the breadth of content available. From movies and TV shows to live sports and music, the variety is staggering. Leading devices, like Roku, Amazon Fire Stick, Apple TV, and Google Chromecast, offer extensive libraries of apps and channels, catering to all interests and preferences.

But it's not just about quantity. The user experience offered by modern streaming devices is remarkable, thanks to their advanced user interfaces and AI-powered recommendations. Based on your viewing history, these devices can suggest new content you're likely to enjoy. As you continue to use them, the recommendations become more fine-tuned, evolving in tandem with your tastes.

Let's delve into how these streaming devices work. Most require an HDMI connection to your TV and access to a Wi-Fi network. Once connected, setting up involves linking the device to your various streaming service accounts. Many devices also offer voice control functionality, allowing you to navigate through commands like "play next episode" or "find comedy movies."

For those looking to create a seamless smart home ecosystem, the interoperability of streaming devices with other smart home gadgets is a massive plus. Whether it's dimming the lights via voice command while watching a movie or automating your TV to turn off when you leave the room, the collaborative potential is tremendous. Google Chromecast integrates well with Google Home devices, while Apple TV works seamlessly with HomeKit. Amazon Fire Stick, naturally, pairs efficiently with Alexa.

Voice control is taking center stage in streaming device technology. Voice assistants like Alexa, Google Assistant, and Siri are embedded into these devices, giving you an added layer of convenience. Imagine saying, "Alexa, play the latest episode of my favorite show," and having it start without lifting a finger. It's not just a novelty; it significantly enhances accessibility and ease of use.

Beyond basic streaming, many of these devices offer additional features like gaming and smart home controls. Apple TV, for instance, allows you to download various games and use compatible controllers to play. Amazon Fire Stick gives you access to thousands of Alexa skills, enabling you to control smart home devices, check the weather, or even hear a joke while you watch TV. Google Chromecast offers casting capabilities, allowing you to mirror your smartphone, tablet, or computer screen onto your TV, expanding the functionality considerably.

The technological backbone of these streaming devices is impressive. They support high-definition resolutions, often up to 4K, and boast high dynamic range (HDR) imaging, ensuring that your viewing experience is vibrant and crystal clear. Additionally, most devices support Dolby Atmos and Dolby Vision, providing an immersive audio-visual experience akin to a mini home theater setup.

Even though these devices are designed for simplicity, it's worth noting the differences in user interfaces and the platforms they support. Roku stands out for its simple, grid-based interface and vast platform-agnostic library. Apple TV's interface is sleek and integrates effortlessly into the Apple ecosystem. Amazon Fire Stick's interface revolves around emphasizing Amazon Prime content, although it supports numerous other platforms. Google Chromecast tends to focus on casting media from other devices and integrates strongly with Google services.

Given their capabilities, choosing the right streaming device can hinge on several factors. First, consider the ecosystem you're already part of. If you use Alexa for smart home control, an Amazon Fire Stick might be a better fit. Conversely, if you're deeply entrenched in Apple products, Apple TV would offer unparalleled synergy. Likewise, Google enthusiasts might find Chromecast more appealing.

Additionally, assess the device's compatibility with your current technology. Factors like 4K support, HDR compatibility, and available ports can affect your choice, especially if you have a high-end TV and sound system. It's essential to ensure your chosen streaming device can maximize your existing setup's potential.

Security and privacy are also critical considerations. Streaming devices, like all connected gadgets, can be vulnerable to breaches if not properly secured. Regular software updates, secure passwords, and setting up a secure Wi-Fi network are essential measures to protect your digital sanctuary. Devices often offer parental controls, ensuring that your children can enjoy a safe viewing experience, free from inappropriate content.

It's not just about individual device capabilities. The transformative power of streaming devices lies in their integration within your broader smart home infrastructure. Picture a scenario where your lights dim, your thermostat sets to a cozy temperature, and your TV starts playing your favorite movie—all through a single command. This scenario is not just futuristic but entirely feasible with a well-integrated setup.

On the horizon, the evolution of streaming devices shows no signs of slowing. Advances like 8K resolution, deeper AI integration for even more personalized experiences, and enhanced interactivity through augmented and virtual reality are just the beginning. As technology progresses, these devices will continue to expand their roles, becoming even more integral to the smart home ecosystem.

Streaming devices are an essential cog in the wheel of smart home entertainment. By merging advanced technology with user-friendly design, they offer a seamless, immersive, and customizable media consumption experience. As you explore which device best fits your lifestyle, consider how they interact with your broader smart home setup to create a harmonious, high-tech living environment that caters specifically to your preferences and needs.

CHAPTER 9:
KITCHEN AUTOMATION

Stepping into the world of kitchen automation is like opening a door to unparalleled efficiency and convenience, powered by artificial intelligence. Imagine a refrigerator that not only keeps your groceries fresh but also tracks their expiration dates, sending alerts when it's time to replenish. Smart ovens now come with recipe databases that can automatically adjust cooking times and temperatures based on what you're preparing. For those who juggle busy schedules, automated cooking assistants can take over meal prep, following your favorite recipes to the tee. Inventory management becomes a breeze as AI systems monitor your pantry and create shopping lists tailored to your dietary preferences and cooking habits. By integrating these advanced technologies into our kitchens, we aren't just creating a smarter home; we're laying the groundwork for healthier, more efficient living spaces that adapt to our daily needs and routines.

Smart Appliances

In the modern quest for a seamlessly automated kitchen, smart appliances are the linchpins that hold everything together. These devices transcend traditional functionality, offering features that cater to both efficiency and convenience. They work synergistically with the broader smart home ecosystem, connecting through hubs and voice assistants to streamline everything from meal preparation to cleaning. The profound impact of smart appliances in kitchen automation goes beyond mere gadgetry; it's about enhancing a lifestyle, promoting sustainability, and making everyday activities as frictionless as possible.

At the core of kitchen automation, smart refrigerators are worth their weight in gold. Imagine a fridge that not only stores your food but also keeps track of your inventory, suggests recipes based on available ingredients, and even orders groceries for you when supplies run low. Equipped with internal cameras, these next-generation refrigerators allow you to peek inside your fridge while you're grocery shopping, ensuring you never miss an essential ingredient again. Integrating this with AI algorithms, the refrigerator can even learn your consumption habits over time, optimizing energy use and reducing waste.

Ovens and stovetops have also evolved significantly with the advent of smart technology. Modern smart ovens can be preheated remotely via a smartphone app, have precise temperature controls, and feature multiple cooking modes to ensure your meals are cooked to perfection every time. Some models include a built-in AI-powered cooking assistant that can guide you through recipes step by step, employing sensors to adjust cooking times and temperatures for optimal results. Smart stovetops, on the other hand, can automatically turn off when they sense overheating or are left unattended for too long, providing an additional layer of safety in your kitchen.

Another standout in the realm of kitchen automation is the smart dishwasher. These appliances come with sensors that detect how dirty the dishes are and adjust the water pressure and temperature accordingly. Advanced models can be controlled via smartphone apps, allowing you to schedule wash cycles at your convenience. Additionally, many smart dishwashers are designed to work efficiently with minimal water and energy, contributing to a more sustainable household.

Moving on to smaller but equally impactful devices, smart coffee makers and toasters have brought a new level of customization and ease to our mornings. A smart coffee maker can grind beans to your preferred coarseness, brew coffee at your desired strength, and even have your morning cup ready and waiting when you wake up. Some models are compatible with voice assistants, so you can start brewing with a simple voice command. Smart toasters, similarly, can remember your preferred browning settings, ensuring your toast is just the way you like it every time. These devices often come with a range of preset modes for different types of bread, bagels, or pastries.

Blending traditional kitchen tools with modern technology, smart scales, and mixers offer precise measurements and hands-free operation, making them invaluable for anyone who loves baking. Smart scales can sync with recipe apps to provide accurate ingredient measurements and adjust quantities based on the number of servings you need. They take the guesswork out of baking, leading to more consistent and delicious results. Smart mixers, on the other hand, often include preset programs for different tasks like kneading dough or whipping cream, making these repetitive tasks simpler and faster.

Beyond individual smart appliances, the integration of these devices creates a cohesive and highly efficient environment. For instance, you could set up a cooking routine where your oven preheats while your smart coffee maker brews your coffee, saving you precious minutes during your morning rush. Home automation platforms enable these devices to communicate with each other, creating scenarios where the smart refrigerator signals the dishwasher to start its cycle after dinner, orchestrating a well-timed, harmonious workflow.

These transformative technologies are particularly beneficial for those with busy lifestyles, but they also present opportunities for fostering more inclusive and accessible homes. For example, senior citizens or individuals with disabilities might find that smart appliances significantly enhance their autonomy. Voice-controlled functionality and automation can minimize the physical effort required for daily tasks, allowing people to maintain their independence while ensuring their safety.

Moreover, the data analytics capabilities provided by smart appliances can offer actionable insights that drive better decisions. For instance, analyzing consumption patterns from your smart refrigerator can guide you in reducing food waste and managing your grocery budget more effectively. Smart ovens can offer health-centric suggestions based on your dietary preferences, helping you to achieve your well-being goals without compromising on taste.

It's also essential to mention that as more people adopt these technologies, the ecosystem of compatible appliances continues to expand. This broadening scope makes it easier to find devices that fit your specific needs and preferences. As these technologies become more widespread, economies of scale will likely drive prices down, making smart kitchen appliances more accessible to the average consumer.

However, it's not enough for an appliance to be smart; it must also be secure. With the convenience of connectivity comes the risk of potential security vulnerabilities. Ensuring that your smart kitchen appliances have robust security features is paramount. This includes using strong, unique passwords for device access, keeping firmware updated, and regularly monitoring for any suspicious activity. Manufacturers are continually improving security protocols, but staying informed and proactive is crucial for protecting your smart home environment.

The future of smart kitchen appliances also holds promise for even deeper integration and innovation. We're starting to see advancements in AI that allow appliances to interact more naturally with users. Soon, you might have a kitchen assistant capable of holding a conversation, offering cooking tips, nutritional advice, and even mood-based meal recommendations. With the integration of machine learning, your kitchen appliances will not just be reactive but predictive, adapting to your behaviors and anticipatory needs.

In essence, incorporating smart appliances into your kitchen isn't just about adopting the latest trends; it's about building a space that enhances your quality of life and aligns with your evolving needs. These devices bridge the gap between routine kitchen tasks and a truly connected home environment, paving the way for a future where every meal is a little easier, every chore a bit simpler, and every day a lot more delightful.

Automated Cooking Assistants

The kitchen has long been considered the heart of the home. Yet, it is also a space that can benefit immensely from the advancements in artificial intelligence and automation. One fascinating aspect of kitchen automation is the advent of automated cooking assistants. These assistive technologies are transforming the traditional cooking experience into something quicker, more efficient, and even more enjoyable.

Imagine coming home after a long day, craving a nutritious meal but feeling too exhausted to cook. Here is where an automated cooking assistant steps in. This system can plan meals, handle ingredient preparation, and guide you through the cooking process. Some advanced models can even cook the meal for you, alleviating the need to stand over a hot stove for hours. These assistants make use of intricate machine learning algorithms to predict your culinary preferences, thereby providing a highly personalized cooking experience.

Automated cooking assistants come in many forms, from countertop devices to complex integrated systems. Countertop appliances like the Instant Pot or Thermomix have built-in cooking programs that allow you to set it and forget it. Simply add the ingredients, select a recipe, and let the machine do the work. More integrated systems, such as those from companies like Moley Robotics, take automation a step further. They encompass robotic arms capable of emulating the movements of a skilled chef, thus providing an entire cooking solution from start to finish.

The backbone of these smart cooking systems is often a combination of sophisticated cameras, sensors, and artificial intelligence algorithms. Cameras and sensors help to accurately measure ingredients and monitor the cooking process, ensuring that everything is prepared to perfection. AI, on the other hand, helps in recipe selection and customization, taking into account dietary restrictions, ingredient availability, and personal taste preferences. These are not just pie-in-the-sky features but tangible advancements that are already making their way into many modern homes.

For those interested in integrating these technologies, it's essential to understand the setup required. Most automated cooking assistants are part of a broader ecosystem of smart kitchen appliances. Therefore, they work best when integrated with other smart devices such as intelligent fridges, ovens, and even voice assistants. This entire ecosystem can be controlled via a central hub or an app, allowing for seamless interaction between different devices. Imagine saying, "Alexa, I'm craving spaghetti carbonara," and having your voice assistant coordinate the oven, fridge, and the smart pan to create that dish while you relax.

Aside from convenience, automated cooking assistants significantly aid in meal planning and ingredient management. Many of these systems include features that can scan your pantry and fridge to track ingredient levels. Advanced AI can suggest recipes based on the ingredients you have on hand, reducing food waste and the need for last-minute grocery runs. Moreover, nutritional information is often readily available, making it easier to maintain a balanced diet.

The dietary and health benefits can't be overstated. These systems often come with built-in nutritional analytics, providing real-time feedback on the nutritional content of meals. This is particularly useful for individuals managing specific health conditions, such as diabetes or hypertension. Automated cooking assistants can tailor recipes to meet dietary requirements, ensuring that both taste and health are given priority.

In the context of families, especially those with children, automated cooking assistants can be a godsend. They help in introducing children to the process of cooking in a supervised, safe manner. With guided tutorials and automated steps, parents can engage their kids in culinary activities without worrying about typical kitchen hazards. Moreover, parents can be assured that nutritional guidelines are being followed thanks to the AI's smart recommendations.

Furthermore, one must consider the potential for advanced customization. Future iterations of automated cooking assistants are likely to incorporate more granular personalization. Through machine learning, these systems could understand and predict changes in your dietary preferences over time, thereby evolving with you. Whether you decide to go vegan or explore a keto diet, your assistant will be able to adapt and provide relevant recommendations seamlessly.

Integration with smart home networks also ensures that these devices are up-to-date with the latest software and recipes. Connectivity through Wi-Fi or even newer protocols like Zigbee and Z-Wave ensures that your cooking assistant can fetch the latest updates, download new recipes, and even troubleshoot issues remotely. The concept extends beyond mere cooking; it's about creating an all-encompassing culinary ecosystem that evolves with technology.

Let's not forget the emotional and psychological benefits. The convenience afforded by these systems often translates to reduced stress and more family time. With an automated cooking assistant handling the meal prep, you have more freedom to engage in meaningful activities with loved ones. The kitchen transforms from a place of labor to one of leisure and interaction. Imagine a Sunday evening where you're not bogged down with cooking, but instead, enjoying quality time while a smart assistant prepares a delicious meal.

Though the initial investment in automated cooking assistants and their associated ecosystem may seem steep, the long-term benefits often outweigh the cost. Reduced food waste, improved health, saved time, and enhanced family experiences bring substantial value. Also, many of these devices are designed to last years, ensuring that you get the most out of your investment.

In conclusion, automated cooking assistants are rapidly becoming an integral part of modern kitchen automation. They offer immense benefits ranging from convenience and efficiency to health and peace of mind. By integrating these systems into your home, you're not only embracing cutting-edge technology, but also creating a smarter, more connected living space that enhances your quality of life.

Inventory Management

Imagine reaching for a box of spaghetti only to realize you're out. An automated kitchen using AI obliterates these inconveniences by revolutionizing inventory management. This isn't just about avoiding last-minute grocery runs; it's about transforming the way we interact with food, possibly even reducing food waste along the way. Inventory management in a smart kitchen integrates various technologies to keep track of what you have, what you need, and what's about to expire.

To truly understand the benefits, it's essential to start with the basics: smart fridges, pantries, and cabinets. Modern smart fridges can scan barcodes of items as they're placed inside and suggest recipes based on current contents. These appliances often feature internal cameras, so you can view what's inside without opening the door—and they update your inventory when items are removed.

But smart fridges are just the beginning. Automated pantries and smart cabinets use similar technology to keep track of what's inside. Sensors can weigh items to determine how much is left. Some systems can even link with online grocery stores to reorder items automatically when you're running low. This level of automation ensures that you're always in sync with your kitchen's inventory, making meal planning and cooking much simpler.

Different AI algorithms can analyze your consumption patterns over time to anticipate which items you'll need and when. For instance, if the system learns you bake frequently, it might alert you when you're running low on flour and sugar, or suggest a sale on chocolate chips. This predictive capability saves time and ensures that your kitchen is always prepared for any culinary adventure.

Effective inventory management also involves strategizing around expiration dates to minimize food waste. Smart kitchen systems can keep track of when items were purchased and provide reminders before they spoil. This could revolutionize your meal planning, encouraging you to use items that are nearing their expiration date sooner. It's a small change with a potentially large impact on reducing household food waste.

The beauty of automated inventory management is that it also integrates seamlessly with other smart kitchen solutions. For instance, automated cooking assistants could offer recipe suggestions based on available ingredients, adjusting portion sizes according to what's left. Smart appliances like ovens or mixers could then pre-program settings for those recipes, creating a fully integrated and efficient cooking experience.

Don't overlook the role of mobile apps in this ecosystem. Many smart kitchen appliances come with companion apps that make inventory management accessible even when you're not at home. You could be at the grocery store and check your app to see if you need eggs or milk. Many apps also allow you to scan items as you purchase them, keeping your inventory perpetually updated.

Moreover, AI-powered analytics go a step further by offering insights into your shopping habits and consumption patterns. Over time, these systems can advise you on more cost-effective or sustainable choices. They could suggest buying in bulk for items you use frequently or choosing seasonal produce to save money and support local agriculture.

For those concerned about privacy, it's crucial to know that most smart kitchen systems now include robust security features to protect your data. Data is generally encrypted, and users have controls to manage their privacy settings, ensuring that their personal habits and preferences remain secure.

The integration of smart home assistants like Amazon's Alexa or Google Assistant adds another layer of convenience. You can manage your kitchen inventory using simple voice commands, asking for updates or instructing the system to add or remove items. This hands-free management is particularly useful when you're in the middle of cooking or have your hands full.

This is not just a futuristic vision; many households have already begun incorporating these technologies with great success. While upfront costs and the complexity of smart appliances can be a barrier, the long-term benefits in terms of efficiency, convenience, and reduced waste make a compelling case for adopting smart kitchen inventory management systems.

Transitioning your kitchen to a smart, automated inventory system involves several steps. Start small by integrating one or two smart devices, such as a smart fridge or pantry. Over time, as you become more comfortable, you can add additional layers of automation, perhaps linking your appliances and integrating with voice assistants. This phased approach helps manage costs and allows for gradual adjustment to the new system.

Ultimately, smart kitchen inventory management embodies the perfect blend of convenience and innovation. It leverages technology to streamline your daily routines, ensuring that your kitchen always operates at peak efficiency. Whether you're an avid cook, a busy professional, or someone looking to make more sustainable choices, automated inventory management could be the key to a smarter, more efficient, and more enjoyable kitchen experience.

Chapter 10:
Health and Wellness

Integrating artificial intelligence into health and wellness within the smart home ecosystem isn't just about convenience—it's a transformative approach to living better and longer. AI-powered wearables can monitor your vitals in real time, providing insights and alerts that may prevent potential health issues before they escalate. Smart health devices like connected scales, blood pressure monitors, and even glucose sensors offer seamless data synchronization, helping you keep track of your health metrics with ease. When this data is integrated within your smart home, it allows for a holistic view of your well-being, enabling personalized adjustments to your daily routine, such as modifying lighting to improve sleep or altering thermostat settings to optimize your comfort. This chapter delves into the ways AI can create a more proactive, health-centric environment, empowering you to make informed decisions and ultimately enhancing your overall quality of life.

AI in Wearables

As we delve into the realm of health and wellness, we can't overlook the growing influence of AI in wearables. These are not merely accessories but sophisticated monitoring devices that bridge the gap between casual fitness tracking and professional health management. Seamlessly integrated into various forms like smartwatches, fitness bands, and even smart clothing, AI wearables have become an integral part of our daily lives.

The capabilities of AI in wearables extend beyond counting steps or tracking sleep. Advanced algorithms analyze a plethora of data points to provide comprehensive health insights. Imagine a smartwatch alerting you to abnormal heart rate variations, or suggesting a change in your exercise routine based on fatigue levels detected by measuring heart rate variability (HRV). These insights can preemptively identify potential health issues, allowing timely interventions and, consequently, better health outcomes.

One of the most compelling features of AI in wearables is their ability to offer personalized recommendations. No two individuals are the same, and therefore, generic advice often falls short. AI wearables adapt to your unique biometrics, lifestyle habits, and fitness levels to create customized wellness plans. These devices learn from your patterns over time, continually refining their recommendations. Whether it's suggesting an optimal time for a workout or reminding you to stay hydrated, the advice is always tailored to you.

Beyond fitness and wellness, AI wearables play a crucial role in medical applications. Continuous glucose monitors (CGMs) equipped with AI can assist diabetics in better managing their blood sugar levels by predicting trends and suggesting insulin doses. These devices employ complex machine learning algorithms to analyze blood glucose data against factors like food intake, physical activity, and stress levels, providing a far more comprehensive overview than traditional methods.

Even mental health isn't beyond the reach of AI wearables. Devices can monitor psychological markers like stress and anxiety through physiological signs, such as changes in skin conductivity (electrodermal activity) or irregular breathing patterns. Over time, AI can recognize patterns and anticipate potential mental health triggers, offering coping strategies or recommending mindfulness exercises. This proactive approach can significantly improve mental well-being by addressing issues before they escalate.

One transformative innovation in AI wearables is their role in managing chronic diseases. These devices are capable of continuous monitoring, making them invaluable for individuals with conditions like hypertension, asthma, or cardiac disorders. AI algorithms can detect anomalies in real-time and send immediate alerts to both the user and healthcare providers. This continuous monitoring can lead to early diagnosis and more effective treatment plans, significantly improving the quality of life for people with chronic ailments.

The advent of AI in wearables has led to a surge in the collection and analysis of health data. While this data is a goldmine for personalized health insights, it also raises questions about privacy and security. Manufacturers are increasingly focusing on creating robust data protection protocols, ensuring that sensitive health information remains secure. Encryption, secure networks, and compliance with healthcare privacy regulations are fundamental in fostering trust among users.

Incorporation of AI in wearables also enhances user engagement. These devices often include gamified elements, such as setting daily activity goals, rewarding achievements, or competing with friends, which encourage consistent use. By integrating social features and interactive challenges, wearables make the journey towards health and wellness more engaging and enjoyable.

AI wearables also shine in the context of emergency situations. Fall detection algorithms in smartwatches can identify when a user has fallen and cannot get up, prompting the device to send a help alert to emergency contacts. Similarly, advanced smart clothing can monitor vital signs and automatically notify medical professionals in case of significant anomalies. These features are particularly beneficial for elderly individuals or those living alone, offering peace of mind to both the users and their loved ones.

Interoperability is another cornerstone of AI in wearables. These devices do not function in isolation but can sync with other smart home systems to create a comprehensive ecosystem for health and wellness. For instance, data from a wearable can integrate with a smart home hub to adjust ambient settings like lighting or temperature, creating an optimal environment for sleep or relaxation. This holistic approach ensures all elements of home and health are in harmony.

The development and evolution of AI wearables are closely linked to advancements in sensor technology. As sensors become more accurate and less intrusive, the capability of wearables to provide real-time, actionable health insights improves exponentially. Companies are continually innovating, incorporating nanotechnology and smart fabrics to ensure that future wearables are more comfortable, accurate, and versatile.

It's clear that AI in wearables represents a significant leap towards a more connected, efficient, and healthier lifestyle. The fusion of AI with wearable tech doesn't just augment our day-to-day activities but makes proactive health management a seamless part of our lives. With continuous advancements in AI algorithms and sensor technology, the future of wellness looks more promising than ever.

In summary, AI wearables are revolutionizing the landscape of personal health and wellness. From fitness tracking and chronic disease management to mental health monitoring and emergency response, these devices offer unmatched levels of convenience and insight. As we move forward, the integration of AI in wearables will only deepen, providing us with smarter, more intuitive tools to manage our health. It's an exciting time to embrace this technology, not just for its novelty, but for its profound potential to transform how we live and care for ourselves.

Smart Health Devices

In the rapidly evolving landscape of health and wellness, smart health devices are transforming our living spaces into hubs of personalized care. These gadgets, equipped with cutting-edge AI technology, offer unprecedented insights into our physical well-being. They help us monitor health metrics continuously, predict potential health issues before they escalate, and even suggest activities to improve our health. For anyone interested in integrating AI into their homes, smart health devices are an essential component of a connected, efficient, and secure living environment.

One of the most popular examples of smart health devices is the smart scale. Unlike traditional scales, these advanced versions do more than just measure weight. They often come with features such as body composition analysis, measuring metrics like body fat percentage, muscle mass, and bone density. Some even offer multi-user functionality, recognizing different family members and customizing their health insights accordingly. By tracking these metrics over time, users can gain a nuanced understanding of their body's changes and adjust their lifestyles accordingly.

Smart blood pressure monitors are another valuable addition to modern homes. These devices not only measure blood pressure but often sync with mobile apps to log readings and monitor trends. Many of them send alerts if readings fall outside of the normal range, prompting timely medical consultations. This proactive approach to managing cardiovascular health can make a significant difference, particularly for those with chronic conditions.

Wearables, such as smartwatches, are perhaps the most ubiquitous smart health devices. These gadgets have come a long way from simple pedometers. Today's wearables can track heart rate, monitor sleep patterns, count steps, and even measure oxygen levels in the blood. Advanced models come with ECG capabilities and fall detection features, offering an added layer of security for the elderly or those with pre-existing conditions. These devices also integrate seamlessly with other smart home systems, enabling a holistic approach to health management.

For those focused on respiratory health, smart air purifiers equipped with AI bring a breath of fresh air. These devices not only filter out pollutants but also analyze air quality in real-time, adjusting their settings to ensure optimal air purity. Some models can even sync with personal health data, adjusting their performance based on individual needs, such as asthma or allergies. By maintaining a cleaner home environment, these purifiers can significantly improve respiratory health and overall well-being.

Nutritional health is another area where smart devices shine. Smart kitchen scales, for instance, can weigh food with precision and provide nutritional information through integrated apps. They can suggest recipes based on available ingredients and dietary preferences. Additionally, smart fridges keep track of food inventory and expiration dates, reducing food waste and helping users adhere to their dietary plans. These devices promote healthier eating habits by making nutritional information readily accessible.

Sleep is a critical component of health, and smart sleep devices aim to optimize it. Smart mattresses, for example, can adjust their firmness based on the user's sleep position and provide gentle adjustments to reduce snoring. Sleep trackers placed under the mattress measure sleep quality, including metrics like REM cycles and restlessness. This data can be invaluable for understanding and improving sleep patterns, contributing to better overall health.

Smart robots and AI-driven companions are emerging as compassionate caretakers in our homes. These devices are particularly useful for elderly individuals or those with limited mobility. They can remind users to take their medications, assist with daily tasks, and even provide companionship. Some advanced models feature AI algorithms that can detect unusual behavior or potential health issues, ensuring timely intervention. The sense of security and comfort these devices bring can be life-changing.

Mental health is also gaining attention in the realm of smart health devices. AI-enabled apps and devices now offer mindfulness and meditation sessions tailored to individual stress levels and emotional states. Some wearables can detect stress through heart rate variability and send prompts to take a break or engage in calming activities. These interventions can help users manage stress better and maintain mental well-being.

The integration of smart health devices extends to family health management. Family health tracking systems can compile data from multiple devices, giving a comprehensive picture of the household's well-being. Parents can monitor their children's activities, sleep patterns, and even screen time, ensuring a balanced lifestyle. Such systems foster a proactive approach to health, making it easier to maintain a healthy and harmonious household.

However, the adoption of smart health devices is not without challenges. Data privacy is a major concern; users need to ensure their health data is securely stored and shared only with trusted entities. It is crucial to use devices from reputable manufacturers with strong privacy policies. Regular firmware updates and secure connections are also essential to safeguard personal health information.

The benefits of smart health devices are undeniable. They offer real-time health insights, enable proactive health management, and foster a healthier living environment. By incorporating AI into our daily lives, these devices make it easier to stay on top of our health and well-being. As technology continues to advance, the potential for even more innovative and personalized health solutions is immense.

Integrating smart health devices into your home doesn't have to be overwhelming. Start with devices that address your immediate health needs and gradually expand your smart health ecosystem. With each new addition, you'll find that managing your health becomes more streamlined and effective.

Ultimately, the goal of smart health devices is to empower individuals to take control of their health. By providing timely, accurate information and actionable insights, these devices enhance our ability to make informed health decisions. They bridge the gap between traditional healthcare and modern technology, creating a harmonious blend that supports our overall well-being.

Incorporating smart health devices into your home is a step towards a more connected, efficient, and healthier lifestyle. Embrace the potential of AI-driven health solutions, and experience the transformative impact on your daily life. The future of health and wellness is smart, and it's time to make your home a part of this exciting journey.

Integrating Health Data

In the age of smart homes, the integration of health data stands as one of the most impactful applications of artificial intelligence (AI). Where once our homes were merely places of refuge, they are becoming hubs for generating and analyzing real-time health information that can significantly improve our quality of life. This transformation allows for continuous health monitoring, early detection of potential issues, and more personalized healthcare experiences. The blending of health data with home automation technologies not only supports a more proactive approach to health management but also fosters a level of convenience and precision previously unattainable.

At the heart of integrating health data within a smart home ecosystem are wearables and smart health devices. These innovations can track a multitude of metrics including heart rate, blood pressure, glucose levels, sleep patterns, and physical activity. Devices like smartwatches and fitness trackers serve as continuous monitors, seamlessly syncing with home hubs and specialized healthcare platforms. The collected data can provide insights into daily routines, uncover patterns, and help set personalized health goals. Such detailed, granular data is invaluable for both users and healthcare providers.

Think about a scenario where your smartwatch alerts you that it has detected irregular heart rhythms in the past week. This information is automatically shared with your healthcare provider, who can then advise on preventive measures or schedule a check-up. It's like having a personal health assistant that never sleeps, ensuring continuous monitoring and timely interventions. Furthermore, smart scales and blood pressure monitors can contribute to this ecosystem, providing key health metrics that are essential for a comprehensive view of one's health.

Data integration becomes particularly powerful when combined with AI's predictive capabilities. For example, machine learning algorithms can analyze historical health data to predict potential issues before they become critical. Suppose an AI system recognizes a pattern of elevated stress levels, poor sleep quality, and irregular exercise routines. In that case, it might recommend adjustments in lifestyle or even alert a healthcare provider to preempt more serious conditions. The potential for AI-powered predictive analytics to improve health outcomes is immense, allowing individuals to take preventive steps well in advance.

However, the integration of health data isn't without its challenges. Privacy and security remain significant concerns. Health data is sensitive and personal, and breaches can have severe repercussions. Therefore, any smart home system dealing with health data must adhere to strict privacy laws and undergo rigorous security measures. End-to-end encryption, secure authentication protocols, and regular updates are essential. Moreover, users should have full control over who can access their health data, ensuring transparency and trust.

To instill confidence, smart home systems must comply with established standards like HIPAA (Health Insurance Portability and Accountability Act) in the United States. Compliance ensures that health data management practices meet legal requirements for protecting sensitive information. Furthermore, educating users about how their data is stored, processed, and shared can significantly enhance trust and adoption of these technologies. Transparency in data practices is not just a regulatory requirement but a cornerstone of a trustworthy system.

Interoperability is another crucial aspect of integrating health data. A smart home consists of a myriad of devices from different manufacturers, each generating valuable data. Ensuring that these devices and the data they produce can effectively communicate with each other is critical. Platforms like Apple HealthKit, Google Fit, and Samsung Health aim to provide this interoperability, acting as central repositories where diverse health data can be aggregated, analyzed, and utilized. Creating an ecosystem where data flows seamlessly between devices and platforms unlocks the full potential of a connected, health-centric smart home.

Let's delve into how integration specifically benefits different groups of individuals. For the elderly, smart home technologies paired with health data can play an essential role in making independent living safer and more feasible. Devices such as fall detectors and medication monitors can alert family members or caregivers in case of an emergency. AI can analyze patterns and recognize anomalies in daily activities, providing timely alerts for potential issues. Such systems ensure that seniors can enjoy an independent life without compromising their safety.

Parents of young children can also reap significant benefits. Smart baby monitors, wearable tags, and even smart thermometers can continuously track vital signs and environmental conditions, sending alerts if anything seems amiss. The data collected can help parents maintain optimal living conditions for their children, from ensuring they sleep in the right temperature to detecting early signs of illness. It's about creating a safer and more nurturing environment through data-driven insights.

Lastly, fitness enthusiasts and those combating chronic conditions stand to gain immensely from integrated health data. Real-time monitoring paired with AI-driven insights provide a comprehensive overview of their health, helping them optimize workout routines, dietary plans, and medication schedules. The feedback loop created by continuous data collection and AI analysis enables more personalized, effective health management. Whether it's optimizing athletic performance or managing diabetes, the integration of health data transforms intentions into actionable plans.

Despite the numerous benefits, the journey doesn't end with integrating existing health devices and data. The future holds promise for even more sophisticated health AI applications. Imagine an AI system that not only tracks your physical health but also gauges your mental well-being. Advances in AI-driven sentiment analysis can already track mood changes through interactions with home devices and biometric data. Combining such insights with traditional health metrics can give a fuller picture of your overall well-being.

Ongoing advancements in natural language processing (NLP) can further enhance how we interact with our smart homes. Voice-assisted AI could serve as a conversational health advisor, providing real-time responses and reminders based on ongoing health data. For instance, a voice assistant might remind you to take your medication, suggest a breathing exercise when it spots rising stress levels, or offer dietary advice based on your tracked nutrition. The more intuitive interactions become, the more seamlessly integrated these systems will feel in our daily lives.

As we integrate health data into our smart homes, it's essential to remain conscious of ethical considerations. Transparency, consent, and the right to forget should be foundational principles. Users should always have the ability to revoke data sharing permissions and have their data deleted. AI should be an enabler, providing tools and insights, but not crossing the line into intrusive or coercive practices.

In closing, integrating health data within a smart home ecosystem is more than just a technological advancement; it's a step towards a healthier, more proactive lifestyle. It offers incredible opportunities for enhancing how we monitor and maintain our health, providing us with real-time insights and recommendations tailored to our unique needs. Leveraging AI and health data within the comfort of our homes turns this vision into reality. As we embrace these technologies, we move closer to a future where enhanced health and well-being are not just goals but everyday experiences.

CHAPTER 11:
ENERGY MANAGEMENT

Managing energy in a smart home involves more than just flipping a switch; it's about creating a balance between convenience and efficiency. By integrating AI-powered smart plugs and switches, homeowners can monitor and control energy consumption in real-time, leading to noticeable savings on utility bills. Imagine your home intuitively adjusting lights and appliances to optimize energy usage based on your daily routines. With advanced energy monitoring tools, it's easier than ever to identify which devices are energy hogs and make informed decisions to enhance efficiency. Automation is key—AI algorithms can learn your habits and automatically adjust settings, ensuring that your home runs smoothly while reducing waste. Through intelligent energy management, not only do you contribute to a greener planet, but you also create a more economically efficient living environment.

Smart Plugs and Switches

For those on a mission to enhance energy management within their smart homes, the integration of smart plugs and switches offers one of the most straightforward and impactful solutions. These devices serve as conduits to convert traditional appliances and lighting into intelligent entities capable of remote control, automation, and energy monitoring. Essentially, they act as the bridge between everyday devices and the intricate network that defines a smart home.

The compelling advantage of smart plugs and switches is their simplicity of installation. Most smart plugs just need to be inserted into any standard power outlet, while smart switches replace existing wall switches with relative ease. They don't require extensive rewiring or professional installation services. Yet, despite their easy setup, these small devices can deliver substantial changes in your household's energy efficiency and convenience.

Imagine being able to turn off all unnecessary appliances with a single voice command or a tap on your smartphone. Smart plugs provide this utility by allowing for remote control over devices plugged into them. Not only does this enhance convenience, but it also serves a critical role in energy conservation. Devices left on standby can be a significant drain on energy resources, contributing to what is known as "vampire power." By using smart plugs, homeowners can cut this waste entirely by scheduling these plugs to turn off when devices are not in use.

Furthermore, smart switches can automate your lighting systems, making it possible to dim lights or even turn them on and off based on specific schedules or occupancy detection. This kind of control eliminates the ever-present worry of leaving lights on when they're not needed. And it's not just about the lights; smart switches can also integrate with other home systems to create complex automation routines, such as setting scenes that adjust lighting, climate, and entertainment systems simultaneously. For example, a "movie night" button could dim the lights, adjust the thermostat, and turn on the TV to your favorite streaming app—all through one switch.

Energy monitoring is another powerful feature of many smart plugs and switches. By providing real-time data on the electricity consumption of connected devices, homeowners gain valuable insights into their energy usage patterns. This data is typically accessible through user-friendly mobile apps, making it easy to identify high-consumption devices and take steps to reduce unnecessary energy usage. Such detailed monitoring allows users to make informed decisions, contributing to a more sustainable lifestyle without sacrificing convenience.

The integration of voice assistants further augments the utility of smart plugs and switches. Devices like Amazon Echo, Google Home, and Apple's HomePod can seamlessly connect with these systems, offering voice commands for control. The charm of telling a virtual assistant to turn off the lights or switch on the coffee maker cannot be overstated; it brings a level of convenience that was once the stuff of science fiction. This hands-free operation is particularly beneficial for people with limited mobility, making smart homes more accessible and user-friendly.

Importantly, smart plugs and switches also fit seamlessly into broader home automation systems. They can be incorporated into routines and scenes managed by central hubs, giving users the ability to craft highly personalized and efficient home environments. For instance, linking a smart switch to a smart thermostat and motion sensors can create an advanced energy management setup that adjusts in real-time based on human presence and activity levels in the home.

From a usability perspective, leading brands have focused on making their smart plugs and switches as intuitive as possible. Many devices come with straightforward apps that guide users through initial setup, allowing even those with minimal technical know-how to have their smart homes up and running in no time. The flexibility of these units means they can be controlled, monitored, and automated not just individually, but also as part of integrated systems that maximize home efficiency.

When considering security, manufacturers have built multiple layers of encryption and protection into these devices to safeguard against potential cyber threats. This builds user confidence and ensures that they can trust their smart plugs and switches not only to perform tasks effectively but also to maintain the integrity of their home networks.

The competitive market has driven innovation, leading to a plethora of options ranging from basic models with just on/off capabilities to advanced versions featuring energy monitoring and Alexa or Google Assistant compatibility. The affordability of these devices also makes them an excellent entry point for individuals new to smart home technologies, providing a low-risk, high-reward investment in home automation and energy management.

Moreover, as renewable energy sources become more integrated into residential power systems, smart plugs and switches can optimize the use of solar panels or wind turbines. Sophisticated algorithms can manage when devices draw power from renewable versus grid sources, maximizing efficiency and reducing overall energy costs. Thus, smart plugs and switches aren't just making our homes more convenient—they're playing a crucial role in the shift toward more sustainable living practices.

While the current capabilities are already impressive, the future promises even more advanced functionalities. Next-generation smart plugs and switches are likely to feature AI-driven predictive algorithms that learn from user habits, adapting their operations to further enhance efficiency and comfort. Imagine a home where the lights adjust brightness based on the time of day and natural light levels, or a switch that automatically powers down all unnecessary devices as you leave the house, adapting each day to your unique schedule.

Overall, smart plugs and switches represent a gateway to sophisticated energy management and home automation. They offer a blend of simplicity, functionality, and expansive potential that makes them indispensable in the modern smart home ecosystem. As technology continues to evolve, their role will undoubtedly expand, delivering even greater levels of convenience and efficiency to homeowners striving for a smarter and greener lifestyle.

Energy Monitoring

Energy monitoring is the cornerstone of an intelligent and efficient smart home. It enables homeowners to understand their energy consumption patterns, identify waste, and implement strategies to reduce electricity bills. In the era of climate change and rising energy costs, the importance of energy monitoring can't be overstated. This chapter delves into the technologies and practices that make energy monitoring feasible and effective in a modern smart home.

At its core, energy monitoring involves tracking the usage of electrical devices and systems within the home. This usually starts with smart meters, which are installed by utility companies but can be supplemented by a variety of smart plugs and switches that provide more granular data. These devices can measure the energy consumption of individual appliances, allowing homeowners to pinpoint exactly where their power is going.

One of the major advantages of energy monitoring is the ability to visualize data in a meaningful way. Many smart home hubs and energy monitoring platforms offer user-friendly dashboards that display real-time and historical energy usage. This data can be segmented by device, room, or time of day, offering valuable insights that can lead to smarter energy usage. For instance, spotting patterns such as a spike in power usage at certain times can help you figure out whether devices are being left on unnecessarily.

Advanced energy monitoring systems incorporate machine learning algorithms to predict future energy needs based on past behavior and external factors like weather conditions. By analyzing these patterns, the system can make recommendations or even take actions automatically to optimize energy use. For example, during a hot summer day, the system might suggest pre-cooling the house slightly before peak hours to minimize air conditioning usage when electricity rates are higher.

Integration with other smart home systems enhances the benefits of energy monitoring. When paired with smart thermostats, for instance, homeowners can not only see how much energy their heating and cooling systems consume but also adjust settings to maximize efficiency. Similarly, integrating with smart lighting solutions can provide insights into which rooms are consuming more energy and enable automatic adjustments based on occupancy.

One of the key features of modern energy monitoring solutions is their ability to send alerts and notifications. These updates can inform homeowners about unusual spikes in energy usage, potential faults in appliances, or times when they've exceeded a certain energy threshold. With this information, swift action can be taken to address any issues, avoiding unnecessary costs and potential hazards.

But energy monitoring isn't just about cutting costs; it's also about contributing to a more sustainable environment. By maximizing energy efficiency and reducing waste, homeowners can significantly lower their carbon footprint. This environmental benefit is becoming an increasingly important consideration for many people when they choose to invest in smart home technologies.

Energy monitoring also plays a crucial role in making renewable energy more viable. For homes equipped with solar panels or wind turbines, monitoring systems provide essential data on energy production and consumption. This helps homeowners understand how much of their energy needs are being met by renewable sources and optimize their usage accordingly. In some cases, excess energy can even be sold back to the grid, further offsetting costs.

Moreover, energy monitoring technologies continue to evolve, with new developments making them more accessible and affordable. Wireless energy monitors, for example, can be easily installed without the need for complex electrical work. These devices communicate with a central hub or smartphone app, providing real-time data with incredible accuracy. Battery-operated options ensure continuous monitoring even during power outages.

For households with electric vehicles (EVs), energy monitoring takes on an added layer of importance. Charging an EV can be one of the most significant electricity expenses in a home. Energy monitoring systems can schedule charging during off-peak hours, taking advantage of lower electricity rates and reducing the overall cost of vehicle ownership.

The integration of energy monitoring with home automation systems allows for automated adjustments that optimize energy use. For example, if a room's lights are left on and the space is unoccupied, the system can automatically turn them off. Similarly, it can adjust thermostatic settings when it detects that no one is home, ensuring that energy isn't wasted on climate control.

Investing in energy monitoring tools and practices provides both immediate and long-term benefits. Not only can you see a reduction in your monthly utility bills, but you can also contribute to broader environmental goals by curbing excessive energy use. Additionally, as AI and machine learning applications continue to evolve, the benefits and capabilities of energy monitoring systems will only increase, making them an essential component of any smart home.

Lastly, the journey towards a fully optimized home doesn't end with just installing these systems. Continuous engagement, tweaking settings, and utilizing the insights provided by energy monitoring platforms will help you maintain an efficient and sustainable household in the long run. By embracing these technologies and practices, you're taking a significant step toward not just a smarter home, but a smarter planet.

Automation for Efficiency

When discussing energy management within the context of a smart home, one cannot overemphasize the importance of automating processes to boost efficiency. Automation is the driving force that transforms ordinary households into intelligent, responsive environments. By implementing sophisticated algorithms and machine learning, smart homes can perform tasks autonomously, adjusting and optimizing energy use in real-time. This capability not only reduces energy waste but can lead to significant cost savings over time.

One of the primary benefits of automation is the ability to set predefined conditions that trigger specific actions. For instance, consider a home where the lights turn off automatically when no movement is detected for a certain period. This simple yet powerful automation can lead to substantial energy savings. Similarly, smart thermostats can be programmed to adjust heating or cooling based on occupancy patterns detected through motion sensors or even the GPS location of the residents' smartphones.

Now, imagine a home where every device communicates seamlessly. This communication enables your smart hub to aggregate data and make more informed decisions about energy consumption. For example, a well-integrated smart home can lower the thermostat if the system predicts that everyone will be out for the next several hours. These cutting-edge algorithms are always learning from user behavior, making your household increasingly efficient over time.

Furthermore, automation allows for granular control of energy usage. Instead of having a single switch for all lights in a room, smart lighting solutions let you control individual bulbs. This level of precision means that you can light specific areas without wasting energy on unnecessary spaces. Automation can even go a step further by adjusting brightness levels based on natural light availability, reducing the need for artificial lighting during the daytime.

Consider also the automation of large appliances, such as washing machines, dishwashers, and ovens. These devices can be scheduled to run during off-peak hours when energy costs are typically lower. Smart meters play a crucial role here by monitoring real-time energy consumption and providing feedback to optimize usage. For example, based on electricity rates, the system might decide to postpone a load of laundry until the price drops.

Another exciting aspect of automation is its integration with renewable energy sources like solar panels. Smart homes equipped with solar energy systems can intelligently control when to draw power from the grid or when to utilize stored solar energy. This capability ensures that renewable energy is used efficiently and that supply aligns with demand. By automating this process, homeowners can also contribute to broader energy grid stability, helping to prevent blackouts and reduce carbon footprints.

Automated energy management systems often come with energy monitoring platforms that offer real-time insights into consumption patterns. These platforms use predictive analytics to suggest optimizations, such as identifying energy-hungry appliances or recommending the optimal times for running specific devices. With these insights, homeowners can take prompt action to manage their energy use better, often receiving automatic alerts for unusual activities that may indicate a problem.

Smart plugs and switches are small, often overlooked components that can have a big impact on energy management. These devices allow you to control appliances remotely and monitor their energy consumption. Automation software can be set to turn off devices that aren't in use after a certain period, preventing phantom energy drain—a common issue where devices continue to consume power even when they're off.

Automation's role in efficiency isn't just limited to energy savings—it's about enhancing the overall quality of life. By reducing the cognitive load associated with managing various home systems, automation allows residents more time to focus on things that truly matter, whether that's spending time with family, pursuing hobbies, or simply relaxing. An intelligently automated home knows when to lower the lights for a movie, adjust the thermostat for bedtime, and even remind you if the garage door is left open.

Moving beyond individual devices, the concept of automation extends to entire ecosystems within the home. With comprehensive automation, different systems—lighting, climate control, security, and entertainment—operate in harmony, learning from each other to create a cohesive, efficient, and comfortable living environment. For instance, a smart security system can communicate with smart lights and speakers when it senses unauthorized entry, not only alerting residents but also creating an effective deterrent by simulating occupancy.

Moreover, AI-powered home automation systems can run complex scenarios that would be impossible to manage manually. Picture a home that adjusts its climate settings not only based on the immediate weather forecast but also on longer-term climate predictions and the thermal properties of the building. These nuanced adjustments can lead to significant energy savings by anticipating heating or cooling needs well in advance.

Automation also brings a new dimension to energy efficiency through adaptive learning. Initially, the system might require input and configuration, but over time it evolves. It learns your schedule, preferences, and even the nuances of how your home reacts to different conditions. For example, it might know that your living room heats up quickly in the afternoon sun and adjusts the blinds and air conditioning preemptively. This sort of advanced automation ensures energy use is finely tuned to minimize waste while maximizing comfort.

Another area where automation shines is in maintaining optimal performance of home energy systems. For example, automated systems can monitor HVAC filters and notify residents when it's time for a replacement, ensuring that the system operates efficiently. This not only helps in conserving energy but also extends the lifespan of costly equipment, thereby providing financial benefits in the long run.

Lastly, it's worth mentioning that automation for efficiency often comes with the added benefit of scalability. As new technologies emerge and more smart devices enter the market, they're typically designed to integrate easily with existing systems. This flexibility ensures that your home automation framework can grow and adapt over time, continually improving efficiency without requiring a complete overhaul.

In essence, automation for efficiency transforms how we think about and interact with our living spaces. It turns passive elements of our home into dynamic, responsive entities that actively contribute to improving our quality of life while conserving resources. The integration of AI-driven automation in energy management is not just a trend but a necessity for a sustainable, augmented future where homes are not just smart but truly intelligent.

CHAPTER 12:
SMART HOME CLEANING SOLUTIONS

Imagine coming home to a spotless house without lifting a finger—that's the promise of smart home cleaning solutions. Robotic vacuums like the Roomba have paved the way, offering automated floor cleaning that handles both carpets and hard floors with remarkable precision. In addition to indoor cleaning, automated lawn care systems keep your grass impeccably trimmed, while robotic pool cleaners ensure your swimming pool stays pristine. These devices, powered by advanced sensors and AI algorithms, can adapt to your home's layout and your habits, providing personalized cleaning schedules. Integrating these smart cleaning solutions into your living space does more than just save you time; it turns a traditionally labor-intensive chore into a seamless, efficient process, allowing you to focus on what matters most. By leveraging these technologies, you're not just cleaning your home—you're revolutionizing how you maintain your living environment.

Robotic Vacuums

Robotic vacuums have become an essential component of modern smart home cleaning solutions. They offer a convenient and efficient way to maintain cleanliness without dedicating valuable personal time to mundane chores. These devices have undergone significant advancements, powered by cutting-edge artificial intelligence and machine learning algorithms that make them smarter, more efficient, and increasingly user-friendly.

The genesis of robotic vacuums can be traced back to their inception as simple, pre-programmed devices. Early models essentially followed a pre-determined pattern, often bumping into obstacles and ricocheting off in random directions. Fast forward to today, and modern robotic vacuums are far more sophisticated. Equipped with advanced sensors, mapping technologies, and the ability to learn and adapt over time, robotic vacuums now offer exceptional cleaning performance and intuitive operation.

One of the standout features of contemporary robotic vacuums is their advanced navigation systems. These devices utilize a mix of laser sensors, cameras, and infrared technology to create detailed maps of your home. By constantly updating these maps, robotic vacuums can efficiently move through rooms, avoiding obstacles and systematically covering every inch of floor space. Some models even come with the ability to detect the type of floor surface they're cleaning, adjusting their suction power accordingly.

Another key aspect is the integration of AI-driven software. Modern robotic vacuums utilize machine learning algorithms to improve their cleaning efficiency. For instance, after a few rounds of cleaning, the device learns the layout of your home, the location of furniture, and even areas that typically accumulate more dirt. This adaptive learning capability ensures that your floors are cleaned more thoroughly over time.

Remote control and scheduling are vital features for a smart home cleaning solution. Most robotic vacuums come with dedicated mobile apps, allowing users to control them from anywhere in the world. Whether you're at work or on vacation, you can easily start, stop, or schedule cleaning sessions with just a few taps on your smartphone. These apps often provide real-time status updates and detailed cleaning reports, offering complete control and transparency.

Robotic vacuums are also notable for their compatibility with other smart home systems. Integration with voice assistants like Amazon Alexa and Google Assistant means you can start or schedule your vacuum with simple voice commands. For instance, you can say, "Alexa, start the vacuum," and your robotic friend will spring into action. This seamless integration enhances the user experience and makes it easier to incorporate robotic vacuums into your existing smart home ecosystem.

While robotic vacuums are tremendously effective at sweeping and vacuuming, some models also feature mopping functions. These hybrid devices come equipped with water tanks and mopping pads, allowing them to perform a wet clean on hard floors. By integrating sweeping, vacuuming, and mopping into a single device, these robots provide a comprehensive cleaning solution for various floor types in a single run.

Battery life is a crucial consideration when evaluating robotic vacuums. Modern units are designed to clean large areas on a single charge, with many capable of returning to their docking stations autonomously to recharge. After charging, they can resume cleaning from the exact spot where they left off, ensuring uninterrupted and efficient cleaning cycles. Some high-end models even offer the ability to detect low battery levels and head back to their charging docks independently before resuming their tasks.

Maintenance of these robotic marvels is straightforward but essential for optimal performance. Features like self-emptying dustbins reduce the manual intervention needed, as the robot can automatically empty its dustbin into a larger canister located at the docking station. This integration minimizes the need to frequently empty the robot manually. Additionally, routine maintenance, such as cleaning the sensors and brushes, is typically simple and can be managed through the manufacturer's guidelines and tutorials.

From an environmental perspective, robotic vacuums contribute to a sustainable lifestyle. These devices are generally energy-efficient, using significantly less power compared to traditional vacuum cleaners. Their ability to schedule cleanings means they can operate during off-peak hours, further reducing their environmental footprint. Moreover, some models are designed with eco-friendly materials, aligning with the broader goal of sustainable smart home solutions.

The future of robotic vacuums looks promising, with ongoing innovations aimed at making them even more autonomous and smarter. Emerging technologies such as artificial general intelligence (AGI), enhanced machine learning capabilities, and more advanced sensor systems promise to push the boundaries of what robotic vacuums can achieve. Additionally, the development of better integration with other smart home systems will further enhance their utility and adaptability.

Investing in a robotic vacuum represents more than just a commitment to a cleaner home—it's a step towards a more convenient and efficient lifestyle. The ability to automate this repetitive task frees up time that can be better spent on other activities, whether for leisure or productivity. Additionally, the convenience provided by these devices allows for consistent maintenance of cleanliness, contributing to a healthier living environment.

As we move forward in the age of smart homes, the role of robotic vacuums will likely expand and evolve. Alongside other smart cleaning solutions, they will continue to play a pivotal role in transforming home maintenance tasks. By embracing these advanced technologies, users can look forward to a future where maintaining a clean home is not just easier but also more intelligent and efficient.

Automated Lawn Care

Automated lawn care is a game changer for anyone looking to maintain a pristine lawn with minimal effort. This AI-powered solution brings together advanced technology and practical applications to create a seamless experience that keeps your exterior as smart as your interior. With the development of sophisticated robotic lawn mowers and integrated smart irrigation systems, your lawn can now receive the customized care it deserves without the traditional time investment.

Let's start with robotic lawn mowers. These nifty devices have transformed the labor-intensive task of mowing the lawn into a simple push of a button—or even better, an automated routine that you can set and forget. Modern robotic mowers are equipped with advanced sensors, GPS navigation, and AI algorithms that enable them to navigate your yard with precision. They can detect obstacles, adjust their cutting patterns to avoid uneven patches, and even return to their charging stations autonomously. The convenience these mowers offer is unparalleled, saving you time and effort while keeping your lawn consistently well-manicured.

Another crucial aspect of automated lawn care is irrigation. Proper watering is key to maintaining a healthy lawn, but traditional sprinkler systems often fall short of delivering the right amount of water at the right time. Smart irrigation systems, however, take the guesswork out of the equation. These systems utilize weather data, soil moisture levels, and plant-specific requirements to determine the optimal watering schedule. By ensuring that your lawn receives just the right amount of water, smart irrigation systems help conserve water and reduce your utility bills while promoting lush, green growth.

Imagine having a lawn that's always picture-perfect, without having to spend your weekends pushing a mower or fiddling with sprinkler settings. Automated lawn care solutions make this possible by integrating seamlessly into your smart home ecosystem. You can control and monitor your lawn care devices through a single app, whether you're home or away. Schedule your robotic mower to trim the grass while you're at work, or adjust your irrigation settings based on real-time weather forecasts—it's all at your fingertips.

Integration with other smart home devices further enhances the capabilities of your automated lawn care system. For instance, you can use voice commands via your smart assistant to start or stop the robotic mower, or receive notifications about your lawn's watering schedule. Smart cameras can provide visual feedback, allowing you to monitor your lawn's condition and make adjustments as needed. The synergy between different smart devices creates a cohesive and efficient lawn care system that's truly intelligent.

The environmental impact of automated lawn care should not be overlooked. Traditional lawn care equipment, such as gas-powered mowers, contributes to pollution and greenhouse gas emissions. By switching to electric robotic mowers and water-efficient irrigation systems, you can significantly reduce your carbon footprint. Additionally, smart irrigation systems help prevent water waste by delivering precise amounts of water based on real-time data, contributing to more sustainable water usage.

Maintenance is another area where automated lawn care solutions excel. Robotic mowers are easy to maintain, requiring only periodic blade replacements and routine cleanings to keep them in top shape. Smart irrigation systems usually come with features like leak detection and automatic shutoff, which help identify and resolve issues before they become significant problems. These systems can also notify you of maintenance needs, ensuring that your equipment remains operational and efficient throughout the year.

Cost is often a concern when considering new technology, and it's no different for automated lawn care. However, while the initial investment might be higher than traditional lawn care tools, the long-term benefits often justify the expense. Reduced water and energy consumption, lower maintenance costs, and the value of your time saved all contribute to the overall return on investment. Moreover, the market for AI-driven lawn care solutions is growing, leading to more competitive pricing and a wider range of options to suit different budgets.

So, how do you get started with automated lawn care? Begin by evaluating your specific needs and the layout of your lawn. Consider factors like lawn size, terrain complexity, and the types of plants you have. Research different robotic mower models and smart irrigation systems to find the ones that best fit your requirements. Look for features like GPS navigation, obstacle detection, weather integration, and app compatibility. Once you've chosen your devices, setting them up is usually straightforward, with most systems offering user-friendly installation guides and customer support.

To maximize the benefits of your automated lawn care system, take advantage of the customization options available. Set up tailored mowing and watering schedules based on your lawn's unique needs, and adjust these settings as necessary based on seasonal changes or specific weather conditions. Regularly monitor the performance of your devices through your smart home app, and be proactive about maintenance to ensure longevity and efficiency.

The potential for further innovation in automated lawn care is vast. Future advancements could include even smarter AI algorithms that learn and adapt to your lawn's growth patterns over time, more robust integration with other smart home devices, and enhanced sustainability features. As these technologies evolve, maintaining a beautiful lawn will become increasingly effortless, allowing you to enjoy more leisure time while your smart home takes care of the hard work.

In conclusion, automated lawn care is a powerful component of smart home cleaning solutions that offers significant benefits in terms of convenience, efficiency, and sustainability. By embracing AI-powered robotic mowers and smart irrigation systems, you can achieve a consistently well-maintained lawn with minimal effort, while also contributing to a greener planet. As these technologies continue to advance, the future of lawn care looks promising, making it an exciting time to invest in and explore the possibilities of automated solutions for your home.

Pool Maintenance

As you integrate artificial intelligence into various aspects of your home, pool maintenance represents another domain where smart technologies bring significant ease and efficiency. Traditionally, maintaining a swimming pool can be a high-maintenance endeavor that requires regular monitoring and cleaning. A smart pool system automates many of these tasks, allowing you more time to enjoy the water rather than fuss over it. By integrating AI into your pool maintenance routine, you're taking another step forward in creating a home that's not only smart but also incredibly convenient.

Imagine waking up each morning to a pool that's already been vacuumed, with water at the perfect temperature and balanced chemical levels, all without lifting a finger. This scenario isn't just a fantasy; it's entirely possible with smart pool solutions. Automated systems can handle virtually all aspects of pool upkeep, from routine cleaning to real-time chemical monitoring and adjustments. These systems come equipped with a suite of sensors and connected devices that communicate with an AI-powered hub to keep your pool in pristine condition.

One of the critical components of smart pool maintenance is robotic pool cleaners. These robots can scrub and vacuum the pool floor, walls, and even the waterline. Equipped with advanced algorithms, they ensure that every nook and cranny is cleaned efficiently. Unlike manual pool cleaning tools, these robots can be scheduled to operate at optimal times, often during the night or when the pool is not in use. The result? A spotless pool that's always ready for a dip.

Another crucial aspect is water quality management. Maintaining proper pH levels in your pool is paramount for both safety and enjoyment. Smart chemical monitors continually analyze the water, providing precise data on pH, chlorine, alkalinity, and other metrics. When adjustments are needed, automated chemical feeders can dispense precise amounts of chemicals to balance the water. This automated process not only ensures crystal-clear water but also minimizes the use of potentially harmful substances, making the pool safer for everyone.

Temperature control is another area where AI shines. Automated pool heaters and covers work in tandem with weather forecasting algorithms to maintain an ideal swimming temperature. These systems can adjust heating schedules based on anticipated weather conditions, ensuring energy efficiency and optimal comfort. Additionally, covers can be automatically deployed to reduce heat loss and prevent debris from entering the pool, further decreasing the need for manual cleaning.

Integrating these systems may seem daunting, but in reality, many smart pool solutions are designed to be user-friendly. They often come with companion apps that provide real-time updates and controls at your fingertips. From your smartphone, you can check the status of your pool cleaner, monitor water quality, adjust temperature settings, and even start or stop certain tasks remotely. This centralized control simplifies pool maintenance, allowing you to focus on relaxation and fun.

Security and safety also benefit from smart technologies. Motion sensors and cameras strategically placed around the pool can alert you to unauthorized access, ensuring that children or pets don't enter the pool area unsupervised. Some systems can even integrate with your broader home security network, providing seamless coordination between different smart home components.

Energy efficiency is enhanced through AI-driven optimization. Smart pumps, for instance, can adjust their speed based on the pool's needs, lowering energy consumption without compromising water circulation. Automated lighting systems can turn pool lights on and off based on schedules or ambient light levels, reducing unnecessary power use. These energy-saving measures not only decrease operating costs but also contribute to a more sustainable household.

For those who enjoy a more hands-on approach, smart systems still offer tremendous value. With detailed data and analytics, you can gain insights into your pool's health and performance. This information can help inform better maintenance practices, such as identifying trends that might indicate a looming issue before it escalates. Thus, even in manual interventions, AI serves as a valuable assistant.

As far as installation goes, modern smart pool systems are increasingly designed for easy integration with existing pool setups. Many components are plug-and-play, requiring minimal modifications to your current pool infrastructure. Professional installation services can also provide a seamless transition, ensuring that all elements of the system are optimally configured.

Smart pool maintenance is not just about the technology; it's about enhancing your lifestyle. It transforms pool care from a series of labor-intensive tasks into an almost invisible service that happens in the background. The result is a more enjoyable, low-maintenance pool experience that lets you focus on what really matters: spending quality time with family and friends.

Overall, integrating AI into your pool maintenance regimen is a game-changer. It reduces the manual labor involved, yields better results, and offers peace of mind through improved safety and efficiency. By leveraging advancements in AI and connected devices, you're converting your pool into a smarter, more user-friendly component of your smart home ecosystem. The future of pool maintenance is here, and it's both intelligent and intuitive.

As you continue on this journey of smart home integration, remember that these technologies are designed to enhance your quality of life. In pool maintenance, as in other areas of home management, AI serves as a powerful ally, providing convenience, efficiency, and security. Embrace these innovations and transform your pool into a hassle-free oasis.

CHAPTER 13:
AI IN HOME MAINTENANCE

Integrating AI into home maintenance redefines the way we care for our living spaces, making upkeep almost effortless through predictive maintenance, smart diagnosis, and routine automation. Imagine your home's systems being able to anticipate issues before they turn into costly repairs, alerting you to potential problems and even scheduling fixes autonomously. Predictive maintenance leverages machine learning algorithms to monitor the health of appliances, alerting you to service needs before a breakdown occurs. Smart diagnosis tools can instantly identify issues with your HVAC system or kitchen appliances, offering solutions in real-time, thus saving time and reducing stress. Routine automation takes care of mundane tasks like filter replacements or gutter cleaning, ensuring that your home runs smoothly without you having to lift a finger. Together, these technologies not only enhance the efficiency and reliability of our homes but also give us peace of mind, allowing us to focus on enjoying our living spaces rather than constantly managing them. By adopting AI in home maintenance, we step into a future where home care is proactive, seamless, and smarter than ever before.

Predictive Maintenance

In the bustling world of home maintenance, predictive maintenance powered by artificial intelligence (AI) emerges as a groundbreaking solution. It transforms the way we approach the upkeep and longevity of our home systems, redefining efficiency and preemptive care. At its core, predictive maintenance leverages AI algorithms to forecast potential failures before they become inconvenient or costly problems. This forward-thinking approach ensures fewer breakdowns, increases the lifespan of home appliances, and enhances the overall comfort and convenience of your living space.

The concept is akin to having a personal handyman with a crystal ball. By employing sensors and machine learning algorithms, AI analyzes data streams from various home systems—be it HVAC units, plumbing, or electrical circuits—to detect anomalies and predict issues before they escalate. Imagine getting alerted to a slow refrigerator compressor before it stops working entirely or identifying a minor plumbing leak before it floods your kitchen. These preemptive measures save homeowners not only money but also the stress and inconvenience associated with sudden, unexpected repairs.

Given the data-driven nature of AI, predictive maintenance involves continuous monitoring of systems, thus ensuring a constant check on the health and efficiency of appliances. For example, an AI-powered HVAC system would continually assess variables such as temperature fluctuations, filter status, and airflow efficiency. By gathering and analyzing this data, the system can predict when a filter needs replacing or if an impending mechanical failure looms. This kind of monitoring isn't just about recognizing faults but about optimizing performance, ensuring that the systems run at their highest efficiency, thereby conserving energy and reducing costs.

One of the most compelling aspects of predictive maintenance is its ability to integrate with smart home ecosystems seamlessly. Through platforms like Amazon Alexa, Google Home, or Apple HomeKit, predictive maintenance solutions can communicate directly with homeowners. You'll receive instant updates via your smart devices, notifying you of potential issues along with recommendations for action. This real-time interaction makes managing home maintenance tasks more intuitive and less labor-intensive.

From a broader perspective, integrating predictive maintenance into a smart home ecosystem facilitates a more proactive and holistic approach to home care. It's not just about fixing things that break; it's about creating a resilient environment where malfunctions are rare and quickly resolved. Enhanced with AI, home maintenance shifts from a reactive to a proactive model, fundamentally transforming how we interact with our living spaces.

Another interesting facet of predictive maintenance is its potential to extend beyond standalone systems and into more complex integrations. Consider a scenario where your smart refrigerator not only monitors its own functional health but also communicates with the electrical grid. By knowing the best times to run self-diagnostic tests (such as during periods of low electricity tariff), it can optimize both its performance and your energy bills.

For appliance manufacturers, the benefits of predictive maintenance are multifold. They can offer enhanced warranties and after-sales services, reinforcing their brand's reliability while cultivating a loyal customer base. Predictive analytics also provide valuable insights into product performance, helping manufacturers design more durable and efficient appliances in the future.

The path to adopting predictive maintenance isn't particularly cumbersome either. Most modern appliances already come equipped with smart capabilities that can be easily connected to your home network. Retrofitting older systems might require additional sensors or smart plugs, but the investment is often offset by the convenience and savings achieved through predictive maintenance. Even older homes can benefit, with a range of retrofit solutions available that integrate seamlessly into existing infrastructures.

There's also an important consideration for the environment. By optimizing the performance of home appliances, predictive maintenance reduces the need for replacements and disposals, leading to less waste. With better-maintained systems operating at peak efficiency, energy consumption is also minimized, contributing to a lower carbon footprint. Thus, predictive maintenance aligns well with the broader goals of sustainability and responsible living.

Potential challenges in adopting predictive maintenance include the initial costs and the need for a certain level of tech-savviness. However, as the technology matures and becomes more ubiquitous, these barriers are expected to diminish. Tech companies are continually improving the user interface and user experience, making it easier for even non-tech-savvy individuals to benefit from these advancements.

For instance, AI algorithms are designed to learn and adapt over time, so the more they monitor your home systems, the more accurate and reliable they become. This learning capability can adjust for unique characteristics of your home environment, providing customized maintenance schedules and alerts. Therefore, the longer you use predictive maintenance, the more efficient and tailored it becomes to your specific needs.

As we look to the future, the role of AI in predictive maintenance will only grow more integral. Emerging technologies like edge computing, combined with more robust neural networks, will allow for even faster data processing and more sophisticated analysis. This development means even quicker response times and more precise predictive capabilities, solidifying AI's role in making homes smarter and more efficient.

In conclusion, predictive maintenance is not just an optional enhancement to a smart home—it's a vital component that offers peace of mind, cost savings, and a more comfortable living environment. It aligns perfectly with the goals of convenience, efficiency, and security, making it an invaluable asset for anyone looking to modernize their home. Embracing predictive maintenance powered by AI represents a forward-thinking approach to home care, one that promises to make our lives smarter and more streamlined.

Smart Diagnosis

One of the often-overlooked marvels of integrating artificial intelligence into home maintenance is its capability for smart diagnosis. At its core, smart diagnosis entails utilizing AI algorithms and machine learning models to identify, predict, and troubleshoot issues within the home environment. This isn't merely a futuristic concept; it's a practical application that provides significant convenience and efficiency to homeowners today. Let's delve into the layers of this fascinating technology.

Imagine having an AI system that can alert you about a potential malfunction in your HVAC system before it breaks down. Smart diagnosis leverages a network of sensors spread throughout your home, collecting data in real-time. These sensors monitor the operational status of various devices and systems, from your refrigerator to your water heater, and transmit this data to a central AI hub for analysis. Through continuous learning, the AI system can discern patterns and detect anomalies that may indicate a developing problem.

At its most basic level, the function of smart diagnosis can be likened to a "health check" for your home's appliances and systems. Let's break down how it actually works. A multitude of sensors collect data on temperature, humidity, vibrations, and even sound patterns. For instance, an unusual vibration detected in your washing machine motor could signal an impending failure. The AI system processes this input and cross-references it against a database of known issues, thereby issuing a preliminary diagnosis.

Take, for example, a smart washing machine equipped with these diagnostic sensors. The washing machine can continuously monitor its own performance, providing updates to the homeowner via a connected app. If it detects a problem—such as an imbalance in the drum or a blocked water inlet—the device can not only alert the user but even recommend immediate actions to resolve the issue. This proactive approach can prevent minor issues from escalating into costly repairs or replacements.

The predictive capabilities of smart diagnosis make it an invaluable asset for long-term home maintenance. Not only can it identify current problems, but it can also foresee potential issues based on historical data and usage patterns. For example, a smart water heater with diagnostic features can predict component wear-and-tear, indicating when it's time for preventive maintenance or part replacements. This foresight can significantly extend the lifespan of appliances and ensure they operate at peak efficiency.

Moreover, integrating smart diagnosis into home maintenance can lead to substantial energy and cost savings. By detecting and addressing small inefficiencies, such as air leaks in HVAC ductwork or sediment buildup in plumbing, homeowners can reduce energy consumption and utility bills. These savings alone can often offset the initial investment in smart diagnostic systems, making them a financially sound choice.

Another key aspect of smart diagnosis is its integration with other AI-enabled home systems. For example, an AI-driven thermostat that senses an issue with the HVAC system could automatically adjust the temperature settings to prevent overuse and notify a repair service if necessary. Or consider a smart oven that detects a fault in its heating element and emails the manufacturer's service team directly, initiating a service request before you even realize there's a problem.

Furthermore, smart diagnosis systems can offer a layer of security, particularly against environmental hazards. Smoke detectors and carbon monoxide sensors are traditional tools, but AI-enhanced versions can take their functionality to the next level. They can analyze the air quality in real-time and trigger ventilation systems if harmful levels are detected, ensuring not only timely alerts but also immediate, automated responses to mitigate risk.

Another sector benefiting from smart diagnostic systems is water management. Through AI-enabled leak detection sensors placed at strategic points around a home, the system can monitor water flow and pressure. If an unusual variance is detected, such as a steady decrease in water pressure which might indicate a hidden leak, the system can immediately alert the homeowner and even shut off the water supply to prevent damage while the issue is being addressed.

Consider also the possibilities in lighting systems. Intelligent lighting solutions equipped with diagnostic capabilities can monitor their usage and performance over time. If a light fixture starts flickering or loses brightness, it may indicate an issue with the electrical wiring or the bulb itself. The system can then alert the homeowner to replace the bulb or consult an electrician, preventing potential electrical hazards.

Another compelling feature of smart diagnosis is its potential to integrate with voice assistants. Imagine being able to ask your digital assistant for a health report of your home. A simple query like, "What's the status of my home systems?" could prompt a comprehensive summary of current diagnostics, alerts for any detected issues, and suggested actions to maintain optimal performance. It's a seamless blend of convenience and efficiency, putting the power of AI right at your fingertips.

For those concerned about data privacy, it's essential to note that many smart diagnosis tools are designed with robust security measures. Data encryption, secure networks, and stringent access controls ensure that the information collected by these systems remains confidential and is used solely for the purpose of home maintenance. Manufacturers are increasingly transparent about their data policies, and many offer options for users to manage their data preferences directly.

Looking ahead, the integration and advancement of AI in smart diagnostics promise to bring even more innovative features. Future developments may include more sophisticated machine learning models capable of diagnosing and rectifying issues autonomously, without any human intervention. Virtual repair assistants, augmented reality maintenance guides, and real-time video consultations with technicians are just a few possibilities on the horizon.

In summary, smart diagnosis represents a monumental leap forward in home maintenance. It's not just about fixing problems as they arise, but about fostering a proactive, preventative approach to home care. With the ability to predict issues before they become critical, optimize the efficiency of home systems, and provide actionable insights, smart diagnosis stands as a cornerstone of the modern, AI-enhanced home.

The inclusion of smart diagnosis systems in your home ecosystem can dramatically improve the convenience, efficiency, and security of your living space. As AI technology continues to evolve, these systems will become even more intuitive, integrated, and indispensable, truly transforming the way we manage and maintain our homes.

Routine Automation

Routine automation in the context of AI in home maintenance brings the promise of transforming daily chores into a seamless, efficient flow of tasks managed by smart systems. Imagine waking up to a home where the mundane, repetitive tasks are all taken care of without you lifting a finger. This is not just a futuristic dream but a present-day reality thanks to advancements in artificial intelligence and its integration into our living spaces.

One of the significant benefits of routine automation is the time saved by automating repetitive tasks. Procedures that typically consume portions of your day—like vacuuming, adjusting the thermostat, or even watering your plants—can be handled by AI-powered devices. For instance, robotic vacuums equipped with AI algorithms can navigate your home, avoiding obstacles, and clean your floors on a schedule that suits you. These devices learn your home's layout over time, optimizing their cleaning paths and ensuring no spot is missed.

Routine automation also contributes to energy efficiency. AI systems can monitor and manage your home's energy consumption more effectively than any human could. Smart thermostats like the Nest Learning Thermostat analyze your schedule and adjust heating and cooling settings to conserve energy when you're not home. Over time, they learn your preferences and adjust accordingly, ensuring comfort and efficiency. An intelligent sprinkler system can adjust water usage based on local weather patterns, soil moisture levels, and the type of plants in your garden, significantly reducing water waste.

Beyond energy savings, AI in routine automation also enhances security. Consider a scenario where your smart home coordinates various security devices—such as smart locks, cameras, and motion sensors—to create a secure environment tailored to your habits. For example, setting your home's alarm system automatically when you leave for work or ensuring all windows and doors are locked at bedtime can provide peace of mind without requiring daily manual checks. Even more, AI can provide real-time alerts and video feeds to your phone if an unusual activity is detected, allowing you to act promptly.

Another compelling facet of routine automation is its role in maintaining your home's overall condition. AI-powered systems can send you reminders for routine upkeep tasks such as changing HVAC filters, servicing home appliances, or even checking for leaks in plumbing systems. Advanced sensors and machine learning can predict when a gadget is likely to malfunction based on its usage patterns, enabling preemptive maintenance and ultimately extending the life of your appliances.

Health and wellness can also benefit significantly from routine automation. Smart health devices can monitor your vitals and track daily activities, providing recommendations to improve your lifestyle. Imagine having a smart mirror that analyzes your skin condition and suggests skincare routines or a smart mattress that adjusts to provide optimal sleep conditions based on your sleep patterns. Even dietary habits can be automated with smart kitchen devices that create meal plans and grocery lists, ensuring a balanced diet without the need for exhaustive planning.

The beauty of AI-driven routine automation lies in its adaptability. AI systems grow smarter over time as they collect and analyze data. Your home becomes an extension of your behavior, adapting to your changing routines and preferences. For families, this means that the AI can cater to different members' schedules and preferences, creating a harmonious living environment. For instance, lights can be programmed to adjust their intensity according to the time of day and individual needs, or music can follow you room by room, shifting genres based on who's present.

In fostering a more connected home environment, routine automation champions the concept of "set it and forget it." Once your preferences are set, these smart systems take over, offering you the luxury of focusing on what truly matters while they handle the daily grind. They bring a level of personalization that feels bespoke, crafted specifically for your lifestyle. And as these systems become more ingrained in the fabric of our homes, the boundary between task and leisure continues to blur, offering us more downtime and less time in maintenance mode.

However, with great power comes great responsibility. As we rely more on AI to manage our daily routines, concerns about data privacy and security become paramount. Routine automation requires the collection and analysis of large amounts of personal data. Ensuring that this data is protected and used ethically is crucial to maintaining trust in these systems. Secure networks, strong encryption, and transparent data policies are essential in safeguarding your private information.

Imagine a future where smart homes are not just reactive but proactive. Your AI system might recognize early signs of wear in your plumbing, alerting you before a pipe bursts, or it might detect small changes in your home's electrical consumption, indicating a malfunctioning appliance. The potential of routine automation stretches far beyond mere convenience; it ushers in an era of predictive maintenance and enhanced home care.

Integrating routine automation in our homes is akin to adding an invisible workforce that functions tirelessly behind the scenes. These systems offer a blend of efficiency, security, and convenience. It's about creating a living space that responds dynamically to your daily routines, learns from them, and continuously adapts to serve you better. It's a testament to how far we've come in the evolution of smart homes, and it hints at a future where our living spaces are not just smart but intuitively intelligent.

To truly harness the power of routine automation, one must be willing to invest time in the initial setup and customization of these technologies. The key is to start with small, manageable steps—like setting up automated lighting or a smart thermostat—and gradually expand to more complex systems. As you do so, you'll find that the AI's capacity to manage and optimize your home's functions grows, providing ever-increasing benefits.

The transformative potential of AI in routine automation is boundless. By embracing these technologies, we're not only simplifying our daily chores but also stepping into a future where our homes are guardians of our wellbeing, efficiency, and even our happiness. Let the AI handle the routine, so you can focus on what makes your home truly yours.

CHAPTER 14:
HOME OFFICE AND PRODUCTIVITY

In an era where remote work is more prevalent than ever, transforming your home office into a productivity powerhouse is key to maintaining efficiency and focus. AI tools can seamlessly manage your work tasks, from scheduling to virtual meetings, making your day flow effortlessly. Smart office equipment like AI-powered printers and voice-activated assistants create a hands-free experience, allowing you to concentrate on what truly matters. Automation extends to scheduling, where intelligent systems can coordinate your calendar, set reminders, and even suggest optimal work times based on your productivity patterns. By integrating these technologies into your home office, you're not just enhancing convenience, but creating an environment that fosters creativity and peak performance.

AI Tools for Managing Work

As the trend of remote work and home offices continues to rise, integrating AI tools for managing work within your home can significantly enhance productivity. These tools can streamline communication, automate repetitive tasks, and provide insights to optimize your workflow. In this section, we'll explore some of the most effective AI-powered solutions designed to help you manage your work efficiently and seamlessly from home.

First, let's talk about AI-powered project management tools. Platforms like Trello and Asana have AI features that can predict task completion times, recommend task assignments, and automate project updates. With the click of a button, you can delegate tasks, set deadlines, and communicate project statuses without sending multiple emails or holding unnecessary meetings.

Communication is a vital part of any work environment, and AI can enhance this aspect through tools like predictive text and smart email categorization. For instance, Gmail's Smart Compose uses machine learning to suggest complete sentences as you type, helping you write emails faster and more efficiently. Similarly, AI-driven tools like Grammarly not only correct spelling and grammar errors but also offer stylistic suggestions to improve the clarity and effectiveness of your communication.

Moreover, AI-driven virtual assistants like Clara and x.ai can schedule meetings for you. These AI tools scan your calendar for availability, coordinate with other participants, and send out invitations, all without human intervention. The result is a significant reduction in the time spent on scheduling work, allowing you to focus on more important tasks.

For those who need to keep a close eye on their time management, AI time-tracking tools like RescueTime can be invaluable. RescueTime automatically tracks the time you spend on applications and websites, then provides detailed reports on where your time is going. With this information, you can identify productivity bottlenecks and make informed changes to your daily routine.

In addition, AI can help manage your workload through intelligent document processing. Tools like Microsoft's AI-driven Office 365 suite offer features like automatic data extraction from documents, predictive text in Excel, and advanced grammar checking in Word. These functionalities can save you hours of manual work and reduce the likelihood of errors, making your documents more reliable and professional.

Data analysis and reporting are other areas where AI excels. Tools like Tableau and Power BI use machine learning algorithms to analyze data sets and generate insightful visualizations. By leveraging these tools, you can quickly transform raw data into actionable insights, which can be a game-changer for strategic planning and decision-making.

Another innovative use of AI in managing work is in customer relationship management (CRM). Platforms like Salesforce integrate AI to provide sales predictions, identify potential leads, and automate customer follow-ups. This level of automation ensures that you don't miss out on opportunities and can maintain strong customer relationships without the need for constant manual oversight.

The integration of AI in video conferencing tools has also made remote meetings more efficient. Platforms like Zoom and Microsoft Teams use AI for background noise reduction, automatic transcription of meetings, and even real-time translation. These features make it easier to communicate with team members regardless of their location, breaking down barriers to effective collaboration.

AI's contributions to cybersecurity can't be overlooked, especially in a home office setup. AI-based security tools can detect unusual activity, block malware, and send alerts about potential threats. By ensuring that your work environment is secure, these tools let you focus on your tasks with peace of mind.

Another exciting AI tool for managing work is voice recognition software like Dragon NaturallySpeaking. This software can transcribe your voice into text, allowing you to dictate emails, reports, and other documents hands-free. This can be particularly useful for those who need to multitask or have accessibility needs.

Furthermore, AI-driven personal finance tools can be invaluable in managing your work expenses. Platforms like Expensify use AI to scan and categorize receipts automatically, making expense tracking and reporting much simpler. This automation ensures that you can focus on your core responsibilities without getting bogged down by financial admin tasks.

For professionals juggling various projects, AI-driven task prioritization tools can be a game-changer. Tools like Todoist use machine learning to prioritize tasks based on their urgency and importance, helping you focus on what matters most. This can significantly improve your productivity and ensure that you meet your deadlines.

Lastly, AI-enhanced focus tools like Forest and Focus@Will offer personalized recommendations to help you maintain concentration. These tools analyze your behavior and adjust their recommendations to create an optimal work environment, helping you achieve a state of flow where you're most productive.

In summary, AI tools for managing work offer a plethora of features designed to streamline various aspects of your job. From project management and communication to time tracking and data analysis, these tools can transform your home office into a hub of productivity and efficiency. As AI technology continues to advance, the potential for these tools to further enhance your work-life balance and overall productivity is limitless. Embracing these AI solutions can pave the way for a more connected, efficient, and productive work environment right in the comfort of your home.

Smart Office Equipment

As the border between home and office continues to blur, the integration of smart office equipment has emerged as a pivotal element in the quest for a more productive and efficient home workspace. The advent of these innovative tools doesn't just streamline administrative tasks; it fundamentally transforms the way we approach work, allowing us to operate with greater efficiency and creativity.

Imagine walking into your home office, and with a simple voice command, your desk adjusts to your preferred standing height, your computer powers on, and a digital assistant provides you with a briefing of the day's schedule. This is no longer a futuristic fantasy but a present-day reality made possible through smart office equipment. These intelligent devices are designed to work harmoniously to create an ecosystem that anticipates your needs, thereby minimizing distractions and maximizing productivity.

Key among these innovations are smart desks and chairs. Adjustable standing desks, for instance, can simplify switching between sitting and standing at your whim, promoting better posture and reducing health risks associated with prolonged sitting. These desks often come equipped with programmable settings that remember your preferred heights and can even remind you to take breaks or switch positions throughout the day. Smart chairs, on the other hand, can adjust to support your lumbar at the perfect angle, promoting good ergonomic practices without you having to consciously think about it.

But it's not just the furniture that's getting smarter. Multifunctional devices like AI-enhanced printers and all-in-one office hubs can perform a variety of tasks autonomously. Imagine a printer that can order its own ink when levels are low, or an office hub where print, scan, fax, and cloud-based file sharing capabilities are seamlessly integrated into one device. The goal is to remove as much friction as possible from routine tasks, allowing you to focus more on what truly matters—your work. These devices also offer robust data security features to ensure that sensitive documents remain protected.

Speaking of data security, smart office equipment often comes with sophisticated security and management solutions. Devices like biometric scanners and smart locks can ensure that your office space is secure, giving you peace of mind whether you're working in another part of the house or halfway around the world. These solutions integrate effortlessly with other smart home security systems, creating a seamless line of defense against unauthorized access.

Another crucial component is smart lighting. The right lighting can significantly impact your mood and productivity. Smart office lighting systems can be adjusted to mimic the natural progression of daylight, reducing eye strain and boosting concentration. You can also set up specific lighting scenes for different tasks—brighter lights for analytical work and softer tones for brainstorming or creative endeavors. When these systems are integrated with voice assistants, making adjustments becomes as simple as speaking a command.

Furthermore, artificial intelligence plays a significant role in office automation. AI-driven task management systems can help you organize your workflow. Imagine an AI assistant that not only schedules your meetings but also analyzes your habits to suggest the best times for focused work or collaborative sessions. These systems can also automatically set reminders, sort through your emails, and even draft responses based on your communication style.

The benefits of smart office equipment aren't confined to solo workspaces either. For those who frequently collaborate, smart conferencing tools can be a game-changer. Video conferencing systems equipped with AI enhance video and audio quality by focusing on the active speaker and minimizing background noise. Some systems can even provide real-time translations, making international collaborations smoother and more efficient. Additionally, these systems can be integrated with smart whiteboards that digitize your notes and sync them with cloud storage, ensuring no detail is lost.

For content creators, smart office equipment can extend to include tools like AI-powered cameras that can track your movements and ensure you remain in focus during video recordings. There are also smart microphones that can filter out ambient noise and enhance voice clarity, making them ideal for podcasts or conference calls. These devices ensure that you present your best self, whether you're streaming, recording, or attending virtual meetings.

The integration of AI extends to your computer as well. Customizable AI software can monitor your usage patterns to optimize system performance, from managing system resources to predicting and preloading apps based on your behavior. This means fewer interruptions and faster transitions between tasks. Coupled with voice commands, these systems allow for hands-free operation, making multitasking more efficient.

Looking at the peripherals, smart keyboards and mice tailored for ergonomic comfort and efficiency have also entered the market. These accessories can adapt to your work style, offering programmable keys and customizable settings tailored to different applications. Imagine a keyboard that not only reduces strain through ergonomic design but also learns your typing habits to offer predictive text and shortcuts tailored to your workflow.

The same intelligence is applied to smart monitors, which offer features like adjustable brightness and blue light filters based on ambient lighting conditions. Some advanced models can even connect to multiple devices simultaneously, allowing for seamless switching between your computer, phone, or any other connected device. This flexibility promotes an organized and efficient workspace, reducing the clutter of multiple screens and devices.

In a holistic view, smart office equipment extends to environmental control within your workspace. Smart air purifiers, for instance, can ensure that the air quality remains optimal, promoting better health and concentration. Smart thermostats and fans can regulate the room temperature based on your preferences and work schedule, ensuring that your workspace is always comfortable.

Therefore, the integration of smart office equipment in your home isn't just about adopting new tools; it's about creating a cohesive and responsive environment tailored to boost your productivity. By leveraging the power of AI, these devices collectively create a smart office ecosystem that reduces manual input and cognitive load, leaving you more time and energy to focus on your most important tasks.

Automated Scheduling

Automated scheduling in a home office setting can significantly transform the way you manage your time and tasks. In our increasingly connected world, AI-driven systems bring a level of efficiency and organization that's nearly impossible to achieve manually. Imagine waking up to a perfectly calibrated schedule, with meetings, deadlines, and even personal errands neatly sorted out. That's what AI promises when you integrate automated scheduling into your home office.

First and foremost, automated scheduling reduces the cognitive load associated with managing a busy schedule. Instead of juggling multiple calendars and to-do lists, AI-driven systems can consolidate all your activities into a single, coherent plan. These systems can integrate seamlessly with your existing calendar apps, email platforms, and other productivity tools. By analyzing data from these sources, they create a dynamic schedule tailored to your priorities and deadlines.

The power of automated scheduling lies in its adaptability. Unlike static schedule planners, AI systems can adapt in real-time. If a meeting gets canceled or an unexpected task pops up, the system can automatically adjust your schedule, ensuring optimal use of your time. This dynamic adaptation is particularly useful when you're dealing with a mix of professional and personal commitments. An AI-driven schedule doesn't just keep you organized; it keeps you flexible and responsive, ready to tackle changes as they come.

Another advantage of AI-based scheduling is its ability to optimize time slots for productivity. By analyzing data such as your previous work patterns, energy levels at different times of the day, and even the nature of each task, these systems can recommend the best times for focused work, meetings, and breaks. For instance, you might find that your most productive hours are in the morning. The AI can then allocate complex tasks during this period, leaving routine tasks for your less productive hours.

The level of granularity that AI can bring to time management is extraordinary. It can suggest the best time for sending out emails to ensure maximum engagement or remind you of deadlines well in advance. Furthermore, these systems can prioritize tasks based on their urgency and importance, ensuring that critical work doesn't fall through the cracks. This not only helps in achieving a seamless workflow but also in maintaining a balanced workload.

An invaluable feature of automated scheduling is integration with voice assistants and other smart devices. Imagine instructing your voice assistant to "schedule a meeting with John for next Monday at 10 AM," and having it instantly appear in your calendar without you lifting a finger. From setting reminders to managing daily tasks, voice assistants can significantly reduce the time you spend on mundane scheduling activities, making your daily operations smoother and more efficient.

Additionally, these scheduling systems can provide insightful analytics about how you spend your time. By examining patterns and trends, you can identify areas where you might be wasting time or where efficiency can be improved. For instance, if you notice that a lot of your time is spent on low-priority meetings, you can take steps to consolidate or delegate these tasks. The insights gained from these analytics can be a game-changer, allowing you to fine-tune your habits and workflows for maximum efficiency.

Privacy considerations are also crucial when adopting automated scheduling systems. Given the sensitive nature of calendar data, AI systems must ensure robust data protection measures. Always opt for scheduling solutions that emphasize privacy and data security, offering encrypted data storage and strict user control over data sharing. These steps are essential to safeguard your personal and professional information from unauthorized access.

It's also worth considering the collaborative features that AI-driven scheduling systems provide. In a team setting, these systems can streamline scheduling across multiple calendars, ensuring that meetings are set at times convenient for all participants. They can also send automatic reminders and follow-ups, reducing the administrative burden on team members. This makes collaboration smoother, allowing teams to focus more on productive discussions and less on logistical details.

Balancing work and personal life becomes less of a challenge with automated scheduling. By setting clear boundaries within your AI system, you can ensure that work tasks don't encroach on personal time. For instance, you can configure the system to avoid scheduling meetings after a certain hour or during weekends. This helps in maintaining a healthy work-life balance, which is critical for long-term productivity and well-being.

Scheduling systems with AI functionality often include additional productivity tools such as task tracking and project management features. These integrated tools provide a holistic approach to managing your home office. Instead of using separate apps for different tasks, you can have a unified platform where scheduling, task management, and analytics work together seamlessly. This integration eliminates the friction caused by juggling multiple tools, making your workflow more streamlined.

The future of automated scheduling is indeed exciting. With advancements in machine learning and natural language processing, these systems will become even more intuitive and efficient. Imagine a system that can predict potential scheduling conflicts before they arise or suggest changes based on real-time data from your smart devices. These innovations will bring unprecedented levels of convenience and efficiency to your home office.

To sum it up, incorporating automated scheduling into your home office is not just about saving time; it's about transforming your approach to productivity. By leveraging AI, you can achieve a higher level of organization, flexibility, and insight that will empower you to meet your goals more effectively. Whether you're a freelancer juggling multiple projects or a remote worker navigating a hectic schedule, automated scheduling offers a streamlined solution that adapts to your needs.

Chapter 15:
Personalized Home Experiences

Transforming a house into a smart home is just the beginning; personalizing these intelligent spaces takes the experience to an unparalleled level. By leveraging user profiles, you can tailor environments to suit each individual family member's preferences, from lighting and climate settings to media choices. Custom scenes allow you to orchestrate multiple devices with a single command, creating an ambiance for any occasion—whether it's a cozy movie night or a productive work session. But the real magic happens with adaptive learning, where AI algorithms continuously evolve alongside your habits, fine-tuning the home experience in ways that anticipate needs before you even express them. The result is a living space that not only responds to your commands but also proactively enhances your daily life, making every moment at home effortlessly enjoyable.

User Profiles

In the ever-evolving landscape of smart homes, user profiles are a cornerstone for creating truly personalized home experiences. By leveraging artificial intelligence (AI), user profiles enable a dynamic interaction between humans and their living spaces. Imagine walking into your home and everything—lights, thermostat, music, and more—adjusts to suit your preferences seamlessly. This is the power of user profiles.

At its core, a user profile in a smart home consists of a set of preferences, habits, and data points unique to an individual. These profiles can be assigned to each member of the household, ensuring that the home environment adapts fluidly to whoever's present. Each profile can store preferences for lighting, temperature, entertainment, and even security settings. The AI system learns from usage patterns and continuously refines these profiles to offer an increasingly customized experience.

This magic starts with the collection of data. Devices such as smartphones, smartwatches, and voice assistants play a key role in gathering information. For instance, a smart thermostat records the temperature preferences of various users at different times of the day and year. Meanwhile, smart lighting systems track and learn about lighting preferences in different rooms. Even smart speakers capture data related to music, news, and podcast preferences. While the aggregation of this data may initially seem intrusive, it's pivotal to keep in mind that this collected information remains secure and is utilized solely to enhance usability.

So, how does it all come together? The AI system processes the collected data to create and adjust user profiles. It employs algorithms to analyze preferences and behaviors, thereby predicting the next best action without any prompt. For instance, the system may detect that you prefer a specific playlist when you arrive home after work. Consequently, as you walk through the door, your preferred playlist starts playing automatically, setting the perfect welcome atmosphere.

Besides preferences, user profiles also consider context. Contextual awareness is about understanding the state of the user at any given moment. Are you home alone, or is your family with you? Are you working from home, or is it a relaxing weekend? The system may decide to activate a more formal setup in your home office during work hours, while transitioning to a relaxed ambiance on weekends.

This awareness allows for a more nuanced, context-driven approach to personalization.

User profiles go beyond immediate preferences and delve into long-term behaviors as well. As the AI system presents various patterns, it can offer proactive recommendations. Let's take home energy management, for example. By understanding your patterns, the system may suggest optimal settings to conserve energy, saving you money while contributing to environmental sustainability. This proactive aspect contributes to a home that not only meets your current needs but also helps you evolve towards a more efficient lifestyle.

One of the captivating features of user profiles is their ability to incorporate feedback loops. Feedback is crucial in refining and improving the profiles over time. Users can manually tweak settings or provide input through simple commands, which the AI system will then incorporate into the learning process. For example, you might prefer a colder bedroom but occasionally need a warmer setting. A simple voice command like "Make it warmer tonight" helps the system adjust accordingly and learn from your input.

Family dynamics add another layer of complexity that user profiles adeptly handle. In a household with multiple members, each person's preferences must be harmoniously balanced. Smart home systems can differentiate individual preferences effortlessly through voice recognition or device-specific data. Parents can have specific settings tailored to their needs while children have their own profile-controlled environment. For example, parental controls might restrict certain functionalities or content for younger family members, ensuring a safe and age-appropriate experience.

Moreover, guest profiles add an extra layer of interaction. These temporary profiles allow visitors to experience the smart home without disrupting the main user settings. Whether it's a family member visiting or a friend staying over for the weekend, guest profiles ensure they can enjoy a customized experience. The smart home system can provide a level of personalized comfort to guests without compromising the privacy and preferences of the permanent residents.

The evolution of user profiles doesn't stop at simple preferences. With advancements in machine learning and AI, the future points towards even richer personalization. Imagine a home that understands your evolving lifestyle, from fitness routines and dietary habits to mental well-being. Wearables and health monitors can integrate with your user profile to offer seamless health and wellness adaptations. Perhaps after a strenuous workout, your home could adjust the lighting to a more soothing hue and play relaxing music, fostering a recuperative environment.

Security plays a pivotal role when it comes to user profiles. The more data integrated into a user profile, the greater the need for robust security measures to protect that data. Smart homes rely on state-of-the-art encryption techniques to secure personal data. Additionally, user profiles can carry different levels of access control. For instance, you may choose to have a more secure profile for sensitive areas like home offices or security systems, while more relaxed profiles might control day-to-day conveniences like lighting and entertainment.

The dynamic nature of user profiles means they can adapt to long-term changes, such as a new job, a change in daily routines, or even seasonal adjustments. As your situation evolves, the AI system will continuously update and adapt your profile to reflect these changes. This adaptability ensures that personalization remains relevant, making your home an ever-evolving sanctuary tailored to your needs.

It's crucial to recognize the collaborative effort involved in setting up and refining user profiles. While the AI system does a significant amount of heavy lifting, users also play an active role. The initial setup may involve inputting basic preferences and routine patterns. Over time, as the system learns and adapts, users will find that their interaction mainly involves occasional tweaks and commands to finetune their experience. It's a seamless partnership between human input and machine intelligence aimed at creating the most comfortable living environment.

To get the most out of user profiles, it's beneficial to keep all smart home devices updated and integrated. Doing so ensures seamless communication between devices, allowing the AI system to receive and process comprehensive data. Regularly reviewing and updating user preferences and settings also enriches the profile, making it more attuned to your current lifestyle.

In wrapping up, user profiles stand at the heart of personalized home experiences. They're not just about convenience but also about creating an environment that continually adapts to your evolving needs and preferences. As AI technology advances, the scope and capabilities of user profiles will only grow, turning human habitats into responsive, intelligent, and caring spaces that feel uniquely yours.

Custom Scenes

Imagine walking into your home, and with a simple voice command or the press of a button, your living space transforms to perfectly suit your current activity and mood. This is the power of custom scenes—tailored experiences that integrate multiple smart home devices to create the ideal ambiance and functionality for any given moment.

Custom scenes are essentially pre-programmed settings that coordinate various smart devices to perform specific actions simultaneously. These scenes can be designed to fit a myriad of lifestyles, activities, and personal preferences. You might have a "Good

Morning" scene that gradually brightens your lights, starts brewing your coffee, and adjusts the thermostat to a comfortable temperature—all timed perfectly with your morning routine.

Creating custom scenes begins with understanding your daily habits and identifying the moments where automation can add the most value. Start by mapping out your daily routines and pinpointing the activities that can benefit from a seamless, automated experience. Perhaps your evening routine includes winding down with soft lighting, calming music, and a thermostat set to a cooler temperature. A custom "Relax" scene can bring all these elements together at the touch of a button.

One of the most exciting aspects of custom scenes is their adaptability. They aren't just static configurations; they can evolve with your changing needs and preferences. With the integration of machine learning and AI, smart home systems can learn your patterns over time and adjust scenes dynamically. For instance, if you typically watch movies on Friday nights, your smart home can automatically prepare the perfect "Movie Night" scene—dimmed lights, drawing the curtains, and turning on your home entertainment system.

To set up custom scenes, you'll need a central smart home hub or a voice assistant with robust scene configuration capabilities. Popular platforms like Apple HomeKit, Google Home, and Amazon Alexa offer intuitive interfaces for creating and managing scenes. These hubs allow you to link various devices—lights, thermostats, speakers, and more—into cohesive experiences.

While the technical setup might seem daunting at first, most platforms provide user-friendly apps that guide you through the process step by step. Start by naming your scene, then select the devices involved and specify the actions each device should perform. Testing and tweaking are crucial during this phase to ensure everything works harmoniously.

The key to a successful custom scene is in the details. Consider adding conditions to your scenes based on time of day, occupancy, or even weather conditions. For example, your "Coming Home" scene can activate differently if it's dark outside, turning on exterior lights and setting a warm, welcoming glow indoors. Similarly, a "Leave Home" scene might shut off all lights, secure the doors, and lower the thermostat to save energy.

Custom scenes can extend beyond convenience and comfort, playing a vital role in home security. Imagine a "Vacation" scene that simulates your presence by randomly turning lights on and off, playing recorded sounds, and adjusting shades. Such scenes can deter potential intruders, providing peace of mind when you're away from home.

Beyond practical uses, custom scenes also offer a creative outlet to express your personal style. You might create a "Party" scene that syncs dynamic lighting effects with your favorite playlist, instantly transforming your living space into a vibrant gathering spot. Or perhaps a "Study" scene that minimizes distractions by dimming lights, reducing screen glare, and playing soft, focus-enhancing ambient sounds.

Incorporating custom scenes into family routines can foster a more harmonious home environment. Scenes like "Family Dinner" can dim the lights and play soft background music, creating an inviting atmosphere for shared meals and conversations. "Homework Time" might brighten the workspace, turn on desk lamps, and mute non-essential notifications to optimize focus.

Custom scenes are not limited to single-room setups. They can span the entire house, linking multiple rooms and devices for a cohesive experience. For instance, a "Wake Up" scene may start in the bedroom by gently raising blinds and turning on bedside lamps, then proceed to the bathroom with mirror lights turning on, and finally to the kitchen where the coffee maker begins brewing.

Integrating voice control can further enhance the ease and accessibility of custom scenes. With simple commands like "Alexa, activate Movie Night," you can trigger complex sequences without lifting a finger. This hands-free operation is particularly beneficial in moments when convenience is paramount, such as cooking, hosting guests, or relaxing after a long day.

For families with diverse schedules and preferences, user profiles can add an extra layer of personalization to custom scenes. Each family member can have their scenes tailored to their routines, ensuring that the home environment adapts to individual needs seamlessly. Parents might have a "Morning Workout" scene that activates early in the gym, while children enjoy a "Bedtime Story" scene with dimmed lights and soothing sounds.

It's important to periodically review and update your scenes to reflect any changes in your lifestyle or household. As new devices are integrated into your smart home ecosystem, they can be incorporated into existing scenes or inspire the creation of new ones. Continuous refinement ensures that your scenes remain relevant and efficient.

Ultimately, custom scenes are about enhancing the quality of life within your home. They harness the capabilities of AI and smart home technology to create environments that are not just automated, but intelligently responsive to your unique way of living. By investing thought and creativity into your custom scenes, you'll unlock the full potential of your smart home, making everyday tasks smoother, more enjoyable, and tailored to your personal comfort.

The future promises even more sophisticated and intuitive scenes as AI continues to advance. Imagine scenes that not only react to your commands but anticipate your needs based on data and predictive analytics. A truly smart home will offer an unparalleled level of personalization, making it an indispensable partner in your daily life.

If you're new to creating custom scenes, start small with basic configurations and gradually build complexity as you become more comfortable with the process. The beauty of custom scenes lies in their scalability—from simple actions to intricate sequences, there's no limit to how you can tailor your smart home to fit your lifestyle.

In conclusion, custom scenes are the linchpin of a personalized home experience. They bring together the myriad capabilities of smart devices into cohesive, meaningful experiences that enhance convenience, comfort, and security. By thoughtfully designing and implementing custom scenes, you will not only make your home smarter but truly make it your own.

Adaptive Learning

Adaptive learning is pivotal when it comes to creating truly personalized home experiences. It's about more than just programming routines or setting schedules; it's about your home understanding and adapting to your lifestyle dynamically. Imagine a home that doesn't just react to your commands but anticipates your needs even before you realize them. That's the power of adaptive learning.

At its core, adaptive learning relies on continuous data collection and analysis. Your smart home devices are constantly gathering data about everyday activities—when you wake up, how you adjust your thermostat during different times of the day, or which rooms you frequent. This data is then fed into sophisticated AI algorithms designed to discern patterns and predict future behavior.

Consider a scenario where your home knows you like to have the lights dimmed in the living room around 8 PM as you start to wind down. Initially, you might set this manually. Over time, however, your smart lighting system learns this preference and begins to adjust automatically. This kind of intuitive response fosters a sense of comfort and ease, making your home environment more harmonious with your personal rhythms.

But adaptive learning doesn't stop with lighting. It extends to climate control, entertainment, security, and even kitchen management. Smart thermostats, for example, can learn your temperature preferences and adjust them according to the time of day or your presence in the home. This isn't just about comfort but also energy efficiency, as the system avoids heating or cooling an empty house.

In the realm of entertainment, adaptive learning can lead to personalized content recommendations. AI-powered televisions and streaming devices can study your viewing habits and suggest movies or shows you're likely to enjoy, eliminating the often time-consuming task of browsing endlessly through options. This saves time and brings a tailored entertainment experience right to your living room.

For security, adaptive learning enhances the effectiveness of your smart home cameras and other surveillance devices. By analyzing routines, an AI-powered security system can distinguish between normal activities and potential security threats. Whether it's recognizing unusual movements or alerting you when a package is delivered, adaptive learning fortifies the safety of your home.

In the kitchen, adaptive learning transforms how you interact with your appliances. Smart ovens can learn your cooking preferences, such as the way you like your bread toasted or the perfect temperature for baking cookies. Over time, these preferences are stored and can be accessed with a simple voice command or through an app, making meal preparation more efficient and enjoyable.

Adaptive learning also plays a crucial role in energy management. Smart plugs and switches that monitor usage patterns can suggest optimal times for running energy-intensive devices to minimize costs.

They can even turn off appliances left on by accident, ensuring that your home runs both smartly and sustainably.

Moreover, adaptive learning contributes to daily wellness. Wearable health devices integrated with your home system can monitor your physical activity, sleep patterns, and stress levels. This information can then be used to adjust home environments, such as altering lighting and room temperature, to help you achieve a healthier lifestyle.

Imagine a smart mirror that offers you health and wellness advice based on the data it receives from connected health devices. It could suggest a stretching routine if it notices you've had a sedentary day or recommend increased hydration based on your activity levels. Such proactive measures can contribute significantly to your overall wellness journey.

Advanced voice assistants are a cornerstone of adaptive learning in smart homes. They progress beyond the basic commands to understanding context and making inferences. For example, saying "Goodnight" might not only turn off the lights but also lock the doors, adjust the thermostat, and ensure all security systems are active. This contextual understanding makes interactions seamless and intuitive.

Custom scenes are another illustration of adaptive learning. With these, a combination of lighting, climate, and even sound adjustments are set for different parts of your day—be it waking up, unwinding after work, or setting the mood for a dinner party. Once established, these scenes can evolve based on how you adjust them over time, ensuring they remain relevant and useful.

In the workspace, adaptive learning helps in maintaining productivity. Your smart home office can learn to dim the lights and minimize ambient noise as you approach a deadline, or even prompt you to take breaks based on your working patterns. This contributes to mental well-being and better work-life balance.

To get the most out of adaptive learning, initial setup and periodic interaction can't be ignored. It's crucial to spend some time teaching your home about your preferences and routines. While the system will learn and adapt over time, the foundational data you provide will hasten the learning curve, bringing about quicker and more accurate adjustments.

Privacy concerns are natural, given the level of data collection involved. However, most smart home systems come with robust security measures to protect your data. Adopting a mindful approach to data permissions and updating security settings regularly can offer both the benefits of adaptive learning and peace of mind.

Finally, the essence of adaptive learning in a personalized home experience is the transformation of technology from mere tools into collaborative partners. Your smart home, enhanced with adaptive learning capabilities, doesn't just wait for orders but evolves alongside you, making daily life smoother, more efficient, and more enjoyable. As these technologies advance, the synergy between human and machine in the home environment promises to become even more seamless and enriching.

CHAPTER 16:
AI IN HOME DÃ©COR

Imagine a home where the decor isn't just beautiful but also intuitive and responsive. With AI in home décor, this possibility becomes reality. Smart art frames allow you to switch between a myriad of artworks with a simple command, reflecting your mood or the season. Automated blinds adjust themselves based on time of day and weather conditions, offering a seamless combination of privacy and natural light. Lighting scenes can turn your living space into a tranquil haven or a vibrant entertainment area at the push of a button, all while learning your preferences over time. The convergence of technology and aesthetics isn't about replacing human touch but enhancing it, making your living environment more attuned to your lifestyle and needs.

Smart Art Frames

Imagine walking into a room where the art on your walls isn't static but dynamic, changing based on your mood, the time of day, or even the weather outside. Welcome to the world of Smart Art Frames—an innovation in home décor where artificial intelligence meets artistry to transform your living spaces into an ever-evolving gallery.

Smart Art Frames are digital frames that utilize AI algorithms to curate and display art. The beauty lies not just in their ability to showcase high-resolution images but also in their intelligent selection process. These devices can pull from a vast library of artworks, including classical pieces, contemporary photographs, and even personal photos, adjusting the display based on predefined criteria or real-time inputs like your viewing habits or the ambience of the room.

One of the key advantages of Smart Art Frames is their adaptability. Many models come with integrated sensors that detect the room's lighting conditions and adjust the brightness and color temperature of the displayed images accordingly. This ensures that whether it's morning, noon, or night, the displayed art always looks its best. Some advanced models even have motion sensors that can detect when someone enters the room, activating the display to create a welcoming visual experience.

Another fascinating feature is the ability to change the displayed art based on user preferences or moods. Through a connected app, users can indicate their mood or choose from a variety of themes—such as calming landscapes, vibrant modern art, or nostalgic family photos. The AI then curates a selection of images that align with the chosen theme, providing a personalized and emotive touch to home décor.

Smart Art Frames also offer an educational benefit. With built-in AI, these devices can display information about the artwork being shown, including the artist's background, historical context, and related works. This can be particularly beneficial for families with children, serving as both a decorative and an educational tool, sparking curiosity and learning through everyday interactions with art.

Integration with other smart home devices elevates the functionality of Smart Art Frames even further. For instance, they can be synced with smart lighting systems to create cohesive lighting scenes that complement the displayed artwork. If you're throwing a dinner party, you can program your frame to display elegant pieces while dimming the lights, enhancing the atmosphere in your dining room. This seamless integration with other AI-driven home décor elements enables a harmonious living environment tailored to individual needs and occasions.

Customization is another significant feature of Smart Art Frames. Users can upload their own images or create playlists of their favorite artworks. Imagine having a personal slide show that rotates through family photos, vacation snapshots, and digital art pieces—all beautifully presented with optimal lighting and display settings. This level of personalization makes these frames much more than just decorative pieces; they become an integral part of storytelling within the home.

For the environmentally conscious, Smart Art Frames present a sustainable alternative to traditional art displays. Conventional framed artworks often involve resources like paper, ink, and framing materials. In contrast, digital frames can cycle through thousands of images without the need for physical materials, reducing waste and the carbon footprint associated with constant redecorating. Moreover, some Smart Art Frames are designed with energy efficiency in mind, featuring low power consumption and automatic sleep modes when not in use.

Security and privacy are paramount in any AI application, and Smart Art Frames are no exception. Modern frames come equipped with data encryption, secure connections, and privacy settings that allow users to control what art libraries and data the frame can access. This ensures that while your home enjoys the benefits of AI-curated art, your personal information remains protected.

The potential for Smart Art Frames extends beyond individual households. In commercial settings, they can transform the aesthetic experience of offices, hotels, and retail spaces. Imagine walking into a hotel lobby where the artwork changes daily, giving returning guests a fresh visual experience each time they visit. Or consider an office environment where the ambiance of the workspace can be adjusted through dynamic, AI-driven art, thereby influencing employee morale and productivity.

In summary, Smart Art Frames are revolutionizing home décor by merging technology with art in innovative ways. They offer unparalleled flexibility, personalization, and integration with other smart home devices, enhancing the aesthetic and functional aspects of modern living spaces. As AI continues to advance, we can expect Smart Art Frames to become even more intuitive, perhaps predicting our art preferences before we even recognize them ourselves. Whether for educational purposes, personalization, or sustainable living, these intelligent frames are setting new standards for how we experience and interact with art in our homes.

Automated Blinds

Imagine waking up to the sunrise streaming gently into your bedroom, the blinds gradually opening without any effort on your part. Automated blinds, powered by artificial intelligence, offer a seamless blend of convenience and sophistication, transforming the way you interact with your living space. This chapter delves into how these smart innovations not only enhance the aesthetic appeal of your home but also contribute to energy efficiency and overall well-being.

Automated blinds operate via a combination of sensors, smart control systems, and integration with your home network. These systems can be programmed to adjust the blinds based on various factors such as the time of day, room occupancy, and even the weather. The ability to control light exposure with precision can lead to significant energy savings, as your home's heating and cooling requirements are optimized according to natural light levels.

One of the key elements of automated blinds is their seamless integration with voice assistants and smart hubs. By linking your blinds to devices like Amazon Alexa, Google Home, or Apple

HomeKit, you can control them through simple voice commands. This integration extends to creating complex automation scenarios where the blinds work in tandem with other smart devices. For instance, you could set a morning routine that gradually opens the blinds as your alarm goes off, adjusts the thermostat, and starts playing your favorite wake-up playlist.

Beyond convenience, automated blinds enhance home security. By simulating occupancy, your blinds can deter potential intruders when you're not at home. Scheduled to open and close at typical times, they give the impression that someone is always present, adding a layer of security without much thought or effort required from you.

The installation of automated blinds varies based on the model and brand. Some require professional installation while others are designed for DIY enthusiasts. Battery-operated models provide flexibility as they don't necessitate hardwiring, making them easier to install in any room. Some systems are solar-powered, ensuring sustainability and reducing reliance on traditional energy sources.

Customization is another standout feature. With a wide variety of materials, colors, and styles available, you can select blinds that perfectly match your home décor. Advanced systems allow for customization in terms of operation too, enabling you to set different schedules and preferences for each window in your home. Whether you prefer them fully open, partially shaded, or closed, the control is in your hands—or, more accurately, at your command.

Furthermore, automated blinds can significantly contribute to energy management in your home. By using smart blinds to control solar heat gain, you can reduce the burden on your HVAC system. During summer, the blinds can close during the hottest part of the day, keeping your home cooler and reducing air conditioning costs. Conversely, in the winter, opening the blinds can allow more sunlight and warmth to enter, lowering heating expenses.

The health benefits of automated blinds should not be overlooked either. By regulating natural light exposure, they help maintain circadian rhythms, which are crucial for a good night's sleep and overall well-being. This can be especially beneficial in homes located in areas with significant seasonal light variation. Rural or urban, large or small, every home stands to benefit from the nuanced control of light that automated blinds offer.

The impact of natural light on mood and productivity also cannot be overstated. Studies have shown that exposure to natural light improves mood, increases productivity, and enhances alertness. By automating the adjustment of your blinds, you ensure that you get the right amount of light throughout the day, thereby fostering a positive and productive home environment.

As you embark on the journey to integrate automated blinds into your smart home ecosystem, it's crucial to consider not just the technological aspects, but also the aesthetic and functional needs of your living space. Coordinate with interior design elements to create harmony and avoid creating discord with other elements of home décor. With automated blinds, your aim should be to enhance—not overshadow—the overall ambiance of your home.

It's also worth mentioning that the market for automated blinds is rapidly evolving. Innovations such as voice-driven AI and machine learning are making these systems even more intuitive and responsive. Future iterations might include even more advanced features, like predictive adjustments based on your routine and energy consumption data, making them more efficient and smarter than ever before.

In conclusion, automated blinds are not just a luxury but a smart investment in modern living, comfort, and efficiency. By strategically incorporating AI-driven solutions like these into your home, you not only elevate your living experience but also contribute positively to energy conservation and personal well-being. So as you explore other aspects of AI in home décor, consider automated blinds as a pivotal element that ties together convenience, security, and aesthetic excellence.

Lighting Scenes

One of the most transformative aspects of AI in home décor is its ability to create dynamic lighting scenes that can enhance the ambiance and functionality of any living space. Imagine walking into your living room and having the lights automatically adjust to suit your mood, the time of day, or even the activity you are undertaking. Whether you are hosting a dinner party, reading a book, or watching a movie, smart lighting can make your home feel both more inviting and functional.

Lighting scenes allow for tailored illumination setups that are finely tuned to specific needs and occasions. For instance, a bright and vibrant setting might be ideal for morning routines, helping you wake up and energize for the day ahead. Conversely, a warm, dimmed setting might be perfect for winding down in the evening, creating a cozy atmosphere conducive to relaxation. The adaptability of AI-driven lighting systems lies in their ability to seamlessly transition between these various scenes based on pre-set schedules, sensor detections, or voice commands.

Furthermore, the hardware behind these lighting scenes often involves smart bulbs, smart switches, and motion sensors. Modern smart bulbs come equipped with a full spectrum of color options and can be dimmed to precise levels, offering an unparalleled degree of control. Meanwhile, smart switches provide a convenient retrofit solution for existing lighting circuits, allowing regular light fixtures to be brought under the umbrella of smart home control. Motion sensors can add another layer of automation, ensuring that lights respond to your movement, thus saving energy and adding convenience.

The integration of AI apps and assistants simplifies the management of lighting scenes. Voice-controlled platforms like Amazon Alexa, Google Assistant, and Apple's Siri enable homeowners to adjust their lighting with simple spoken commands. These systems can also be programmed to recognize different residents, customizing light settings according to individual preferences.

Moreover, geofencing technology can be utilized to make lighting even more intuitive. Geofencing involves setting up a virtual perimeter around your home. When your phone crosses this boundary—either upon returning home or leaving—the system can trigger specific lighting scenes. Imagine pulling up into your driveway and having your porch lights switch on automatically, welcoming you home. Or, picture leaving the house and being assured that all unnecessary lights have been turned off, contributing to energy conservation.

Lighting scenes can also incorporate advanced AI algorithms to learn and predict your habits and preferences over time. This feature, often referred to as adaptive learning, means your smart lighting will continually refine its performance, tailoring its responses to your evolving needs and routines. Over time, your AI-driven lighting system will become more intuitive and personalized, further enhancing the comfort and efficiency of your home.

For those who love to entertain, customizable lighting scenes can also help set the perfect mood for events. Integrating smart lighting with your home's entertainment system can create immersive experiences. Imagine a movie night scene where the lights automatically dim as the film begins or a party scene where the lights change colors to match the music's rhythm. Through the synchronization of light with other smart devices, the entire ambiance of your home can be tightly choreographed to suit any occasion.

Beyond aesthetics and convenience, smart lighting scenes contribute to home security. A well-lit exterior can deter potential intruders, while interior lights that simulate occupied spaces can give the impression that someone is home even when the house is empty. Smart lighting can be programmed to follow natural patterns of activity, which can make a significant difference when you are away on vacation. Coupled with remote control capabilities, you can manage your home's lighting from anywhere in the world, adding an extra layer of security.

Another remarkable aspect of AI-powered lighting scenes is their impact on well-being. Research has shown that lighting significantly influences our circadian rhythms, which govern sleep-wake cycles and overall health. Smart lighting systems can mimic natural daylight patterns, aiding in better sleep hygiene and overall wellness. For instance, in the morning, the system can gradually increase light intensity to gently wake you up, mimicking a sunrise. At night, it can reduce blue light emissions, helping to prepare your body for rest. These subtle but powerful changes can make a profound difference in how we feel each day.

Seasonal changes are another factor that smart lighting scenes can adapt to. During shorter winter days, for example, enhancing indoor lighting can help combat seasonal affective disorder (SAD). Having your AI system automatically adjust lighting according to the seasons ensures that your home remains both comfortable and energy-efficient year-round.

Creating lighting scenes doesn't have to be complicated. Many platforms offer user-friendly interfaces where you can select from preset scenes or easily create your own. This customization allows you to experiment with different settings and find what works best for your home. It also makes the process of setting up a smart lighting system accessible, even for those who are less tech-savvy.

Moreover, the integration of lighting scenes with other smart home ecosystems elevates the overall user experience. By connecting your lighting system to other smart devices, such as thermostats and blinds, you can create holistic scenes that address multiple comfort needs simultaneously. For example, a 'Good Morning' scene might not only brighten lights but also gradually raise the blinds and adjust the thermostat to your preferred morning temperature.

As AI continues to evolve, so too will the capabilities of smart lighting systems. Future advancements may include more refined artificial intelligence algorithms, enhanced integration with other smart home devices, and even greater user customization options. Imagine a future where your home lighting self-adjusts in real-time based on facial recognition technology, detecting who is in the room and adjusting settings to their preferences without a single word being spoken.

In summary, the potential for AI in creating sophisticated lighting scenes is enormous. From daily routines to special occasions, security to wellness, these intelligent systems offer a customizable and highly efficient way to enhance your living spaces. As we continue to advance into an era of smart homes, the integration of AI-driven lighting will undoubtedly become a fundamental aspect of modern home décor, offering benefits that go well beyond mere illumination. Whether you are looking to simplify your daily routines, enhance your home's security, or just create the perfect atmosphere, smart lighting scenes represent a leap forward in home comfort and efficiency.

CHAPTER 17:
AI AND HOME SAFETY

Integrating AI into home safety systems is transforming the way we protect our living spaces. Advanced hazard detection technologies, such as AI-powered sensors, can now identify potential risks like gas leaks, smoke, or even carbon monoxide, providing warnings before danger escalates. Emergency response mechanisms are also evolving, with AI systems capable of automatically alerting emergency services or designated contacts during critical incidents. This rapid communication ensures timely intervention, mitigating damage and enhancing safety. Additionally, AI-driven communication systems streamline crisis management by providing clear, real-time instructions to residents, reducing panic and improving evacuation procedures. These innovations not only make our homes safer but also offer peace of mind, knowing that potential hazards are continuously monitored and addressed with unparalleled efficiency.

Hazard Detection

In the ever-evolving landscape of smart homes, safety remains a paramount concern. The potential of artificial intelligence (AI) to enhance home safety through hazard detection is not only promising but transformative. Imagine a living space where AI monitors and identifies potential dangers before they escalate, ensuring a safer environment for you and your loved ones.

Hazard detection systems leverage AI's ability to analyze data continuously and make informed decisions in real time. Unlike traditional systems that often rely on human intervention, these AI-driven systems can autonomously detect smoke, gas leaks, water leaks, and other hazards, triggering immediate alerts and mitigating potential damage. This proactive approach significantly reduces response times, enhancing the overall security of your home.

One of the fundamental aspects of AI-driven hazard detection is its integration with various sensors and smart devices. These sensors continuously monitor environmental conditions and anomalies, feeding data back to a central AI system. For instance, smoke detectors and carbon monoxide sensors equipped with AI capabilities can distinguish between normal levels and those indicative of danger. When a threat is detected, the system can alert homeowners through various connected devices, including smartphones, tablets, or even smart TVs.

AI's predictive capabilities play a crucial role in hazard detection. Machine learning algorithms analyze historical data to identify patterns and predict potential risks. For example, predictive maintenance algorithms can anticipate electrical faults or appliance malfunctions before they occur, allowing homeowners to address these issues preemptively. This not only prevents accidents but also extends the lifespan of your home appliances, contributing to overall cost savings.

Integration with other smart home systems amplifies the effectiveness of AI in hazard detection. For example, an AI-powered security system can work in tandem with smart lighting and climate controls to create a comprehensive safety net. If a gas leak is detected, the system can automatically shut off the gas supply, ventilate the area by activating fans, and illuminate exit paths to guide occupants to safety.

Voice assistants, another cornerstone of smart homes, can also play a role in hazard detection. Equipped with AI, these devices can be programmed to recognize emergency phrases or unusual noises and respond accordingly. For instance, if you shout "Help!" your voice assistant could instantly alert emergency services, providing them with vital information about your location and the nature of the emergency.

Moreover, AI-enhanced cameras can analyze visual data to detect potential hazards. These cameras, integrated with image recognition algorithms, can identify smoke, fire, or flooding. When such hazards are detected, the system can notify homeowners and take pre-configured actions like contacting emergency services or activating internal alarms.

Another layer of hazard detection involves the use of smart water leak sensors. Water damage can be incredibly costly and damaging to households. With AI-integrated sensors placed in high-risk areas (like basements, underneath sinks, or near water heaters), these devices can detect even the smallest leaks. When a leak is detected, the AI system can shut off the main water supply to prevent further damage and alert the homeowner about the issue.

The sophistication of AI in hazard detection doesn't stop with individual homes; it extends to community safety as well. By aggregating data from multiple houses within a community, AI can identify broader patterns and predict regional hazards, potentially preventing large-scale disasters. For example, by monitoring air quality data across several homes, AI could predict wildfires or other environmental hazards, coordinating with local authorities for timely intervention.

Privacy and data security are often concerns when it comes to integrating AI into home safety systems. It's essential to ensure that all hazard detection devices operate on secure networks, with robust encryption protocols to protect sensitive data. Manufacturers must prioritize building these security measures into their products to build trust with consumers.

The journey towards an AI-enhanced hazard detection system doesn't require starting from scratch. Many smart home devices are designed to integrate seamlessly with existing systems, making upgrades more accessible and less disruptive. As more homeowners adopt these technologies, the cumulative effect will be a significant reduction in domestic accidents and a dramatic improvement in overall safety standards.

To conclude, AI presents a groundbreaking approach to hazard detection in smart homes. By leveraging real-time data analysis, predictive capabilities, and integration with various smart devices, AI systems offer unparalleled protection and peace of mind. As these technologies continue to evolve, their potential to safeguard homes will only grow, transforming the nature of home safety for years to come.

Emergency Response

The integration of artificial intelligence (AI) into home safety systems has revolutionized how we approach emergency response. By leveraging advanced technologies, homes can now be equipped with intelligent systems capable of not only detecting emergencies but also taking immediate action to mitigate risks. In the realm of home safety, emergency response is about creating a seamless and efficient system that can act faster than human intervention, potentially saving lives and property.

One of the most critical aspects of AI-driven emergency response is the speed and accuracy of hazard detection. Smart sensors placed throughout the home can identify a wide range of potential emergencies, from fires and gas leaks to intrusions and medical emergencies. These sensors are interconnected through a central hub, which continuously monitors data and uses machine learning algorithms to detect anomalies that signify a potential threat.

When a hazardous situation is detected, AI systems can initiate a series of predefined actions. For instance, in the event of a fire, smart smoke detectors can trigger an alarm, send notifications to the homeowner's mobile device, and even communicate directly with emergency services. The integration of AI can enhance this process by predicting the fire's spread and suggesting the best evacuation routes, considering real-time data and environmental conditions.

AI systems can also be programmed to shut down electrical systems or gas lines to prevent further damage. This level of automation minimizes the risk to human life and reduces property damage. In addition, smart home systems can collaborate with smart locks and windows, ensuring that exit pathways are clear and accessible during an emergency.

Medical emergencies represent another area where AI excels in emergency response. Wearable devices such as smartwatches can monitor vital signs and detect irregularities like heart attacks or strokes. These devices can instantly alert emergency contacts and relay critical health information to paramedics en route, vastly improving the chances of a timely and effective medical intervention. In the case of elderly family members or individuals with chronic conditions, AI-powered systems can provide an extra layer of safety and reassurance.

Moreover, communication during emergencies is paramount, and AI can streamline this process through advanced communication systems. Voice assistants, for example, can be integrated into emergency protocols, allowing users to issue voice commands even under stress. With custom commands configured, a simple phrase can alert all connected devices and initiate emergency procedures without the need for physical interaction.

Community-based emergency response is also enhanced through AI integration. Smart home systems can be connected to neighborhood networks, alerting nearby homes of potential hazards and prompting collective action. This kind of community alert system can be particularly useful in situations such as natural disasters, where coordinated efforts significantly improve overall safety.

While the technology itself is impressive, proper setup and maintenance of these emergency response systems are equally crucial. Homeowners should ensure that all sensors and devices are correctly installed and regularly maintained. Devices should be tested frequently to confirm they are functioning as expected, and backup batteries should be in place to guarantee operation during power outages.

Additionally, educating household members on how to interact with AI-powered emergency systems is vital. Everyone should be familiar with the functionality of voice commands, manual overrides, and emergency contacts pre-programmed into the system. Drills and simulations can be conducted to ensure readiness in actual emergency scenarios.

AI-driven emergency response systems also necessitate robust data protection measures. Given the sensitive nature of the data being processed, from health information to real-time environmental monitoring, secure networks and encryption protocols must be in place. Users should regularly update firmware and apply patches to protect against potential vulnerabilities.

Besides handling real-time emergencies, AI can also be predictive in its approach to home safety. Machine learning algorithms analyze past data to identify patterns and suggest preventive measures, such as modifying the placement of smoke detectors or reinforcing structural elements vulnerable to natural disasters.

Finally, integration with other smart home features ensures that the emergency response is comprehensive and context-aware. For example, smart lighting systems can illuminate exit paths during a fire alarm, improving visibility and safety. Similarly, smart cameras can provide real-time video feeds to first responders, offering them a clearer picture of the situation before they arrive on the scene.

In conclusion, AI's role in emergency response within the realm of home safety is transformative. By combining rapid hazard detection, automated intervention, and enhanced communication, AI systems create safer living environments. As technology continues to evolve, the potential for further advancements in emergency response is limitless, offering even more sophisticated solutions to keep our homes and loved ones safe.

Communication Systems

When it comes to the integration of artificial intelligence in home safety, communication systems play a pivotal role. The seamless exchange of data and commands between devices is what makes a smart home truly 'smart.' With efficient communication systems, various AI-powered devices can work in unison to create a safer and more responsive living environment.

First, let's dive into the core of communication systems in smart homes: the protocols and networks that bind these devices together. Wi-Fi remains a cornerstone, offering robust connectivity for many smart home gadgets. However, it's not the only option. Zigbee and Z-Wave are two popular alternatives that offer low-power, high-reliability communication, ideal for sensors and other small devices. Mesh networks, such as those used by some Zigbee setups, add an additional layer of reliability, ensuring that even if one node goes down, others can pick up the slack.

At the heart of these communication systems are hubs and bridges that act as intermediaries, translating signals between different protocols. For example, a smart hub can integrate Zigbee sensors, Wi-Fi cameras, and even older wired systems into a single, cohesive network. This interoperability is vital for ensuring that all devices work together without conflicts or data loss.

The importance of robust communication systems in home safety can't be overstated. Imagine a scenario where your smart smoke detector senses a fire. It immediately sends a signal to your smart hub via Zigbee, which then broadcasts this alert over Wi-Fi to your phone and also triggers other devices like smart locks to unlock doors for an easy exit. The efficiency and reliability of this communication can make the difference between a minor incident and a major disaster.

Furthermore, AI augments these communication systems by providing predictive analytics and automated responses. AI algorithms can analyze patterns in the data generated by these devices to predict potential hazards before they occur. For instance, an AI system can notice that a particular electrical outlet often draws unusually high power and alert you to potential issues such as an impending short circuit, allowing for preventive maintenance.

Emergency response systems are another critical application where communication systems shine. These systems can instantly relay information to emergency services, neighbors, and other relevant parties. Advanced AI algorithms can even make real-time decisions about what type of emergency it is, who to notify, and what actions to take. This could involve shutting off the gas supply in the event of a gas leak or unlocking all doors in case of a fire.

For elderly or disabled home occupants, communication systems enhanced with AI can provide an additional layer of safety and convenience. Voice-activated systems, for instance, allow individuals to call for help without needing to physically reach a phone. AI-driven cameras and sensors can also monitor for falls or unusual behavior, sending alerts to caregivers or family members instantly.

Moreover, the reliability of communication systems is paramount, especially in scenarios involving home security. Smart cameras, motion sensors, and alarms all depend on consistent, real-time data exchange to function effectively. Delays or failures in communication could render these systems less effective or entirely useless in a crisis. Therefore, redundancies such as backup communication channels and fail-safes are often built into these systems to ensure they remain operational even under adverse conditions.

In summary, communication systems form the backbone of AI-driven home safety solutions. From fire detection to emergency response, the seamless interaction between various devices ensures a coordinated and effective approach to home safety. As these systems continue to evolve, they'll become even more integral to creating safer, smarter living environments. With the combination of reliable communication protocols, AI analytics, and automated responses, the future looks promising for homes that are more responsive to our safety needs than ever before.

Ultimately, the goal is to create an ecosystem where all your safety devices—whether they monitor smoke, water, gas, or intrusion—work together seamlessly. When these systems are supported by robust communication networks and smart algorithms, the result is a home that's not just intelligent but also resilient and safe. By investing in effective communication systems, you are laying the groundwork for a home that can anticipate and respond to various safety challenges, ensuring peace of mind for all its occupants.

CHAPTER 18:
PET CARE AUTOMATION

Automation in pet care is transforming how pet owners manage daily tasks and cater to their pets' needs. Imagine a world where smart feeders dispense the right amount of food at scheduled times, ensuring that your pets are fed even when you're not home. These devices can be programmed and monitored through an app, offering push notifications to keep you in the loop. Integrated pet monitoring systems utilize cameras and sensors to track your pet's activities and health, granting peace of mind with real-time video feeds and alerting you to any unusual behavior. Automated play devices further enrich your pet's environment, stimulating both body and mind with programmed routines and interactive features that mimic your presence. Together, these technological advancements create a seamless, effortless way to maintain your pet's well-being, allowing you to focus on enjoying more quality time with your furry friends.

Smart Feeders

In the realm of pet care automation, smart feeders stand out as one of the most revolutionary advancements. Gone are the days when pet owners had to worry about remembering feeding times or fretting over their animals' nutritional intake. With the integration of artificial intelligence, pet feeding has transformed into a seamless, efficient experience that not only benefits the pets but also offers tremendous peace of mind to their owners.

Imagine being able to control your pet's feeding schedule from anywhere in the world. Smart feeders, outfitted with Wi-Fi connectivity and app-based controls, make this convenience possible. These devices allow for remote feeding, portion control, and time scheduling, ensuring that pets are fed the right amount at the right times. No more overfeeding or forgetting to feed your pet while you're stuck at work or away on vacation.

One of the major benefits of smart feeders is their capability to dispense precise portions. Traditional feeding methods often lead to portions that are too generous or too scanty. Consistent overfeeding can lead to obesity, while underfeeding can cause malnutrition. Smart feeders eliminate this uncertainty by measuring out specific amounts of food based on the pet's dietary needs. The system can even be fine-tuned for different types of pets, from cats and dogs to more exotic animals.

Advanced models come equipped with sensors and cameras, offering real-time monitoring of feeding times and consumption habits. Owners can watch live streams or review recorded footage to ensure that their pets are eating properly. If the feeder detects irregularities such as skipped meals or food hoarding, it can send alerts to the owner's smartphone, prompting a timely intervention.

Integration with other smart home devices further elevates the functionality of smart feeders. Voice assistants like Amazon Alexa, Google Assistant, and Apple's Siri can be linked to these devices, allowing for voice-activated feeding or status checks. Imagine saying, "Alexa, feed Bella," and knowing that your furry friend is being fed the exact amount prescribed by the vet, without lifting a finger.

Moreover, AI-powered smart feeders offer predictive analytics that can be crucial for maintaining a pet's health. By analyzing the data collected from feeding patterns, these devices can provide insights into your pet's dietary needs and make recommendations accordingly. If a pet consistently eats less than usual, the system can alert the owner to potential health issues, enabling early detection and treatment.

The setup and configuration of smart feeders are straightforward, even for those who aren't tech-savvy. Most come with user-friendly apps that guide you through the setup process, from connecting to Wi-Fi to setting feeding schedules. Manuals often include detailed instructions with visuals, ensuring a smooth installation experience. The convenience of having a reliable, automated feeding system far outweighs the minor learning curve associated with setting it up.

A particularly innovative feature in some models is the ability to manage multiple pets. With individual profiles that can be created for each pet, the feeder can dispense different portions and types of food as required. This is especially useful in households with pets that have varied dietary needs. No longer will you need separate feeding stations or different feeding times; a well-configured smart feeder can handle it all.

While the practical benefits are plentiful, the peace of mind that comes from knowing your pet's dietary needs are being met is immeasurable. Many pet owners experience guilt or anxiety when they can't be home to feed their pets at regular intervals. Smart feeders serve as a reliable surrogate, ensuring pets receive their meals on time, every time.

It's important to select a smart feeder that is compatible with your other home automation devices. Integration isn't just about convenience but also about creating a cohesive ecosystem where all your smart devices can 'talk' to each other. For example, some smart feeders can be programmed to coordinate with automated pet doors, ensuring that only certain pets have access to the feeder at specific times.

Furthermore, the materials and design of smart feeders are generally pet-safe and durable. Food compartments are made from BPA-free plastics and stainless steel to ensure hygiene. The mechanisms are designed to prevent jamming, and many models feature backup battery options to keep them operational during power outages.

Incorporating smart feeders doesn't just streamline the process of feeding pets; it enhances the overall quality of care they receive. When coupled with other pet care technologies like automated play systems and pet monitoring devices, the smart feeder becomes part of a comprehensive care package that benefits both pets and their owners.

The future of smart feeders holds even more promise. Innovations such as machine learning algorithms and improved sensor technologies could soon offer features like automatic adjustment of feeding schedules based on an individual pet's changing needs. Imagine a feeder that adapts to your pet's growth or health status, delivering tailored nutrition without any manual intervention.

In conclusion, smart feeders are more than just a convenience—they are a powerful tool in the modern pet owner's arsenal, bridging the gap between loving care and cutting-edge technology. By integrating these devices into your smart home setup, you're investing in the long-term health and happiness of your pets. Whether you're a busy professional, frequent traveler, or simply someone who wants the best for their feline or canine companion, a smart feeder is a game-changer.

With the evolution of pet care automation, smart feeders stand at the forefront, exemplifying how AI can make daily responsibilities easier and more efficient. Embrace this technology, and you'll not only enhance your pet's life but also gain invaluable peace of mind.

Pet Monitoring

In a fast-paced world where many of us are occupied with work and other commitments, ensuring the well-being of our pets can sometimes be challenging. This is where AI-driven pet monitoring systems come into play, offering an unprecedented level of care and security for our furry friends. With advanced technologies integrated into our homes, keeping an eye on pets has never been easier or more effective. Let's delve into how AI can transform pet monitoring to provide a safer, healthier, and happier environment for our pets.

One of the primary benefits of AI in pet care is real-time monitoring. Cameras equipped with AI can recognize pets and track their movements throughout the house. These cameras are more than simple recording devices; they come with features like motion detection, night vision, and two-way audio. This enables pet owners to not only see their pets but also interact with them while away. Imagine your cat lounging comfortably in the living room or your dog playing in the backyard—each moment captured and accessible through a smart device.

Beyond visual monitoring, AI systems can learn and recognize your pet's habits over time. For instance, if your dog has a routine of napping in the afternoon or if your cat tends to roam the house at night, the system can notify you if there is anything unusual. Such predictive monitoring ensures that any deviations in behavior—possibly indicative of health issues—are detected promptly. Coupled with other smart home devices, these systems create a network of care that is always vigilant, always on duty.

Furthermore, integrating AI with smart collars takes pet monitoring to another level. Smart collars can track various health metrics like heart rate, temperature, and activity levels. When linked with an AI platform, the data collected can be analyzed to provide insights into your pet's health and behavior. Alerts can be set up to notify you if your pet's vital signs fall out of the normal range, enabling timely interventions. Such proactive measures are invaluable, potentially catching health issues before they become critical.

When it comes to safety, AI-powered systems can also detect and alert you to environmental hazards that may pose a risk to your pets. Whether it's a sudden drop in temperature, a fire, or even a gas leak, these systems are designed to keep your home—and your pets—safe. Some advanced setups can even coordinate with other smart devices to take action, such as turning off gas valves or unlocking pet doors to facilitate an escape in emergencies.

Another fascinating aspect of AI in pet monitoring is the use of facial recognition technology. While this technology is commonly associated with security systems, it has a unique application in pet care. Facial recognition can be used to track individual pets in multi-pet households, ensuring each pet is accounted for and monitored accurately. This feature is especially useful in large homes or when pets have access to outdoor spaces, providing peace of mind that each furry family member is safe and sound.

Pet monitoring also extends to automatic pet feeders and water dispensers, which can be controlled and monitored through AI. These devices ensure that your pets are fed on time and in the right quantities, even when you're not home. Some advanced models can even adjust feeding schedules and portions based on the pet's activity levels and health data. This integration of AI into feeding routines not only ensures consistent nutrition but also prevents overfeeding, which can lead to obesity and other health issues.

AI can also be employed in monitoring behavioral changes. For example, excessive barking, scratching, or other signs of distress can be detected by AI systems, triggering alerts to pet owners. Early detection of such behaviors can lead to quicker diagnosis and treatment of underlying issues, be they medical or environmental. In addition, some systems offer interactive features that allow pet owners to engage with their pets remotely, such as through treat dispensers or automated pet toys, ensuring that pets remain stimulated and happy even in their owners' absence.

One of the more innovative uses of AI in pet monitoring involves virtual veterinarians. With real-time health data collected and analyzed by AI, virtual consultations can become incredibly precise and effective. Veterinarians can access a wealth of information about your pet's activity levels, diet, and vital signs, all in real time, allowing for more accurate diagnoses and personalized care plans. This level of detailed, instant access can make a world of difference in managing chronic conditions or catching potential health issues early.

Finally, the peace of mind that comes from knowing your pets are safe and well-cared for is invaluable. AI-enabled pet monitoring systems can relieve much of the anxiety that pet owners might feel when they're away from home, whether for a short workday or a longer trip. The assurance that AI is keeping a vigilant eye on your pets allows you to focus on your tasks, knowing that an intelligent system will notify you immediately if something isn't right.

In summary, the integration of AI into pet monitoring offers a comprehensive suite of tools designed for the modern pet owner. From real-time video feeds to health tracking and behavioral analysis, the functionalities provided by these advanced systems are transforming how we care for our pets. The seamless integration of AI technology into our homes ensures that our pets are not only safer but also happier and healthier. As AI continues to evolve, we can expect even more innovative solutions to enhance pet care, making our homes more connected, efficient, and secure for every member of the family—human and animal alike.

Automated Play

Understanding the importance of play for pets and integrating that necessity into a smart home platform can bring unprecedented levels of convenience and well-being to your pet care routine. Automated play systems for pets are a burgeoning area of smart home technology that promises not just to keep your furry friends mentally and physically engaged, but also to offer peace of mind when you're away from home.

Automated play systems come in various forms, from robotic toys to smart fetch machines. These devices utilize artificial intelligence to interact with pets in stimulating and engaging ways. Take, for instance, a smart ball; it might seem simple from the outside, but it comes equipped with sensors and learning algorithms that allow it to move around unpredictably, mimicking the erratic movements of prey. This taps into your pet's natural instincts, offering a more fulfilling playtime experience.

This technology isn't just limited to physical exercise. Mental stimulation is just as vital for your pets as it is for humans. Many automated play systems incorporate puzzle games and other brain-teasing activities that challenge your pet to think and solve problems for rewards like treats. These systems not only keep your pet occupied but also contribute to its cognitive development, making for a happier and healthier pet.

One significant advantage of automated play systems is their ability to adapt to your pet's behavior through machine learning. These devices continuously gather data on your pet's interactions, learning what keeps them most engaged and modifying their activities accordingly. Such advancement enables a customized experience tailored precisely to your pet's preferences, ensuring that the novelty of the toy or gadget doesn't wear off quickly.

Another important feature of automated play devices is remote operability. With mobile applications, you can control and monitor these gadgets from anywhere. Imagine being at work and being able to initiate a play session for your pet at home with just a few taps on your smartphone. Schedules can be set to automate playtimes throughout the day, ensuring your pet gets adequate exercise and stimulation regardless of your availability.

It's crucial to consider the safety aspects as well. Many automated play devices are designed with multiple safety features to prevent injuries. For example, some robotic toys have sensors that detect obstacles, ensuring they don't get stuck or cause harm to your pet or home furnishings. Additionally, materials used are often pet-safe, non-toxic, and durable to withstand the wear and tear of energetic play.

The ecological perspective is not overlooked either. Many manufacturers of automated play devices are making concerted efforts to employ sustainable materials and energy-efficient designs. Some devices come with rechargeable batteries or energy-saving modes which contribute to a more eco-friendly and cost-effective operation.

Integrating automated play systems into your smart home setup usually isn't complex. Compatibility with existing smart home ecosystems like Google Home, Amazon Alexa, or Apple HomeKit can simplify control and improve user experience. You can include play sessions in your home's daily automation routines, alongside other activities like feeding and monitoring, offering seamless integration that makes holistic pet care easier than ever.

For those who enjoy tinkering, there are even DIY kits available that allow you to build and customize automated play setups. These kits come equipped with components like Arduino boards, motors, and sensors, along with detailed instructions. Such projects can be incredibly rewarding, giving you a deeper understanding of smart home technology and providing a bespoke solution tailored exactly to your pet's needs.

Moreover, the market for such technologies is rapidly advancing, with new products continually entering the scene. Innovations like AI companions that combine features of automated play, feeding, and monitoring are being developed, promising to revolutionize pet care. Thus, keeping informed about new advancements can help you make choices that best fit your home and your pet's unique requirements.

As you look to incorporate or expand automated play into your pet care arsenal, remember too that your involvement remains valuable. While technology can assist remarkably, spending time interacting with your pet is irreplaceable. Automated play systems should complement, not replace, the human-animal bond that is crucial for pet satisfaction and well-being.

In summary, automated play systems present an innovative, efficient, and engaging way to ensure that your pets receive the exercise and mental stimulation they need. By effectively integrating these systems into your smart home, you achieve a harmonious balance that enhances the quality of life for both you and your pets. After all, a well-stimulated pet is a happy pet, and a happy pet contributes to a happier home.

CHAPTER 19:
CHILD SAFETY AND CONVENIENCE

Integrating AI into your smart home to enhance child safety and convenience offers a transformative way to ensure that both kids and parents enjoy a secure and efficient living environment. Smart baby monitors provide real-time video and health analytics straight to your devices, allowing you to keep an eye on your little ones no matter where you are in the house. Child-friendly devices, such as AI-powered toys and educational tools, add an enriching layer to their learning experiences while keeping them entertained. Parental controls on various smart devices offer an extra layer of protection, enabling you to monitor and regulate screen time, access to content, and even the physical security of your home. This seamless integration not only fosters a safer home but also offers the peace of mind every parent seeks in today's fast-paced world. Whether it's through intuitive voice commands or automated routines, the blend of child safety and convenience through AI makes managing your family's needs simpler and more effective.

Smart Baby Monitors

In the realm of child safety and convenience, smart baby monitors have emerged as indispensable tools for modern parents. These devices integrate seamlessly into the fabric of smart homes, leveraging artificial intelligence to provide a level of oversight and peace of mind that was previously unattainable. Unlike traditional baby monitors, smart baby monitors offer real-time video, audio streaming, and even advanced analytics that keep parents connected to their little ones in unprecedented ways.

The most compelling feature of smart baby monitors is their ability to deliver real-time alerts. These monitors can detect a wide range of activities and notify parents instantly through their smartphones. For instance, they can alert you if your baby rolls over, starts crying, or even if the room temperature changes. Such capabilities ensure that parents can respond immediately to any potential issues, thereby enhancing the safety and comfort of their children.

Integrating advanced AI algorithms, smart baby monitors can differentiate between a baby's various cries—whether it's hunger, discomfort, or just needing a little attention. This means you're not just alerted to any sound, but you also get a clearer understanding of your baby's needs. This feature becomes particularly valuable during the middle of the night when distinguishing between a mere whimper and a genuine cry for help can mean the difference between a peaceful night and unnecessary anxiety.

Alongside real-time notifications, these monitors come equipped with high-definition cameras that provide crystal-clear visual feeds. Many smart baby monitors also offer night vision, allowing parents to keep an eye on their child even in low-light conditions. The video feeds can be accessed remotely, giving working parents the flexibility to check in on their toddlers from the office or while traveling. Moreover, some smart baby monitors come with pan, tilt, and zoom functions, enabling comprehensive coverage of the room.

Two-way audio communication is another monumental feature of smart baby monitors. This allows parents to talk to their baby or play soothing lullabies through the monitor, offering comfort even when they are not physically present in the room. The ability to communicate instantly can be reassuring for both the child and the parents, fostering a sense of closeness and security.

The use of AI extends to features such as sleep tracking and breathing monitoring. Some advanced models can analyze your baby's sleep patterns and provide insights into their sleep quality and duration. Breathing monitoring capabilities can alert parents to any irregularities, allowing them to take prompt action if needed. These functionalities can be life-saving, offering an extra layer of protection for infants who are particularly vulnerable.

Furthermore, many smart baby monitors are equipped with temperature and humidity sensors. These sensors help ensure that the room environment remains within a comfortable and safe range for your baby. Parents receive notifications if conditions deviate from the set parameters, allowing them to make adjustments as needed.

Interconnectivity with other smart home devices is another major advantage of smart baby monitors. For instance, they can be integrated with smart lighting systems to automatically adjust the room lighting based on the time of day and the baby's sleep schedule. Integration with smart thermostats can also ensure that the room temperature remains optimal. This level of automation not only enhances child safety but also offers significant convenience in managing the household environment.

Privacy and security are paramount when it comes to using smart baby monitors. Manufacturers are increasingly focusing on robust security measures to ensure that video feeds and data streams are encrypted and protected against unauthorized access. Parents should opt for monitors that offer strong password protection, secure data encryption, and regular software updates to safeguard their family's privacy.

Despite their advanced capabilities, setting up a smart baby monitor is straightforward. Most models come with user-friendly apps that guide parents through the installation process step-by-step. Once set up, these monitors can be easily managed and controlled through smartphone apps, providing a centralized platform for monitoring and managing the device.

Additionally, many smart baby monitors are compatible with popular voice assistants like Amazon Alexa and Google Assistant. This allows parents to use voice commands to check the camera feed, adjust settings, or play recorded lullabies. Integrating voice control enhances ease of use and adds another layer of convenience to the parenting experience.

When selecting a smart baby monitor, parents should consider factors such as video quality, range of coverage, battery life, and ease of installation. Reviews and user feedback can be invaluable in making an informed decision. By choosing a reliable and well-reviewed monitor, parents can ensure that they are investing in a device that will provide consistent and accurate performance.

Smart baby monitors are not just about providing immediate safety; they also contribute to long-term parenting strategies. By leveraging data and insights provided by these devices, parents can better understand their child's habits and needs, enabling them to create more effective routines and caregiving strategies. This data-driven approach fosters a more informed and proactive parenting style.

The evolution of smart baby monitors embodies the merging of technology and caregiving, highlighting the potential of AI to enhance both safety and convenience. As these devices continue to advance, they promise to offer even more sophisticated features, making parenting easier and more connected than ever before. The integration of smart baby monitors into the smart home ecosystem not only addresses immediate safety concerns but also lays the foundation for intelligent and informed parenting, ensuring that children grow up in a secure and nurturing environment.

In conclusion, smart baby monitors are a significant advancement in the field of child safety and convenience. Their array of features—ranging from real-time alerts and high-definition video feeds to sleep tracking and environmental monitoring—offer parents the peace of mind and control they need to ensure the well-being of their children. By embracing these intelligent devices, parents can create a safer, more responsive, and ultimately more nurturing home environment for their little ones.

Child-Friendly Devices

When incorporating artificial intelligence into your home, ensuring that the youngest members of your family are safe and comfortable is paramount. Child-friendly devices aim to provide additional layers of safety, convenience, and even education, making your smart home not only more efficient but also kid-friendly. These devices can range from smart cameras and monitors to interactive learning gadgets, all designed with children's special needs in mind.

One of the primary categories of child-friendly devices includes smart baby monitors. Modern AI-powered baby monitors do much more than simply stream video to a parent's smartphone. Advanced models can track your baby's sleep patterns, analyze crying sounds to determine why your baby might be distressed, and even monitor the room's temperature and humidity levels. These features allow parents to be more proactive in taking care of their infants, offering peace of mind and, most importantly, ensuring the child's well-being.

Another useful device in the child-friendly domain is the smart speaker designed specifically for kids. While adults enjoy features like virtual assistants and music streaming, kids' versions often come with parental controls, filtered content, and educational games. In addition to being a source of entertainment, these devices can help children improve their language skills, learn about various subjects, and even practice mindfulness and relaxation techniques.

Moving on to child-friendly lighting solutions, the right kind of smart lighting can create an ambience that's both calming and secure. For instance, programmable night lights can help children who are afraid of the dark, while color-changing bulbs can be set to 'study mode' to promote better concentration during homework time. These lighting solutions can be controlled remotely, allowing parents to ensure their child's environment is optimal for any activity, all through a smartphone app or voice command.

Smart thermostats also play a role in child safety and convenience. Kids are particularly sensitive to temperature fluctuations, and an AI-powered thermostat can create a comfortable environment by adjusting heating or cooling based on the room's occupancy and the child's routine. Some advanced models come with additional sensors that can be placed in different rooms, ensuring consistent comfort throughout the home.

Safety is a paramount concern, and child-friendly devices often incorporate robust security features to keep kids safe. For example, AI-driven smart locks can ensure that children can't accidentally wander outside without adult supervision. Some smart locks even allow parents to set up temporary access codes for babysitters or caregivers, enhancing security while maintaining convenience.

Integrated home security systems often come with child-specific features as well. Motion sensors can be programmed to alert parents if certain areas of the house, like the front door or the stairway, are accessed during specific times of the day. This proactive approach can prevent accidents and ensure that children are always within safe boundaries.

Educational benefits can't be overstated when it comes to child-friendly devices. Interactive smart screens or tablets designed for learning come equipped with a plethora of educational apps, games, and e-books. These devices often include parental controls to restrict screen time and access to certain content, ensuring a balanced approach to learning and leisure.

Additionally, wearable devices designed for children offer another layer of safety and convenience. Smartwatches for kids often come with GPS tracking, allowing parents to know their child's location at all times. Some models even offer features like calling and text messaging, so children can reach out to their parents instantly in case of an emergency.

Voice assistants designed for children serve as helpful companions for kids as they grow and learn. These devices can tell bedtime stories, answer endless questions, and even help with day-to-day tasks like setting reminders for homework or chores. With child-specific voice recognition, these assistants can interact with kids in a way that's both engaging and educational, making them invaluable tools for modern parenting.

Voice-controlled smart home hubs can also be child-friendly. They can help children with morning routines by playing wake-up songs or reminding them to brush their teeth. The routines can be fully customizable, making it easier for kids to get into good habits even when parents are busy.

Furthermore, child-friendly devices often integrate seamlessly with existing smart home systems. For instance, a child's smartwatch can be connected to the home's AI system to notify parents if the child leaves a designated safe area. Such integrations ensure that all aspects of child safety and convenience are covered, providing seamless experiences that adapt to your child's needs.

In terms of fun, there are many AI-powered toys that foster creativity and learning. These toys can help children learn coding fundamentals, solve puzzles, or even interact with AI companions that respond to their emotional and social needs. Such toys not only provide entertainment but also contribute to the developmental milestones that are crucial in early childhood.

All in all, child-friendly devices integrate seamlessly into the broader context of a smart home, ensuring that while your home gets smarter, it also becomes a safer, more nurturing environment for your children. From monitoring their well-being and ensuring their safety to offering educational and entertainment opportunities, these devices are geared to address various aspects of your child's needs, enhancing both their and your experience in the smart home ecosystem.

Parental Controls

In the increasingly connected, AI-driven world of smart homes, keeping the youngest members of the family safe is a paramount concern. Parental controls serve as a crucial feature in creating a secure and child-friendly environment within the home. The variety of devices and systems under the umbrella of smart home technology can be overwhelming, but at their core, parental controls are designed to give parents peace of mind and a greater sense of control over what their children can access and interact with.

One of the primary benefits of integrating AI into parental controls is the ability to customize and monitor access levels in real-time. Smart hubs and voice assistants like Amazon Alexa and Google Nest can be configured to limit what children can do and see. For example, you can set up guidelines for screen time, restrict certain types of content, and even manage the overall usage of connected devices through simple voice commands or mobile app interfaces.

The seamless integration of AI with smart home systems means that parental controls are not just about blocking or restricting access, but also about proactively creating a safer environment. Advanced AI algorithms can identify potential hazards or inappropriate content and alert parents immediately. For instance, smart speakers can be programmed to mute themselves if they detect language or content that's deemed unsuitable for children. This allows parents to stay one step ahead in managing their children's exposure to various media forms.

Additionally, smart cameras and monitoring systems have made great strides in terms of integrating parental controls. Beyond just keeping an eye on kids' activities, modern AI-powered cameras can recognize and differentiate between different people, pets, and objects in the home. Parents can receive instant notifications if their child is approaching an unsafe area, such as the kitchen or the swimming pool. This level of real-time monitoring and situational awareness can significantly reduce risks and make home life more stress-free for parents.

Another dimension where parental controls shine is in regulating internet access. Routers and mesh networks enhanced with AI capabilities can limit children's online activity to specific hours, ensuring they don't stay up late browsing or playing online games. These systems can also filter out harmful websites and restrict access to unsafe content. Many of these controls can be adjusted remotely, giving parents the flexibility to manage settings even when they're not at home.

For parents who are concerned about screen time, AI offers intelligent solutions that go beyond simple time limits. AI-driven parental controls can encourage kids to take breaks, suggest educational content, and even track how screen time is being spent. By analyzing usage patterns, AI can recommend more balanced ways for children to interact with their devices, promoting healthier digital habits.

Integrating parental controls within a smart home extends to physical devices as well. Smart locks, for example, can be programmed to restrict access to certain rooms, ensuring that children can't get into areas that may pose a danger, like workshops or home gyms. Parents can set these restrictions based on schedules or specific criteria, allowing for dynamic and adaptable control over the home environment.

The ability to monitor and regulate interactions with smart devices doesn't just stop at safety concerns. It can also be used to foster learning and development. For instance, AI can recommend educational apps and content based on the child's interests and age. This not only enriches the child's learning experience but also ensures that screen time becomes a productive and valuable part of their day.

Moreover, AI can help to create a more harmonious household by recognizing and adapting to the unique needs and routines of each family member. For families with multiple children, AI systems can individualize settings for each child, helping to manage everything from bedtime routines to homework schedules. These personalized insights are invaluable for making life more manageable and organized, allowing parents to focus on what matters most.

But it's not just about imposing limits and controls; parental controls integrated with AI also offer insights and analytics that can be incredibly beneficial for parents. Detailed reports on what your children are accessing, how they are spending their time, and any potential risks can provide a comprehensive view of your child's digital life. This data can be invaluable for having informed conversations about internet safety and responsible behavior.

As with any technology, the effectiveness of parental controls is dependent on how they are implemented and used. Parents should take the time to learn about the various features and capabilities of their smart home systems, ensuring they are configured to meet their specific needs. It's also crucial to keep the lines of communication open with children, explaining why certain controls are in place and encouraging responsible use of technology.

While AI-powered parental controls add an essential layer of security and management, it's also important to recognize that they are just tools. They should complement, not replace, active and engaged parenting. Using AI to its full potential means leveraging its capabilities to create a safer, more intelligent home environment where children can thrive, learn, and grow safely.

In closing, the integration of AI into parental controls offers a comprehensive, proactive way to ensure child safety and convenience within the smart home. The adaptive, intuitive nature of AI makes it an indispensable ally for parents, providing peace of mind and enabling a balanced and secure home environment. So, as you continue to navigate the landscape of AI-driven smart homes, remember that parental controls are a vital tool, helping to make your home not just smarter, but fundamentally safer for your children.

CHAPTER 20:
SUSTAINABLE SMART HOMES

The concept of sustainable smart homes marries the latest advancements in artificial intelligence with ecological responsibility, creating living spaces that are not only intelligent but also environmentally conscious. Imagine a home where every device is fine-tuned to minimize energy consumption without sacrificing comfort or convenience. Energy-efficient devices seamlessly integrate with water conservation systems, creating a balanced ecosystem that reduces waste and enhances efficiency. Additionally, sustainable building materials, often sourced responsibly or recycled, are increasingly utilized in smart home construction, strengthening the home's commitment to environmental stewardship. As AI continues to evolve, these smart, sustainable homes will increasingly become the norm, offering inspirational models for future living that prioritize both tech-savvy convenience and ecological integrity.

Energy-Efficient Devices

One of the most compelling aspects of integrating artificial intelligence into modern home environments is the promise and practice of energy efficiency. For anyone interested in sustainable living, energy-efficient devices represent the confluence of technology and environmental stewardship. AI-powered smart homes have the capacity to revolutionize how we interact with and conserve energy, significantly impacting both our monthly utility bills and our broader carbon footprint.

At the forefront of energy-efficient devices are smart thermostats. These advanced climate control units go beyond mere temperature regulation by learning household patterns and adjusting settings autonomously to optimize energy consumption. Unlike traditional thermostats, smart versions use machine learning algorithms to predict and adapt to your lifestyle. This means that over time, they get better at predicting when you're at home, away, awake, or asleep. This adaptability ensures that energy is used only when necessary, providing substantial savings and a more comfortable living environment.

Another noteworthy device is the smart plug. While they may seem unassuming, smart plugs play a crucial role in managing energy consumption across various appliances. These devices allow users to monitor and control plugged-in appliances via smartphone apps. The ability to turn off appliances remotely or schedule them to shut down during non-peak hours can lead to significant energy savings. Additionally, many smart plugs come equipped with energy monitoring features, providing insights into which devices are consuming the most power and enabling more informed decisions about energy use.

Lighting also represents a significant portion of household energy usage, and here, smart lighting solutions shine—literally and figuratively. Smart bulbs and lighting systems go beyond mere brightness adjustments; they provide options for dimming, color changes, and even automation based on time of day or occupancy. Automated scheduling can ensure that lights are turned off when rooms are unoccupied, while motion sensors can trigger lighting only when needed. Smart lighting systems are often connected to central hubs or voice assistants, offering an integrated approach to energy management.

In the realm of kitchen automation, smart appliances such as energy-efficient refrigerators, dishwashers, and ovens are gaining traction. These devices are designed not only to perform their primary functions but also to optimize their energy consumption. For example, smart refrigerators can adjust their cooling cycles based on the time of day or whether the door has been frequently opened. Similarly, smart dishwashers can schedule wash cycles during off-peak hours, reducing the load on the power grid and consequently lowering energy costs.

The integration of solar power into smart homes is another aspect that can't be overlooked. AI-powered solar panels are now capable of maximizing energy capture by adjusting their angles and positioning throughout the day. Coupled with smart battery storage systems, these panels can store excess energy for use during cloudy days or nighttime, providing a sustainable and reliable energy supply. Many such systems also allow homeowners to monitor solar energy production and consumption through user-friendly apps, offering real-time data and insights for better energy management.

Automation for efficiency doesn't stop with appliances and lighting. Smart home systems are increasingly incorporating AI capabilities to manage overall energy usage more holistically. Through energy management dashboards, residents can get an aggregate view of their household's energy consumption, identifying patterns and areas for improvement. These systems often provide recommendations for optimizing energy use, such as adjusting thermostat settings, scheduling appliance use, or even suggesting alternative energy sources.

Beyond individual devices, entire smart home ecosystems can be designed with energy efficiency in mind. Home automation platforms can integrate various energy-efficient devices and manage them in unison. For instance, coordinating between smart thermostats, lighting, and smart plugs can ensure a seamless and comprehensive approach to reducing energy consumption. These platforms often include AI-driven analytics that provide actionable insights, making it easier for homeowners to understand and improve their energy efficiency.

Moreover, smart windows and shading solutions contribute to reducing the energy needed for heating and cooling. Automated blinds and smart windows can adjust their transparency or opacity based on external weather conditions and internal room temperatures. By doing this, they help maintain an optimal indoor climate, reducing the need for artificial heating or cooling. Such systems can be programmed to operate in sync with other smart devices like thermostats, further enhancing energy efficiency.

While these technologies are already making strides, the future promises even more sophisticated and efficient solutions. Advancements in AI and machine learning continually enhance the predictive capabilities of energy-efficient devices, making them smarter and more effective. The integration of renewable energy sources with AI technologies will further revolutionize the landscape, pushing us closer to truly sustainable smart homes.

In conclusion, the implementation of energy-efficient devices within a smart home is more than just a trend; it's a fundamental shift towards a more sustainable and cost-effective way of living. By leveraging AI and advanced technologies, we can create homes that not only cater to our immediate needs but also contribute to the broader goal of environmental conservation. These devices, from smart thermostats to intelligent lighting and beyond, collectively make a significant impact on our energy footprint, showcasing the true potential of sustainable smart living.

Water Conservation

In the quest for a sustainable smart home, water conservation stands as a pivotal area with immense potential. It's not merely about reducing utility bills—though that's a notable benefit—but about making a meaningful ecological impact. Every drop conserved translates into a reduced burden on our natural water resources, invaluable especially in areas suffering from drought or water shortages.

Smart homes offer ingenious solutions to water conservation through the integration of advanced technologies. One of the primary tools for achieving this is smart irrigation systems. Traditional sprinkler systems often operate on a timer without regard to current weather or soil moisture. In stark contrast, smart irrigation systems utilize weather data and soil sensors to optimize water usage. These systems can adjust watering schedules based on real-time precipitation, temperature, and even the type of plants being watered. For instance, if it rains, the system automatically skips the scheduled irrigation, preventing unnecessary water usage.

These smart irrigation systems also offer zone-specific customization. Homeowners can tailor the watering schedule to different areas of their gardens, ensuring that plants with varying water needs receive appropriate care. Additionally, such systems can be controlled via a smartphone app, giving users the flexibility to manage their gardens remotely and adjust settings on the fly. This automated precision not only conserves water but also promotes healthier plant growth by providing them with the right amount of water.

Another impactful technology for water conservation in smart homes is the automated leak detection system. Water leaks, both visible and hidden, can lead to a significant amount of wasted water over time. Automated leak detection systems use sensors strategically placed around the home—such as under sinks, near water heaters, and along pipelines—to monitor for any signs of leaks. When a leak is detected, these systems can immediately alert homeowners via a mobile app or even shut off the water supply to prevent further waste and potential damage.

Advanced leak detection systems come equipped with machine learning capabilities. Over time, they learn the normal water usage patterns of the household, allowing them to more accurately identify anomalies that may indicate a leak. Some systems integrate with the smart home ecosystem, enabling coordinated responses; for instance, if a leak is detected, the system could trigger alerts, shut off water valves, and even contact a plumber.

Smart water heaters are another game-changer in residential water conservation. Traditional water heaters constantly keep a large volume of water heated, often wasting energy when hot water is not needed. Smart water heaters, on the other hand, use on-demand heating principles, warming water only when required. This not only conserves water by eliminating the need to run taps waiting for hot water but also reduces energy consumption considerably. Many of these systems can be programmed to heat water during off-peak hours, taking advantage of lower electricity rates, further optimizing household energy use.

Moreover, integrating smart water meters into the home ecosystem provides real-time data on water consumption. These meters enable homeowners to track usage patterns and identify areas where water is being wasted. Detailed insights reveal specific activities consuming large amounts of water, helping residents make informed decisions about their water usage habits. Monthly reports generated by these meters can offer suggestions for improving water efficiency, thereby educating users about their consumption behaviors.

In addition to technological gadgets, software solutions play a crucial role in promoting water conservation. Smart home platforms often offer water conservation programs, integrating with various devices to create a comprehensive water management system. For example, a smart home assistant could deliver reminders based on water consumption goals or even simulate a consultation with a water conservation expert, providing tailored advice and actionable steps to improve efficiency.

Future advancements hold even more promise for water conservation in smart homes. Emerging technologies like AI-powered water quality sensors are capable of monitoring and improving the quality of water usage. These sensors can detect contaminants and automatically signal water treatment devices to correct any issues. Using AI algorithms, these systems can also predict potential water-related problems based on historical and real-time data, offering preemptive solutions before issues escalate.

The integration of smart home technology with municipal water management systems offers additional benefits. Some cities are experimenting with AI-driven water distribution networks that optimize the delivery of water to households based on demand and availability. These systems could eventually allow for collaborative water conservation efforts between individual homes and their municipalities, fostering a more sustainable community-wide approach.

Ultimately, the significance of water conservation in sustainable smart homes cannot be overstated. By leveraging a combination of advanced irrigation systems, leak detection, smart water heaters, and real-time consumption monitoring, smart homes can drastically reduce their water footprint. The integration of these technologies not only ensures responsible water usage but also transforms how we interact with our natural resources, instilling a sense of stewardship in every resident.

Adopting water-saving technologies in smart homes is more than just about embracing innovation; it's about contributing to a sustainable future. Whether it's through smart irrigation systems that ensure optimal watering, leak detectors that prevent wastage, or real-time data that informs better habits, the tools are in place to make significant strides in water conservation. What remains is the collective will to implement these solutions and champion a more water-conscious lifestyle.

In conclusion, transforming our homes into intelligent, water-efficient sanctuaries is not just feasible—it's essential. As we harness the power of artificial intelligence and smart technologies, we're paving the way for a more sustainable and ecologically responsible future. Embracing these advancements will help ensure that we're doing our part in conserving one of Earth's most vital resources.

Sustainable Building Materials

In today's world, sustainability isn't just a trend; it's a necessity. As we integrate artificial intelligence into our living spaces for enhanced convenience, efficiency, and security, it's vital to consider the sustainability aspect of the materials used to build these smart homes. Sustainable building materials aren't only pivotal for reducing the carbon footprint during the construction phase, but they also ensure long-term benefits both for homeowners and the environment.

Firstly, let's delve into what qualifies as sustainable building materials. Generally, these materials are divided into a few key categories: natural, renewable, recycled, and locally sourced. Natural materials include options like wood, bamboo, and stone, which are minimally processed and have a low environmental impact. Renewable materials, such as bamboo, grow quickly and can be replenished within a short period. Recycled materials involve repurposing used materials, such as reclaimed wood or recycled metal, thereby reducing the demand for virgin resources. Locally sourced materials lower the carbon footprint associated with transportation and support local economies.

Wood and bamboo are two of the most prominent sustainable materials. Wood, when sourced responsibly from certified forests, provides a renewable option that's also excellent for insulation, thus reducing energy consumption for heating and cooling. Bamboo, often dubbed as the eco-friendly alternative to wood, grows rapidly and has impressive strength and durability. Given its fast growth cycle and minimal need for pesticides or fertilizers, bamboo is a prime candidate for sustainable construction.

Utilizing recycled materials can significantly contribute to a smart home's sustainability profile. Imagine using recycled steel, which requires considerably less energy to produce compared to raw steel. This not only reduces energy consumption during the construction phase but also minimizes waste. Another example is reclaimed wood. Each piece of reclaimed wood carries its own history and character, adding a unique aesthetic to your home while reducing the need for new timber.

Straw bales may sound antiquated, but they're making a comeback as sustainable building materials. They provide excellent insulation and are highly energy-efficient. Straw bales can be sourced from agricultural waste, making them both cost-effective and environmentally friendly. When combined with smart climate control systems, such homes can achieve remarkable energy efficiency.

Furthermore, sustainable building materials can seamlessly integrate with smart home technologies to enhance efficiency. For instance, smart windows made from electrochromic glass can adjust their tint based on the exterior light conditions, reducing the need for artificial lighting and climate control. The materials used to produce these windows are often recyclable or have a lower environmental impact compared to traditional glass.

The choice of materials also extends to insulation, where options like sheep's wool, cellulose fibers from recycled paper, and even denim, have shown to be excellent. These materials not only offer significant insulation properties but are biodegradable and non-toxic, aligning perfectly with the sustainability ethos.

Insulated concrete forms (ICFs), which utilize a combination of concrete and insulating material, are another noteworthy example. They provide durability and substantial energy savings by offering better insulation compared to traditional wood frames. Their composition can often include recycled materials, thereby adding another layer of sustainability.

Incorporating locally sourced materials can further enhance the sustainability of smart homes. By choosing materials available within the local vicinity, the carbon footprint associated with transportation can be significantly reduced. This practice also supports local businesses and economies, creating a ripple effect of positive impacts on the community.

Beyond individual materials, the concept of modular construction and prefabricated elements is revolutionizing sustainable building practices. Modular homes are built in sections in a factory setting and then transported to the site for assembly. This method greatly minimizes waste, optimizes resource use, and shortens the construction timeline—crucial benefits when building sustainable smart homes.

While sustainable building materials offer a myriad of advantages, it's crucial to consider the lifecycle impact of each material. This requires examining not just the sourcing and production but also how the material will be disposed of or repurposed at the end of its life cycle. Cradle-to-cradle certification is one approach to evaluating materials based on their sustainability throughout their entire lifecycle.

Additionally, the integration of AI in the selection and management of sustainable materials can lead to more informed and efficient choices. AI algorithms can analyze the environmental impact of various materials, helping builders and homeowners to make decisions aligned with their sustainability goals. For example, AI can optimize the combination of materials to achieve the best thermal performance and energy efficiency, reducing the overall environmental footprint of the home.

It's also worth noting that sustainable building materials can contribute to healthier indoor environments. Many conventional materials, like certain paints and finishes, release volatile organic compounds (VOCs) that can affect indoor air quality. Sustainable alternatives, such as low-VOC paints and natural finishes, offer a safer choice for building smart homes.

In summary, sustainable building materials are an integral component of creating eco-friendly smart homes. They offer a blend of environmental benefits, economic efficiency, and enhanced living conditions. By thoughtfully choosing materials like wood, bamboo, recycled metals, and locally sourced options, alongside innovative technologies like smart windows and prefabricated elements, homeowners can significantly reduce their environmental footprint. Furthermore, the use of AI in optimizing these choices can lead to even greater efficiencies and sustainability outcomes, paving the way for a smarter, greener future.

In this journey towards building more sustainable and intelligent homes, every choice matters. From the foundation materials to the finishing touches, incorporating sustainable building materials is not just an option but a responsibility towards our planet and future generations. Together with the transformative power of AI, we can create homes that are not only smart and secure but also in harmony with our environment.

CHAPTER 21:
CASE STUDIES IN SMART HOME IMPLEMENTATION

Delving into real-world examples, Chapter 21 presents compelling case studies showcasing the successful implementation of smart homes. These narratives reveal not just triumphs but also the inevitable hurdles faced along the journey. We examine diverse scenarios, from urban apartments utilizing integrated AI systems for optimal energy management to sprawling suburban homes enhancing security and comfort through customized automation. Each case encapsulates the complexities and solutions that define modern smart living, offering valuable insights into best practices and innovative strategies. The lessons learned highlight how resilience, creativity, and a user-centric approach can transform theoretical concepts into practical, everyday conveniences, setting the stage for your own smart home aspirations.

Success Stories

In the realm of smart home implementation, success stories abound, showcasing the remarkable impact of AI-driven technologies on daily living. These narratives highlight the transformative power of integrating artificial intelligence into living spaces, resulting in more connected, efficient, and secure homes. Let's explore a few of these inspiring tales that demonstrate the real-world benefits of smart home systems.

The Intelligent Home

One shining example comes from the Martinez family, who transformed their suburban home into a state-of-the-art smart haven. Initially, they were overwhelmed by the plethora of devices on the market. However, after careful research and consultation, they opted for a comprehensive system incorporating popular smart home hubs, smart lighting, climate control, and security systems. The results were nothing short of astounding. Automated lighting saved energy and reduced electric bills, while smart thermostats optimized heating and cooling, enhancing comfort and efficiency.

For the Martinezes, the most significant change was in home security. With integrated smart cameras, motion sensors, and smart locks, they experienced an unparalleled sense of safety. Real-time alerts and remote monitoring allowed them to keep an eye on their home from anywhere, giving them peace of mind. The convenience of controlling all these systems through voice commands added a layer of simplicity that made daily routines more manageable.

Another heartening story is that of Jane Thompson, a single mother living in an urban apartment. Jane faced challenges juggling work, household chores, and parenting her two young children. Embracing smart home technology proved to be a game-changer. With the help of a robust home automation system, Jane streamlined her daily tasks and enhanced her family's wellbeing.

Smart kitchen appliances emerged as Jane's saving grace. Automated cooking assistants not only simplified meal preparation but also ensured nutritious meals. Inventory management features prevented food wastage, saving her both time and money. Integrating health and wellness devices, Jane kept track of her children's health metrics effortlessly, which proved vital in managing their needs more effectively.

One particularly inspiring transformation occurred in the home of Fred and Eleanor Johnson, an elderly couple looking to age in place.

Living independently remained a top priority for them, and smart home technology became their ally in this endeavor. They chose AI-enabled devices that provided not only convenience but also enhanced their safety and connectedness to their family.

Smart health devices played an indispensable role in monitoring chronic conditions and vital signs. Automated reminders for medication adherence reduced the risk of missed doses, while smart wearables enabled continuous monitoring. Their adult children, who lived in different states, found solace in knowing they could receive instant alerts if anything unusual occurred.

Their home was also equipped with voice assistants capable of executing complex commands, a feature that simplified many day-to-day activities. From adjusting blinds to locking doors, the couple could manage their home with simple voice instructions, reducing physical strain and making their living environment more accessible.

The transformation of the Nguyen household provides another compelling success story. With teenage children and demanding careers, managing time efficiently was paramount. Their foray into smart home technology began with smart climate control and evolved into a fully integrated system encompassing various aspects of their daily lives.

AI-powered televisions and smart speakers became central to their home entertainment, delivering personalized content recommendations and enhancing their viewing experiences. Automated scheduling and smart office equipment streamlined their home office setup, boosting productivity for both parents working remotely.

Smart cleaning solutions, such as robotic vacuums, alleviated the burden of household chores, allowing the family to focus on quality time together. The technology extended outdoors with automated lawn care and pool maintenance, further minimizing their manual workload.

Success stories in smart home implementation aren't limited to individual households; entire communities are witnessing remarkable transformations. One such example is the Green Meadows Housing Development, which incorporated sustainable smart home technologies across all its units. This collective adoption underscored the potential of AI-driven innovations to foster sustainability and efficiency on a larger scale.

Energy-efficient devices and water conservation systems collectively reduced the development's carbon footprint, proving that smart homes can be both eco-conscious and cost-effective. Community-wide data sharing facilitated intelligent resource management and predictive maintenance, resulting in extended device lifespans and decreased utility costs.

One particular highlight was the cooperation among residents to enhance safety and security. Smart cameras and motion sensors formed a network of vigilance, effectively deterring potential intruders and ensuring rapid response to emergencies. The integration of communication systems enabled swift dissemination of crucial information, reinforcing a sense of community and shared responsibility.

Each of these stories exemplifies the substantive impact of smart home technologies when thoughtfully implemented. They underscore the importance of customized solutions tailored to individual needs and lifestyles. While the specifics of each case vary, common threads of convenience, efficiency, and security weave through these narratives, showcasing the transformative potential of AI-driven homes.

As we delve deeper into the challenges overcome and lessons learned, it's clear that the journey toward an intelligent living environment is continuous. The key lies in staying informed, adaptable, and open to new innovations that will undoubtedly continue to shape the future of smart homes.

Challenges Overcome

Implementing a smart home solution, while highly rewarding, often comes with its own set of challenges. These challenges vary from technical hurdles to user adoption issues. In our case studies, homes transformed by AI initially faced significant obstacles, but overcoming these hurdles provided valuable lessons and greater satisfaction with the end results.

One major technical challenge that recurs across case studies is the integration of various devices from different manufacturers. Even though standards like Zigbee and Z-Wave exist to facilitate compatibility, each brand frequently modifies these standards to fit their unique systems. This inconsistency leads to difficulties in achieving seamless device communication. For example, in one home, a mix of smart bulbs, thermostats, security cameras, and voice assistants from different companies created a series of connectivity problems that initially seemed insurmountable.

Another prevalent issue is network congestion. Smart homes generate significant network traffic, whether it's for streaming security camera footage, syncing data, or executing voice commands. In one particular scenario, a family equipped their home with numerous smart devices but soon encountered frequent drops in Wi-Fi signals, which rendered some devices useless at critical moments. Upgrading to mesh networks eventually resolved this issue, but it required a thorough understanding of the home's network layout and the points of greatest congestion.

Security and privacy concerns can't be dismissed lightly. Smart homes utilize a vast amount of data that requires careful handling to protect against breaches. In one of our case studies, a homeowner was initially reluctant to adopt smart devices due to fears of hacking and unauthorized data access. It was only after implementing robust security measures, such as secure networks and stringent data permissions, that this concern was mitigated, allowing for a more full-hearted adoption of the technology.

An often overlooked but critical challenge is user comfort and acceptance. Even the most advanced smart home suffers if its users aren't comfortable or proficient in its use. One particular case involved a multi-generational household where the younger members were excited about the upgrade, but older family members found the new technology intimidating. This issue was solved through a series of user-friendly tutorials and gradual implementation of devices, which helped demystify the technology and ease the transition.

Allocating financial resources effectively also influenced the progression of several projects. The cost of smart home devices can add up quickly when considering high-end models and professional installations. One homeowner faced budget constraints but navigated this well by starting with essential devices like smart thermostats and security cameras, and then gradually adding more sophisticated gadgets over time. This phased approach ensured that the household could experience the benefits of their initial investment while planning for future expansions more strategically.

Installation and setup often pose challenges, especially for those who choose the DIY route. Our case studies frequently highlight initial frustrations during device setup, with issues ranging from unintuitive interfaces to vague instruction manuals. In one case, a family faced extensive delays in setting up their smart irrigation system due to unclear guidelines and software bugs. However, this was eventually overcome through persistent troubleshooting and leveraging online communities for support.

Environmental factors can add another layer of complexity. Certain smart devices are sensitive to specific environmental conditions, which can affect their performance. For instance, a family integrating smart irrigation faced challenges when sensors misread soil conditions due to extreme weather fluctuations. They resolved this by combining data from multiple types of sensors and creating a more resilient algorithm to adapt to environmental changes.

Learning to troubleshoot issues on the fly is a skill that many smart home adopters must quickly develop. Our case studies feature numerous instances where initial setups worked flawlessly, only to encounter perplexing issues down the line. These scenarios ranged from software updates causing temporary outages to hardware malfunctions needing immediate attention. Learning how to diagnose these problems effectively and utilize available resources, such as manufacturer support and online forums, proved crucial in maintaining a fully operational smart home.

Device interoperability also remains a significant challenge. New devices are continuously released, each boasting unique features and enhancements, making the task of ensuring that they work harmoniously together more difficult. For example, updating to a new smart lock system revealed compatibility issues with an older generation smart security system in one household. This mismatch required a software patch to resolve, necessitating cooperation from both device manufacturers.

Though largely focused on technical aspects, many of these challenges also highlighted the emotional and psychological components of adopting smart home technologies. It's essential to recognize that the user experience can dramatically impact satisfaction and continued use. For example, overcoming the initial intimidation and frustration of setting up and using these systems led to increased confidence and engagement with future smart home expansions in multiple families.

The journey from encountering these obstacles to overcoming them isn't always linear or straightforward. Many smart home projects required iterative problem-solving approaches, where solutions came through trial and error rather than instant fixes. This willingness to adapt and constantly improve systems exemplifies the resilience required for successful smart home implementation.

As these case studies demonstrate, the path to a fully functional smart home is rarely without its bumps. But the meaningful improvements in convenience, security, and efficiency make navigating these challenges worthwhile. They offer a roadmap of potential pitfalls and the robust solutions that can transform setbacks into stepping stones for any homeowner venturing into the world of smart living.

Lessons Learned

Implementing AI in smart homes offers profound benefits, but it also presents unique challenges and learning opportunities. Each case study reveals both the potential and the pitfalls, providing valuable insights for moving forward. Understanding these lessons can streamline the process for future implementations, making it easier for others to transform their homes into intelligent, efficient, and secure living spaces.

One significant lesson is the importance of selecting the right hub for your smart home ecosystem. The case studies underscored that a compatible and reliable hub is the cornerstone of a functional smart home. Some users faced compatibility issues when they attempted to integrate various devices from different manufacturers. The key takeaway is to conduct thorough research and ensure that all chosen devices can communicate seamlessly through the selected hub.

Network reliability is another crucial factor. Many users experienced connectivity problems that disrupted their smart home's functionality. Opting for a robust Wi-Fi setup or a mesh network can prevent these issues. In some case studies, homeowners found that Zigbee and Z-Wave protocols offered more stable connections for specific devices. Thus, investing time in understanding the networking essentials and choosing the appropriate protocol based on the devices in use can save considerable trouble in the long run.

Security was a recurring theme across the case studies. Users consistently emphasized the necessity of securing their smart home networks to protect against unauthorized access. Many learned the hard way about the vulnerabilities that come with increased connectivity. Therefore, incorporating strong passwords, enabling two-factor authentication, and regularly updating device firmware were strategies frequently highlighted as essential measures to safeguard the home environment.

Voice assistants have transformed user interaction with smart homes, yet they come with their own set of challenges. Privacy concerns emerged as a significant hurdle. Users became acutely aware of how much personal data these assistants could potentially access. Hence, a critical lesson is to judiciously manage permissions and stay informed about the privacy policies of the companies providing these AI solutions.

The journey into smart lighting solutions also brought to light various insights. Users discovered that while smart bulbs and automated lighting schedules offer convenience, they require careful planning to avoid complications. Instances where systems failed due to power outages prompted homeowners to invest in smart hubs with local control capabilities. This ensures basic functionalities remain operational even when internet connectivity is compromised.

Climate control revealed the complexities of integrating multiple devices for harmonized functionality. Users had mixed experiences based on the compatibility of their smart thermostats and climate zones. A critical lesson here is to choose devices that are not only top-rated but also work well together. Understanding the nuances of device integration can lead to a more comfortable and energy-efficient living environment.

Home security systems were commonly noted for the peace of mind they provide. However, some users reported false alarms and integration issues with motion sensors and cameras. To alleviate these problems, it's advisable to regular calibrate sensors and choose systems that integrate seamlessly with the existing smart home network.

In the area of home entertainment, AI-powered televisions and smart speakers offered transformative experiences, yet came with a steep learning curve. Users often grappled with complex setup processes and occasional glitches. The lesson here is persistence; the initial troubleshooting phase is worth it for the long-term convenience and enhanced media experiences.

Kitchen automation proved particularly beneficial, especially in saving time and streamlining daily tasks. Smart appliances and automated cooking assistants illustrated the value of interconnected devices. However, users learned the importance of regularly updating these devices to avoid software bugs and compatibility issues.

The integration of health and wellness devices posed a challenge due to the sensitive nature of health data. Users had to be extremely vigilant about data security, ensuring that their health metrics were safeguarded. Many found that devices offering comprehensive data encryption and secure cloud storage solutions were invaluable.

Energy management through smart devices highlighted the potential for substantial savings. Users who invested in smart plugs and energy monitoring tools often recouped their costs through reduced utility bills. However, they also discovered that optimal results are achieved through incremental adjustments and monitoring to identify the most effective strategies for their home's unique energy usage patterns.

Smart home cleaning solutions brought mixed reviews, especially regarding robotic vacuums. While convenient, they often required adjustments and regular maintenance to function efficiently. Homeowners learned that knowing their home's layout and setting proper boundaries for these devices can greatly enhance their autonomy and effectiveness.

AI in home maintenance introduced predictive maintenance and smart diagnosis, providing peace of mind by preventing potential issues. Users appreciated the automated alerts for routine inspections and repairs, which helped in averting costly damage. A pivotal takeaway is the ongoing value of investing in these predictive tools, aligning immediate costs with the long-term benefits of home upkeep.

Enhancing home office productivity with AI tools showed great promise, especially for remote workers. Users benefited from AI-powered scheduling and automation systems, though there was a learning curve involved. Successful implementation often came down to choosing interoperable tools and dedicating time to master these new systems.

Personalized home experiences emphasized the significance of user profiles and adaptive learning. Homeowners appreciated that their homes could adapt to their routines and preferences. However, they also noted that initial setup could be time-consuming. The lesson here is that customizing user profiles initially can lead to a more intuitive and responsive home environment over time.

AI in home décor, including smart art frames and automated blinds, illustrated that aesthetics and convenience could coalesce beautifully. Users enjoyed the ability to control ambient settings effortlessly, but initial costs were mentioned as potential barriers. To mitigate this, gradual implementation starting with high-impact areas can be a practical approach.

Ensuring home safety through AI application, like hazard detection systems, proved invaluable in creating a secure living environment. Users emphasized the importance of immediate and reliable alerts. Effective communication systems integrated with these safety tools were highlighted as essential, showcasing the intricate balance between technology and peace of mind.

Pet care automation, with smart feeders and monitoring systems, provided immense relief for pet owners. However, some experienced technical issues with device reliability and connectivity. Reiterating the importance of consistent device updates and regular maintenance can't be overstated to ensure pet safety and well-being.

Child safety and convenience highlighted smart baby monitors and child-friendly devices as game-changers for parents. The key lesson was in balancing between cutting-edge technology and its reliability. Parents frequently stressed that dependable devices, possibly endorsed by trustworthy reviews, were worth the investment.

In the pursuit of sustainable smart homes, energy-efficient devices and water conservation techniques struck a chord with eco-conscious homeowners. While the initial setup cost was highlighted as a concern, the long-term benefits in energy savings and sustainability were clear lessons in the ripple effect of initial investments leading to prolonged returns.

In summary, the overarching lessons gleaned from these case studies emphasize the importance of thoughtful planning, rigorous research, and continuous learning. The integration of AI into homes is a dynamic process, evolving with technology advancements and user learning. Embracing the challenges as part of the journey can lead to smarter, safer, and more sustainable living environments.

CHAPTER 22:
THE FUTURE OF AI IN HOMES

The future of AI in homes is poised to transform our living spaces into highly responsive, intelligent environments that anticipate our needs and adapt in real-time. We are on the cusp of seeing emerging technologies, such as advanced machine learning algorithms and enhanced natural language processing, seamlessly integrated into home ecosystems. Predictive trends suggest that our homes will not just be smart but will actively learn from our behaviors, making life more convenient and personalized. While the benefits are tremendous, it's crucial to navigate the complexities of AI ethics and privacy to ensure that these innovations are implemented responsibly and securely. The ongoing dialogue around these issues will shape how we interact with and benefit from AI-powered homes in the future.

Emerging Technologies

As we explore the future of artificial intelligence in homes, it's impossible to overlook the emerging technologies that are reshaping how we interact with our living environments. These technologies hold the promise of making our homes smarter, more efficient, and even more personalized to our unique needs and preferences. From advanced machine learning algorithms to cutting-edge sensors, the landscape of what is possible within a smart home is expanding at a remarkable pace.

One of the most promising areas of development is the rise of more advanced and context-aware AI systems. These systems are not just reactive but proactive, anticipating the needs of homeowners based on a range of data inputs. Imagine a home that can predict when you'll run out of groceries and automatically place an order, or an AI system that knows when you're likely to come home late and adjusts the heating and lighting accordingly. The future is about seamless integration of AI into daily life, creating an environment that adapts to you rather than the other way around.

Another significant trend is the advancement in natural language processing (NLP). While today's voice assistants are quite capable, future iterations will be even more intuitive, understanding not just the words but the intent and context behind them. This means you'll be able to have more natural and complex interactions with your home AI systems, making the experience feel more like interacting with a human and less like communicating with a machine.

Simultaneously, improvements in computer vision technology are making their way into smart homes. Enhanced image recognition capabilities enable better security systems, more effective monitoring of home environments, and even assistive features for daily tasks. For example, a smart fridge could identify the items placed within it and suggest recipes based on available ingredients, or a security system could differentiate between family members, guests, and potential intruders more effectively.

Edge computing is another emerging technology gaining traction in the smart home arena. Traditionally, most AI processing has been done in the cloud, leading to concerns about data privacy and latency. Edge computing brings the processing closer to the devices themselves, reducing the need for data to travel to distant servers. This not only enhances privacy but also improves the speed and responsiveness of smart home systems. For instance, real-time decision-making in security cameras or voice assistants becomes far more efficient.

Energy management is also being revolutionized by AI. Smart grids and AI-driven energy distribution systems can optimize electricity use throughout the home, ensuring that energy is consumed in the most efficient manner possible. This might involve smart switches that turn off devices when they're not needed or AI-driven thermostats that adjust heating and cooling based on occupancy and weather predictions. The ultimate goal is to create homes that are not just smart but also sustainable.

Home robotics is another area where emerging technologies are making a significant impact. From robotic vacuum cleaners to more advanced robots capable of handling a wider array of household chores, the future home will likely see an increasing number of robotic assistants. These machines will integrate with other smart home systems to provide a cohesive and efficient living experience. Imagine a robot that can tidy up before you get home, prepare a meal, and even put away the groceries.

Wearable technology is also expected to play a more integral role in smart homes. Devices like smartwatches and fitness trackers already collect vast amounts of data about our daily activities and health. Future smart homes will be able to use this data to create truly personalized environments. For instance, if your wearable detects higher stress levels, your home could automatically dim the lights, play calming music, and adjust the temperature to help you relax.

Advanced sensor technology will enhance the intelligence and responsiveness of smart home systems. Sensors that can detect things like air quality, humidity, motion, and even changes in room occupancy are becoming more sophisticated and reliable. These sensors will feed into the home's AI, allowing for real-time adjustments to improve comfort, safety, and efficiency. For example, a network of sensors could detect a water leak early, preventing damage and saving resources.

Blockchain technology is another frontier for the future of AI in homes. Blockchain can provide enhanced security and transparency for smart home devices, securing transactions, automations, and data exchanges. This can be particularly useful in managing permissions and ensuring that data privacy is maintained, as blockchain offers a tamper-proof method for tracking and managing data.

Holographic displays and augmented reality (AR) could also become commonplace in smart homes. Imagine using AR glasses to visualize your home's energy consumption in real-time, or having holographic displays that provide interactive, 3D instructions for DIY home projects. These technologies will enhance how we interact with our home environments, providing a richer and more immersive experience.

The convergence of 5G technology with AI will also drive many of these advancements. With the rollout of 5G networks, the increased bandwidth and lower latency will be crucial for the real-time communication and processing required by advanced smart home systems. This will support everything from high-definition video streaming to more responsive AI-driven home automation.

Finally, collaborative AI systems will allow different AI models to work in harmony. In the future, your smart thermostat, security system, and home entertainment might not just operate independently but collaborate to optimize your home environment effectively. This integrated approach will ensure that all your smart home devices work together seamlessly, providing a more cohesive and efficient user experience.

In conclusion, the future of AI in homes is teeming with possibilities, driven by emerging technologies that promise to make our living spaces more intelligent, efficient, and personalized. As these technologies evolve, they will redefine the concept of a smart home, moving beyond mere convenience to create environments that truly enhance our quality of life. The key will be to harness these advancements in a way that is seamless, intuitive, and respectful of our privacy, ensuring that the smart homes of tomorrow are both innovative and trustworthy.

Predictive Trends

In the evolution of AI integration in homes, predictive trends stand out as a monumental shift that's already transforming our living spaces. At its core, predictive AI leverages data to forecast future events or behaviors, allowing for more proactive rather than reactive responses. This transition is particularly poignant in the realm of smart homes, where predictive models can enhance convenience, efficiency, and security in unprecedented ways.

One prominent trend is the rise of personalized environments. As AI algorithms become more advanced, they're increasingly capable of learning individual user preferences and habits. Imagine a home that adjusts the lighting and temperature when you walk in, plays your favorite music, and even suggests meals based on your dietary history. These personalized experiences can not only enhance comfort but also improve overall well-being by reducing the cognitive load of making daily decisions.

Another significant trend is the integration of predictive maintenance. With an array of sensors distributed throughout the home, AI systems can monitor the health and performance of various appliances and infrastructure. They can predict when a light bulb will burn out, when the HVAC system needs servicing, or even when a pipe is likely to leak. This shift from routine scheduled maintenance to needs-based intervention could save homeowners significant time and money, making home upkeep more efficient and less stressful.

Home security is also poised to be revolutionized by predictive AI. Traditional security systems often rely on alarms to alert homeowners to an immediate threat. Predictive algorithms, however, can assess patterns and identify potential threats before they materialize. For instance, unusual movement patterns detected by cameras can trigger alerts suggesting enhanced vigilance or even direct intervention. This predictive capability adds an extra layer of security, offering peace of mind through early detection and prevention.

Voice assistants, which have become ubiquitous in many homes, are set to become even more integrated into our daily lives through predictive analytics. As these systems collect data on user interactions, they can anticipate needs and respond with increasingly relevant suggestions. For instance, at the start of your day, your voice assistant might remind you to grab an umbrella because rain is expected, suggest the quickest route to work based on current traffic conditions, or even recommend a podcast that aligns with your recent listening habits.

Energy management is another area where predictive trends are making substantial strides. AI can analyze usage patterns to optimize energy consumption, reducing waste and lowering bills. For instance, smart thermostats can learn when you typically leave the house and adjust the temperature accordingly, minimizing energy use during vacant periods. Solar power systems can predict daily energy needs and weather patterns to optimize storage and usage, making renewable energy a more viable option for everyday homeowners.

Smart home entertainment is also on the cusp of transformation thanks to predictive AI. Future entertainment systems will not just respond to commands but will anticipate your preferences. Imagine a television that predicts what you might want to watch based on your viewing history, or a sound system that plays music that suits your current mood, assessed through biometric sensors. These experiences promise to make home entertainment more immersive and tailored.

The realm of health and wellness within the home is also benefiting from predictive capabilities. Wearables and smart health devices can collect continuous streams of data, allowing AI to detect early signs of health issues and recommend preventative measures. By predicting the likelihood of conditions such as heart disease or diabetes, these systems can enable earlier intervention, potentially saving lives and improving quality of life.

Even areas like kitchen automation are being affected by predictive trends. Imagine a refrigerator that predicts when you're running low on certain groceries and places an order for you, or a cooking assistant that recommends recipes based on what you have on hand and your dietary preferences. These applications can streamline meal planning and grocery shopping, making everyday tasks more manageable.

Of course, the integration of predictive AI raises questions about data privacy and security, which are critical aspects covered later in this book. Balancing the benefits of predictive capabilities with the need for robust data protection will be a key challenge as these technologies evolve. Ethical considerations, such as transparency and user consent, must be at the forefront of development to ensure that these systems are not only effective but also trustworthy.

The potential for smart homes doesn't end with automation and convenience. Predictive AI could play a crucial role in promoting sustainability. By analyzing water and energy usage patterns, AI can identify inefficiencies and suggest modifications to reduce waste. Smart irrigation systems, for example, can predict the optimal watering schedule for gardens based on weather forecasts, soil conditions, and plant types, conserving water while maintaining plant health.

In terms of home office and productivity, predictive AI can help us manage our work-from-home lives more efficiently. AI tools can anticipate the best time to schedule meetings, block out periods for focused work based on your personal productivity peaks, and even suggest breaks to prevent burnout. This capability ensures that you're not just working hard but also working smart.

As we've seen, predictive trends are ushering in a new era of smart home technology, making our environments more responsive, efficient, and personalized. The implications of these trends do not merely represent incremental improvements but signal a fundamental shift in how we interact with our homes. As we continue to innovate and integrate these technologies, the predictive capacities of AI will likely expand, offering even more ways to enhance our daily lives.

Looking forward, the potential applications of predictive AI in homes seem almost limitless. The adaptability of AI allows it to grow alongside us, continually improving and becoming more attuned to our needs. As AI continues to advance, we can expect a future where our homes not only serve as shelters but also as intelligent companions that support our lifestyles in increasingly sophisticated ways.

AI Ethics and Privacy

The integration of artificial intelligence into our homes comes with a myriad of benefits—enhanced convenience, heightened security, and increased efficiency. However, with these advantages come complex ethical and privacy considerations that can't be overlooked. As we continue to weave AI into the fabric of our living spaces, understanding the ethical ramifications and potential privacy risks is crucial.

First and foremost, the data collected by smart home devices is at the heart of ethical and privacy concerns. These devices amass vast amounts of information about our daily routines, preferences, and behaviors. It's not just about knowing when you turn your lights on or off but also about discerning patterns that provide a deeper insight into your personality and lifestyle. Because these data points can be so personal, questions about who has access to this information, and how it's being used, become ever more pertinent.

One of the primary ethical dilemmas revolves around consent. Are users genuinely aware of the extent to which their data is being collected and utilized? Often, terms of service and privacy agreements are veiled in legal jargon that many users gloss over or don't fully understand. To ethically integrate AI into homes, companies need to make these terms clearer and more accessible. Transparency is key; users should always know what data is being collected, why, and how it will benefit them or improve their experience with the product.

Another critical aspect is data security. Given the sensitivity of the information collected, ensuring robust security measures is non-negotiable. Robust encryption, regular security updates, and strict access controls must be standard practice. A breach in a smart home system doesn't just expose data; it can undermine the trust users place in AI technologies, halting progress and adoption in its tracks.

Additionally, there's the issue of data ownership. Who truly owns the data generated by your smart home devices? Is it you, or is it the company providing the service? Legal precedents in this area are still evolving, and there's an urgent need to establish clearer guidelines and standards. Ideally, users should have full ownership and control over their data, with the ability to easily export, delete, or share it as they see fit.

Ethical AI also calls for fairness and non-discrimination. As AI systems increasingly become part of our lives, we have to ensure that they do not perpetuate biases. This involves carefully designing algorithms and continuously monitoring their outputs to avoid reinforcing stereotypes or discrimination. The goal is to create systems that serve all users equitably, regardless of background, lifestyle, or socioeconomic status.

Moreover, the rise of AI in homes opens the door to the potential misuse of surveillance technologies. While smart cameras and motion sensors improve security, they also have the capacity to infringe on personal freedoms and privacy if mismanaged. It's vital to strike the right balance between safety and surveillance. Homeowners should have granular control over how and when these devices are active, and there should be strict protocols about data storage and access.

In considering privacy and ethics, we also need to address the long-term societal impacts of AI in homes. As these technologies become more ubiquitous, there's a risk that they could exacerbate social inequalities. For instance, those who can afford premium AI services might enjoy significantly enhanced lifestyles compared to those who cannot. Ethical AI integration requires thinking broadly about accessibility, designing products and services that a wide range of people can use and benefit from.

Our relationship with AI must be built on trust, and that trust is cultivated through ethical practices and respect for privacy. Developers and manufacturers bear a significant responsibility in this regard. They must prioritize ethical considerations throughout the design and deployment phases, ensuring their products are not only functional and efficient but also fair and secure.

The incorporation of ethical AI practices into smart homes is an ongoing journey rather than a one-time effort. It demands continuous vigilance, regulation, and adaptation. Policymakers and technologists must work together to establish frameworks that protect users' rights without stifling innovation. It's a delicate balancing act, but one that's essential for the sustainable and equitable growth of smart home technologies.

As AI evolves, so too must our ethical frameworks and privacy safeguards. New technologies will undoubtedly present new challenges, but being proactive rather than reactive will position us to navigate these challenges effectively. For homeowners, this means staying informed and engaged—choosing devices from manufacturers who prioritize ethical standards and understanding the implications of the technologies they embrace.

In conclusion, the future of AI in homes holds immense promise, but realizing this potential in a responsible and ethical manner is imperative. By addressing the ethical and privacy implications head-on, we pave the way for a smarter, safer, and more inclusive digital future. This involves not only advancing the technology itself but also cultivating a culture of transparency, fairness, and trust, which will be the true foundation of AI-enhanced homes.

CHAPTER 23:
DIY SMART HOME PROJECTS

Diving into DIY smart home projects brings a thrilling opportunity to shape your living environment with a personal touch. From simple tasks like automating your lighting to more intricate endeavors involving custom voice commands and seamless device integration, the DIY approach empowers you to take control and fully customize your home automation setup. Imagine creating a tailored morning routine where your lights gently brighten, your favorite music plays, and your coffee starts brewing as you wake. As you delve into these projects, you'll find that merging creativity with technology not only enhances comfort and convenience but also provides a rewarding experience of innovation. Whether you're a novice enthusiast or a seasoned techie, there's an exhilarating project waiting to bring your smart home dreams to life.

Beginner Projects

If you're feeling a bit overwhelmed by the sheer range of smart home projects, fear not—everyone starts somewhere. Beginner projects are a fantastic way to dip your toes into the world of smart home automation without diving into complexities. They offer the perfect blend of simplicity and functionality, gradually helping you get accustomed to integrating artificial intelligence (AI) into your living space.

Let's start with perhaps the most straightforward yet impactful project: setting up smart lighting. Smart bulbs are one of the most accessible entries into home automation. They require minimal technical knowledge to set up, and you can control them through a smartphone app or voice assistant. Imagine arriving home from work to a warmly lit house without lifting a finger. By scheduling your lights or using motion detection, you can enhance daily convenience and even save on energy bills.

Another beginner-friendly project involves voice assistants like Amazon's Alexa, Google Assistant, or Apple's Siri. These AI-powered devices don't just answer questions; they act as the central command hub for your entire smart home setup. Start simple by setting timers, asking for weather updates, or controlling your new smart lights. As you get more comfortable, you can expand to more complex commands and integrations, but the initial setup is blissfully uncomplicated.

Consider a smart plug as your next project. These little devices can transform any ordinary appliance into a smart device. Plug a lamp, a coffee maker, or even a fan into a smart plug, and suddenly, you have the power to control these devices remotely. Turn on the lights without getting out of bed or start brewing your morning coffee while you're still upstairs getting ready. It's a small change, but it makes a big difference.

For those interested in home security but not quite ready to commit to a comprehensive system, a smart camera is an excellent starting project. Many smart cameras are easy to set up and offer real-time video feeds that you can access from your phone. Not only do you enhance your home's security, but you also gain peace of mind. If you travel often or want to keep an eye on pets, this is an easy yet effective solution.

Have you thought about smart thermostats? If climate control is your interest, a smart thermostat is a worthwhile beginner project. These devices learn your schedule and preferences, making automatic adjustments to your home's temperature. Not only does this provide comfort, but it also optimizes energy use, which could lead to savings on your utility bills. It's as simple as replacing your old thermostat with a smart one and following the included setup instructions.

Smart speakers can also serve as entry-level devices that pack a real punch. They do more than play music. With AI integration, they can control other smart devices, provide news updates, or even tell you the weather while you listen to your favorite songs. Setting one up requires little more than plugging it in and connecting it to your home's Wi-Fi.

Adding smart locks to your front and back doors is another straightforward project. Many smart locks are designed for easy installation, replacing your existing deadbolt. These can be controlled via a smartphone app, and some even support voice commands. Imagine never needing to fumble for keys again; simply unlock your door as you approach, using either your phone or a voice command.

If you have children, a smart baby monitor is an excellent project to start with. These monitors offer a range of features from live video streaming to temperature sensors and two-way communication. Easy to set up and invaluable in terms of functionality, they provide peace of mind while integrating seamlessly into your smart home ecosystem.

One area often overlooked is kitchen automation. As a beginner, you can start with something small, like a smart kitchen scale. These scales connect to your phone and help with precise measurements, managing recipes, or even tracking your dietary intake. It's a small gadget that can have a substantial impact on your cooking efficiency.

Looking after pets can also benefit from a dabble into smart home technology. Smart pet feeders are an excellent starting project. These devices can dispense food at scheduled times, ensuring your pet is always fed on time. Some even come with cameras so you can check in on your pet and engage with them, even when you're not at home. Setting one up involves just a few steps and can make pet care much simpler.

Smart water leak detectors are an excellent way to protect your home without diving into intricate setups. Place them under sinks, near water heaters, or in basements, and they'll alert you if they detect water. This simple action can save you from potentially devastating water damage, making it a worthy project for any smart home beginner.

If you're interested in gardening, consider automated irrigation systems as a beginner project. These systems can be simple hose timers connected to a Wi-Fi system or more complex setups controlling multiple zones of your garden. They ensure your plants are watered on schedule, connecting to weather forecasts to adapt watering times based on rain predictions.

For cleanliness and convenience, a robotic vacuum can be your first step into the world of automated cleaning. These smart devices can map your home's layout, schedule cleaning times, and even empty their dustbins, all controlled via a smartphone app. Initial setup is usually straightforward, making it a low-barrier entry into the realm of smart home tech.

Once you get a feel for these beginner projects, you'll find that the possibilities for further smart home integrations and customizations are practically limitless. You can progressively add more devices and functionalities, layering complexity as your confidence and understanding grow. Remember, the key to a successful smart home setup is starting small and scaling up based on your comfort level and needs.

These beginner projects not only provide immediate benefits and conveniences but also lay a solid foundation for more complex undertakings. With each project, you'll develop a greater understanding of how AI can be integrated into your home, preparing you for more advanced setups and customizations down the line. Enjoy the process; each new installment brings you one step closer to creating a home that's not just smart, but also deeply personalized to your lifestyle.

Advanced Customizations

Once you've mastered the basics of integrating smart devices into your home, it's time to delve into advanced customizations. These enhancements allow you to tailor your smart home exactly to your preferences, increasing convenience, efficiency, and security. With a bit of creativity and technical know-how, the possibilities are practically endless.

Advanced customizations often begin with creating custom automation routines that transcend the functionalities provided by the basic setups. For instance, you might want your smart home to perform multiple operations seamlessly such as dimming the lights, adjusting the thermostat, and locking the doors when you say a specific command or it hits a certain time at night. To achieve this, you can use platforms like IFTTT (If This Then That) or more sophisticated rule engines built into your smart home hub.

Another exciting realm of customizations involves using scripts and APIs to extend the capabilities of your smart home devices. By writing custom scripts, you can create unique sequences that integrate various devices in ways that the manufacturer might not have intended. For example, you could use JavaScript on a Raspberry Pi to connect your coffee maker to your smart alarm clock, ensuring a fresh pot of coffee is ready as soon as you wake up.

Customization also involves tweaking hardware. Take, for instance, a scenario where an off-the-shelf smart sensor might not entirely fit your unique requirements. In such cases, you can modify or build your own sensors to suit your needs. Utilizing microcontrollers like Arduino or ESP8266, paired with various sensors, enables you to monitor anything from soil moisture for your plants to detecting whether your mailbox has new mail.

Voice assistants can be customized far beyond simple commands. Platforms such as Amazon Alexa Skills Kit or Google Actions let you create custom skills or actions tailored to your needs. You could design an Alexa skill that turns on specific lights and starts a specific playlist when you say, "Alexa, I'm home." This not only provides a personalized experience but also showcases the true potential of these devices when tapped into with a bit of programming knowledge.

For those comfortable with code, Home Assistant provides an extremely flexible platform for home automation. With Home Assistant, you can integrate almost any smart device, regardless of the manufacturer, to create sophisticated custom routines. Written in Python, Home Assistant offers the advantage of an open ecosystem, empowering you to customize every aspect of your smart home setup.

A major benefit of advanced customizations is the ability to make your home more responsive and personalized. Machine learning models can be integrated to learn and predict your behaviors. For instance, a custom-built model could learn your routine and adjust the home environment (like temperature and lighting) accordingly. Over time, the AI would know when you prefer certain settings and automate them without your input.

Not all customizations require deep technical ability. Many smart home hubs now come with user-friendly interfaces that allow more advanced routines and rules to be set up with just a few taps. For example, a smart home hub might enable you to create a 'movie night' scene that closes your motorized blinds, dims your smart lights, and turns on your home theater system with a single voice command.

Integration of artificial intelligence algorithms into your smart home can elevate your home's efficiency. Consider integrating sentiment analysis to your voice assistant so it can respond to your mood. If you had a tough day, the assistant could play soothing music, lower the lights, and prepare your environment for maximum relaxation.

Furthermore, integrating AI with security systems can bring significant advancements. AI can analyze patterns from security cameras to detect unusual behavior, thereby enhancing your home's security. For instance, your AI system can alert you only if it detects genuinely suspicious activities, reducing false alarms and providing peace of mind.

Advanced customizations can also focus on energy efficiency. Using AI to predict your energy consumption based on historical data, weather forecasts, and your habits can optimize energy usage in your home. This can range from adjusting your thermostat optimally throughout the day to turning off devices that are not in use.

Even the fields of health and wellness can benefit from advanced setups. Imagine an advanced routine where your smart mirror can provide personalized skin care advice based on daily data analytics, or where your home lighting system can help regulate your circadian rhythm by adjusting the hue and intensity over the course of the day.

For the adventurous, integrating augmented reality (AR) with smart home systems can create futuristic interfaces. For example, you could use AR glasses to overlay controls and information onto your physical space, making interactions with your smart home more intuitive and immersive.

Advanced integrations often require enhanced security measures to ensure your home remains safe from cyber threats. Implementing two-factor authentication for accessing your smart home systems and using VPNs for any remote access are approaches to enhance your security.

Beyond security, advanced customizations should also consider the privacy implications of smart home data. Encrypting sensitive data and choosing platforms that prioritize user privacy can help maintain trust while still enabling the sophisticated customizations you value.

As with any technology, advanced customizations in smart homes will continue to evolve. Staying updated with new developments and participating in user communities can provide inspiration and solutions for even more innovative applications. The journey of transforming a simple smart home into an intelligent, responsive living space is both exciting and rewarding, leveraging technology to create a truly personalized and optimized environment.

CHAPTER 24:
TROUBLESHOOTING COMMON ISSUES

Troubleshooting common issues in a smart home can be daunting, but it's essential for maintaining a seamless and efficient living environment. If you're facing connectivity problems, start by checking your Wi-Fi network's signal strength and making sure your devices are within range. For device malfunctions, a simple restart or firmware update can often solve the issue. Voice assistant errors, on the other hand, might require re-training voice recognition or ensuring that the device settings are correctly configured. By systematically addressing each problem—whether it's a network hiccup, a malfunctioning device, or a misunderstood command—you'll create a more reliable and responsive smart home that's better equipped to meet your needs and enhance your daily life.

Connectivity Problems

In a world increasingly dependent on interconnected devices, connectivity problems can be a significant barrier to the smooth functionality of your AI-integrated home. Understanding the common issues can help you troubleshoot and resolve them efficiently.

The first step in resolving connectivity issues is identifying whether the problem lies with your internet service provider (ISP) or within your home network. An easy way to check this is by seeing if other devices connected to the same network are experiencing similar issues.

If multiple devices are having trouble, the culprit is likely the ISP, and you may need to contact them for support.

However, if the issue is isolated to specific devices, it could be related to Wi-Fi signal strength or interference. Walls, floors, and even furniture can obstruct Wi-Fi signals, causing weak connections or frequent drops. One effective solution is placing your router in a central location within your home. Alternatively, you could use Wi-Fi extenders or a mesh network system to enhance coverage.

Network congestion is another common issue, especially in households with numerous smart devices. When too many devices are connected and actively using bandwidth, it can lead to slower speeds and disconnections. Prioritizing traffic through Quality of Service (QoS) settings on your router can help manage bandwidth distribution effectively, ensuring essential devices get the connection they need.

Firmware and software updates should not be overlooked. Keeping your router and other smart devices up-to-date ensures they have the latest security patches and performance improvements. Regular updates can often resolve connectivity issues caused by outdated software.

Interference is another aspect to consider. Other electronic devices, like microwaves and cordless phones, can interfere with Wi-Fi signals. Switching your router to another channel can help mitigate this type of interference. Most modern routers automatically select the best channel, but manual configuration can sometimes yield better results.

Encryption and security settings can also play a role in connectivity problems. Ensuring your Wi-Fi network uses WPA3 or at least WPA2 security protocol will protect against unauthorized access but requiring occasional reauthentication can sometimes disconnect devices. Make sure your devices are configured to reconnect automatically when this security handshake refreshes.

One must also consider the compatibility of different smart devices. Some devices only support specific Wi-Fi frequencies, like 2.4 GHz or 5 GHz. Ensuring that your device and router operate on compatible frequencies can resolve many connectivity issues. Dual-band routers that support both frequencies simultaneously can provide more flexibility and higher reliability.

It's worth noting that Zigbee and Z-Wave, common protocols for smart home devices, have their own connectivity nuances. If you find that Zigbee or Z-Wave devices are having trouble, the issue might be with signal range or interference from other devices operating on similar frequencies. Adding repeaters to your network can extend the range and improve performance.

A less obvious, but equally impactful, issue could be IP address conflicts. Each device on your network needs a unique IP address. If two devices inadvertently share the same IP address, it can cause connectivity problems. Setting your router to automatically assign IP addresses through DHCP can often solve this conflict.

Lastly, integrating new devices into an existing setup can sometimes disrupt the balance of your network. Carefully following the installation instructions and ensuring that the device firmware is updated can minimize these disruptions. If you encounter persistent issues, resetting the device or removing and re-adding it to your network might help.

In conclusion, while connectivity problems can be frustrating, they are often solvable with some basic troubleshooting. By understanding the common causes and applying targeted solutions, you can ensure that your smart home runs smoothly and efficiently.

Device Malfunctions

Even the most advanced technology is not immune to the occasional hiccup, and smart home devices are no exception. Understanding and addressing device malfunctions promptly can save you a lot of frustration and ensure your smart home remains a harmonious haven. This section delves into various common malfunctions you might encounter with AI-driven home devices and provides practical solutions to get them back in working order.

The first step in troubleshooting any device is to accurately identify the problem. Sometimes, it can be as simple as a device refusing to turn on or respond. Most smart devices come equipped with a light or an indicator to show their operational status. A power cycle, which involves turning the device off and then back on, can sometimes resolve the issue.

However, if the problem persists, it's crucial to check the power source. Ensure that your device is plugged in and that the outlet is functioning correctly. For battery-operated devices, replacing the batteries might seem obvious, but it's a step often overlooked. If the device uses a rechargeable battery, make sure it's fully charged.

Software glitches can be another common cause of device malfunctions. These can often be resolved by updating the device's firmware. Most smart home devices nowadays come with easy-to-use companion apps that notify you of available updates. Regularly updating your device's firmware not only squashes bugs but also enhances performance and security.

Network-related issues are another frequent culprit. A device that appears to be malfunctioning might simply be struggling to maintain a stable connection to your home network. Testing the connectivity can involve several steps. Start by ensuring that your Wi-Fi network is up and running. Moving the device closer to the router can help determine if distance is affecting the connection. Additionally, resetting your router can sometimes fix minor network hiccups.

Interference from other wireless devices can also hamper communication. If you have numerous devices operating on the same frequency, you might experience occasional dropouts or slowdowns. Switching to a less crowded frequency band or channel might ease the congestion and improve performance.

Compatibility issues can lead to operational challenges as well. Smart home ecosystems are often composed of devices from various manufacturers. Although these devices are designed to work together, standards can vary. Always check compatibility requirements before adding new devices to your system. If you notice an issue post-installation, refer to your device's manual or the manufacturer's website for compatibility guidelines and recommended configurations.

Voice assistants are a key component of many smart homes and are not immune to their own set of issues. Misunderstanding voice commands or failing to execute tasks properly can be frustrating. Make sure that your voice assistant is updated and that its microphone is not obstructed. Additionally, recalibrating voice recognition can enhance its sensitivity to your commands, reducing the likelihood of errors.

Sensor and Connectivity Problems

Certain smart devices rely heavily on various sensors to perform their functions accurately. If these sensors malfunction, it can severely impact device performance. For instance, smart thermostats use temperature sensors to regulate home climate precisely. If these sensors fail, your thermostat might start making incorrect adjustments. Regular calibration and maintenance can help keep these sensors in optimal condition.

Connectivity problems not only affect individual devices but can also disrupt the ecosystem as a whole. This often manifests in devices dropping off the network sporadically. A quick way to mitigate this is by ensuring your network is optimized. Using range extenders or mesh networks can provide more robust coverage throughout your home.

Automation and Scheduling Issues

Another common issue involves automation and scheduling malfunctions. Devices might not follow pre-set schedules or automate tasks as intended. This could be due to inaccurate time settings or conflicts between different automation rules. Most smart home applications allow you to review and edit your automation rules easily. Regularly revisiting these settings can help you catch and rectify conflicting rules before they become a problem.

More complex systems, like those integrating machine learning algorithms, can sometimes make predictions based on incomplete or erroneous data. Regularly updating your preferences and providing feedback can help the system learn and adapt to your needs better. Remember, AI thrives on data. The more accurate and up-to-date the information it processes, the better it will perform.

Smart Lighting and Climate Control

Glitches in smart lighting systems can manifest in lights flickering or not responding to controls. Similar issues can arise in smart climate control systems, like thermostats and automated vents, where devices might not maintain the desired temperature or humidity levels. One way to address these issues is by verifying that the lighting and climate control schedules do not overlap and cause conflicts.

Smart bulbs, for instance, can fail to update their firmware, leading to unresponsive states. Manufacturer-specific fixes, such as manual resets or firmware reinstallation, can generally resolve these glitches. Documentation and support from your device's manufacturer can be invaluable in these instances. Don't hesitate to leverage these resources.

Software and Integration Problems

Software compatibility and integration issues are a common source of malfunctions. While some problems might be device-specific, others stem from software updates that disrupt established routines. Keeping abreast of software updates and knowing how to roll back changes can be crucial. Many smart home users benefit from maintaining a log of changes made, aiding them in tracing back to what might have caused an issue.

Integrating multiple devices can sometimes result in conflicts. For instance, a home security camera from one manufacturer might not seamlessly integrate with a smart lock from another. Confirming that devices can communicate effectively before purchase can save a lot of headaches. Familiarize yourself with policies for returns or customer support to resolve any potential incompatibilities post-purchase.

Maintaining Device Efficiency

Routine maintenance plays a critical role in preventing malfunctions. Regularly cleaning your devices, checking connections, and updating software can keep them in optimal working condition. Many smart home systems include automated diagnostics tools that can alert you to potential issues before they become serious. Utilizing these tools can help preemptively address minor glitches.

Lastly, don't overlook the importance of manufacturer support and warranty services. Keeping your receipts, maintaining documentation, and understanding the warranty terms can provide you with recourse if a device consistently malfunctions. Manufacturer

The Intelligent Home

hotlines and online support forums can offer problem-specific advice, often resolved faster than DIY troubleshooting.

Persistence and proactive management are key to maintaining a well-functioning smart home. Understanding the common pitfalls and knowing how to address them will make your smart home both a joy to live in and an efficient, reliable assistant in your day-to-day life.

Voice Assistant Errors

Voice assistants are a cornerstone of modern smart homes, offering hands-free control and seamless integration with various smart devices. However, as with any technology, they are not without their quirks and issues. Understanding common voice assistant errors can save you from undue frustration and help you maintain a smoothly functioning smart home ecosystem.

One of the most frequent issues is the voice assistant not recognizing or misinterpreting commands. This can happen for various reasons, including background noise, unclear speech, or the use of non-standard phrasing. To mitigate this, make sure the room is quiet when giving commands, speak clearly, and familiarize yourself with the specific phrases your voice assistant is most responsive to. For example, instead of saying, "turn the lights to a medium brightness," it might respond better to "set lights to 50%."

Another common problem is the voice assistant becoming unresponsive. This often occurs due to connectivity issues. Ensure that your device is connected to a stable Wi-Fi network. If your home network is experiencing interruptions, consider using a mesh network to improve coverage and reliability. Rebooting both your router and the voice assistant can also resolve many connectivity woes.

Compatibility issues can also arise, particularly when integrating new devices into your smart home. Not all devices are compatible with every voice assistant, so it's crucial to check the manufacturer's guidelines for compatibility before making a purchase. If you've already encountered an incompatibility issue, third-party apps and services like IFTTT (If This Then That) can often bridge the gap, enabling different devices to communicate effectively.

Software glitches can be another source of frustration. These can manifest as the voice assistant not updating, getting stuck in a loop, or performing unintended actions. Keeping your voice assistant and connected devices up-to-date with the latest software versions can alleviate many of these problems. Manufacturers frequently release patches and updates to address known issues and improve functionality, so regular updates are essential.

Sometimes, the root cause of voice assistant errors can be traced back to the initial setup process. During setup, ensure that the device is placed in an optimal location, free from obstructions and within good reach of your Wi-Fi signal. Additionally, follow the manufacturer's instructions carefully, and double-check all settings before finalizing the installation.

Privacy settings can also interfere with the smooth operation of voice assistants. If you find that your voice assistant is not responding as expected, check the privacy settings to ensure it has the necessary permissions to perform tasks. Overly restrictive privacy settings can block some functionalities, making the assistant appear unresponsive.

Another aspect to consider is the physical condition of your voice assistant. Dust and debris can clog the microphone or speakers, impacting performance. Regularly clean your device to ensure it remains in good working condition. Use a soft, dry cloth to wipe the exterior and a can of compressed air for any crevices or speaker grills.

User errors are also quite common. We often forget the exact commands or try to multitask, leading to misunderstood instructions.

Reviewing the user's manual or online resources for a list of supported commands can be extremely helpful. Additionally, involve all household members in learning and using the voice assistant effectively to minimize user-related errors.

In multi-lingual households, voice assistants may struggle with recognizing different accents or languages. Most modern voice assistants support multiple languages and even dialects, so configuring the device to recognize the most frequently spoken languages can enhance its accuracy and responsiveness.

Network congestion can be another culprit behind voice assistant errors. If multiple devices are simultaneously using high bandwidth, it can affect the performance of your voice assistant. Consider setting up Quality of Service (QoS) rules on your router to prioritize traffic for your voice assistant and critical smart home devices.

Occasionally, voice assistants may experience server-side issues that are beyond your control. These can occur due to maintenance or technical glitches on the service provider's end. In such cases, keeping an eye on relevant service status pages can inform you whether the issue is widespread and when you can expect a resolution.

For advanced users, fine-tuning the settings via the voice assistant's app can offer more control. Customizing the sensitivity of the wake word, adjusting the response speed, and setting up custom routines can make the interaction smoother and more efficient. Most voice assistants have a companion app where you can monitor device status, manage settings, and troubleshoot issues.

Security is another factor influencing voice assistant performance. Occasionally, security updates can change settings or disable features to enhance security protocols. It's wise to regularly review security settings to balance safety with functionality. Ensure that your voice assistant's firmware is up-to-date to safeguard against vulnerabilities.

If you've tried everything and the issues persist, reaching out to customer support is a sensible next step. Many voice assistant manufacturers offer robust customer service and technical support. Providing them with detailed information about the issue can expedite the resolution process. Documenting error messages, describing the steps you've already taken for troubleshooting, and noting any recent changes in your network or device setup can be immensely helpful.

Lastly, community forums and user groups can be invaluable. Other users often share their experiences and solutions to similar problems, and you might find a workaround that hasn't been documented officially. Engaging with the user community can provide not only solutions but also tips on maximizing the use of your voice assistant.

In summary, while voice assistant errors can be frustrating, they are usually manageable with some diligent troubleshooting and a bit of patience. By understanding the common causes and solutions, you can ensure that your voice assistant remains an effective and reliable component of your smart home ecosystem. Improved convenience, efficiency, and a touch of modern flair are well within your grasp, making the journey towards a smarter home both rewarding and enjoyable.

CHAPTER 25:
ENSURING PRIVACY AND SECURITY

As we embrace the convenience and sophistication of AI-driven smart homes, it's crucial to prioritize privacy and security to safeguard our personal data and maintain a safe living environment. Ensuring robust data protection entails adopting best practices like regularly updating firmware and using strong, unique passwords for all devices. Additionally, securing your home network with encryption protocols and disabling unnecessary features will significantly mitigate potential vulnerabilities. Careful management of permissions, where you regularly review and limit the access of installed apps and devices, further fortifies the security layer. By implementing these strategies, you can enjoy the numerous benefits of a connected home without compromising on privacy and security, transforming your living space into a haven of both innovation and protection.

Data Protection

In the interconnected world of smart homes, data protection stands as a critical pillar in ensuring that your privacy and security are not just desired outcomes but guarantees. The more integrated and sophisticated our homes become with artificial intelligence, the more pertinent it is to safeguard the treasure trove of data they generate. From daily routines to personal preferences, every piece of information collected and processed by smart devices holds immense value. Protecting this data from unauthorized access, breaches, or misuse is paramount.

At the heart of data protection is encryption. Encryption transforms readable data into an unreadable format without the appropriate decryption key, providing a robust first line of defense against cyber intrusions. When setting up your smart home devices, it's essential to opt for products offering strong encryption standards, such as AES-256. Ensuring that communication between devices, hubs, and applications is encrypted helps prevent interception by malicious actors.

Equally important is regular software updating. Manufacturers frequently release firmware updates to patch security vulnerabilities and introduce new protections against emerging threats. Enabling automatic updates on your smart home devices ensures they are always running the latest and most secure software. Neglecting these updates can leave your smart home network exposed to exploitation.

Data protection also involves the strategic management of permissions. Smart devices often require various permissions to operate optimally, but granting unnecessary access can compromise security. Review and adjust the permissions for each device to ensure they have access only to the data and functions they strictly need. It's a proactive measure to minimize exposure and control the flow of information within your smart home ecosystem.

Two-factor authentication (2FA) is another effective measure in safeguarding your smart home. By requiring a second form of verification—such as a text message code or authentication app—2FA adds an extra layer of security that makes it significantly harder for unauthorized users to gain access, even if they manage to obtain your password. Wherever possible, enable 2FA on your smart home accounts and devices.

When thinking about data protection, it's crucial not to overlook data storage practices. Opt for platforms and devices that offer secure, local storage options. While cloud storage provides convenience, storing sensitive information locally can mitigate the risks associated with cloud-based breaches. For data that must be stored in the cloud, make sure the provider has rigorous security protocols and complies with relevant data protection regulations.

Privacy policies and terms of services are often dense and monotonous, but they contain vital information about how your data will be used, stored, and protected. Taking the time to read and understand these documents helps ensure that you are aware of the protections (or lack thereof) in place. Choose service providers and manufacturers that have strong, transparent privacy policies.

In the unfortunate event of a data breach, having a response plan is critical. This plan should outline steps to identify the breach, contain it, and notify relevant parties affected by the breach. Knowing who to contact, what information to gather, and how to mitigate damage can make a significant difference in handling a security incident effectively.

Regular audits of your smart home network can also enhance data protection. Conducting periodic evaluations of device security settings, network integrity, and data access logs helps identify potential vulnerabilities before they can be exploited. Employing third-party security tools or services for thorough inspections can provide an additional layer of assurance.

Educating yourself and household members about basic cybersecurity principles is a valuable line of defense. Practices such as recognizing phishing attempts, understanding the importance of strong, unique passwords, and being cautious with unknown links or devices can collectively enhance the overall security of your smart home.

In the broader scope of data protection, legislative and regulatory frameworks play a vital role. While individual actions are essential, it's equally critical to support and advocate for robust data protection laws that hold companies accountable for safeguarding user information. Staying informed about changes in data protection regulations, such as the General Data Protection Regulation (GDPR) or the California Consumer Privacy Act (CCPA), empowers you to make informed choices regarding the services and devices you use.

As artificial intelligence continues to evolve, so do the tactics and tools of those aiming to exploit data. Staying ahead in this ever-changing landscape requires continuous learning and adapting. Subscribing to cybersecurity news, participating in online courses, and attending workshops or seminars can keep you up-to-date with the latest threats and protection techniques.

In conclusion, data protection is a multi-faceted endeavor that requires a combination of technological measures, vigilant practices, and continuous education. As you integrate more AI-driven devices into your home, keeping data protection at the forefront ensures that your smart home remains a sanctuary of convenience, efficiency, and most importantly, security.

Secure Networks

One of the paramount concerns in embracing AI-powered smart homes is ensuring that the underlying network infrastructure is secure. A secure network forms the backbone of a reliable and safe smart home, especially when it comes to sensitive personal data and the smooth operation of interconnected devices. Given the proliferation of Internet of Things (IoT) devices in homes today, the significance of a robust, secure network cannot be overstated.

Firstly, it's essential to understand the different types of networks that can be employed in a smart home setup. Most smart homes rely on Wi-Fi as the primary method for device communication. However, with the increasing number of connected devices, traditional Wi-Fi networks can become congested and susceptible to interference. This is where mesh networks come into play. Unlike single-router setups, mesh networks utilize multiple nodes scattered throughout your home, ensuring consistent coverage and reducing dead zones. Mesh networks also inherently offer some security advantages. Since data can travel through multiple pathways, it becomes more challenging for unauthorized users to intercept and compromise traffic.

Secure networks are not just about coverage and speed but also about protecting data from potential cyber threats. Enabling WPA3, the latest Wi-Fi security protocol, can add an extra layer of encryption, making it harder for hackers to decrypt traffic. Wi-Fi Protected Access (WPA3) replaces WPA2 and includes stronger data encryption and enhanced protections against brute-force attacks. The transition between WPA2 and WPA3 should be considered for any smart home setup, especially with the increasing number of cyber threats targeting IoT devices.

The implementation of Virtual Private Networks (VPNs) in a smart home is another critical aspect. A VPN can create an encrypted tunnel for data to travel through, ensuring that even if data is intercepted, it remains unreadable to unauthorized parties. Integrating a VPN with your smart home network can obscure your IP address, adding another layer of anonymity and protection from potential threats.

Let's not forget about device authentication. Using strong, unique passwords for each device is paramount. Often, default passwords are easily guessable and provide an easy entry point for malicious actors. Employing a password manager can help generate and store complex passwords, reducing the risk of password-related breaches. Furthermore, enabling multi-factor authentication (MFA) on devices and accounts can drastically minimize the risk of unauthorized access. Multi-factor authentication requires not just a password but also an additional form of verification, such as a text message code or biometric scan, adding another hurdle for intruders.

Firewalls form another line of defense in securing networks. Using a hardware firewall, in combination with your router, can filter out unknown and potentially dangerous data from reaching your devices. Many modern routers come with built-in firewall features, which, when configured correctly, provide essential protection against cyber threats. It's crucial to regularly update the firmware of these routers to patch any vulnerabilities discovered by manufacturers.

Another factor is the segmentation of your smart home network. Network segmentation involves dividing your home network into different segments or 'sub-networks,' each with its access controls. This means that even if one device is compromised, the attacker would not have access to the entire network. For instance, placing your IoT devices on a separate network from your personal computers and smartphones can contain potential breaches and protect sensitive information.

Let's talk about regular updates and patches—a cornerstone of a secure network. Manufacturers of routers and smart home devices frequently release updates to enhance functionality and patch security vulnerabilities. Setting your devices to update automatically ensures they have the latest protections, reducing the risk of exploitation from outdated software. It's a simple measure that can have a significant impact on your network's security.

Lastly, educating every household member about safe online practices is invaluable. Even with the most secure network setup, human error can undermine security measures. Teaching everyone about the risks of phishing attacks, the importance of not sharing passwords, and recognizing suspicious activities can build a culture of security in your home. Regularly reviewing who has access to your network and devices, and promptly revoking access if someone no longer needs it, helps maintain security over time.

In conclusion, creating a secure network goes beyond just having a strong Wi-Fi signal. It involves a multi-faceted approach that includes encryption, authentication, firewalls, network segmentation, regular updates, and continuous education. As AI continues to mold the landscape of modern smart homes, fortifying your network infrastructure safeguards not just your devices, but your privacy and peace of mind.

The next step in our journey will delve into the intricate details of managing permissions, ensuring that every device and user in your smart home has the appropriate level of access, and nothing more. Balance is key, and understanding how to manage permissions effectively can significantly reduce the risk of unauthorized access and potential security breaches.

Managing Permissions

In the digitized realm of smart homes, managing permissions forms the cornerstone of ensuring privacy and security. Just as you wouldn't hand over the keys to your house to strangers, it's crucial to be discerning about what permissions you grant to various smart devices and applications. This section is dedicated to providing you with the knowledge and tools needed to manage permissions effectively, ensuring that your smart home is not just intelligent but also secure.

To start, understand that every connected device in your home—whether it's your smart thermostat, lighting system, or voice assistant—requires certain permissions to function optimally. These permissions may include access to your location, microphone, camera, or even other devices within the network. It's tempting to go through the setup process quickly, but make it a habit to review the permissions requested by each device carefully. Think of it like reading the terms and conditions of software updates, but this time, it directly impacts your home's security.

Next, it's imperative to regularly review and update the permissions granted to your devices. As you integrate new devices or apps, permissions may change over time. Changes in software updates can also alter the scope of permissions given. Using a centralized platform, such as a smart home hub, can simplify the management of these permissions. Most hubs allow you to view and adjust permissions from one interface, making it easier to ensure every device only has the access it absolutely needs.

Another layer of control can be achieved through user-based permissions. In homes with multiple occupants, not everyone needs the same level of access to all devices. For instance, children might not require control over security cameras or climate settings. Setting up user profiles with different permission levels ensures that each member of the household can interact with the smart home environment in a way that's appropriate for their needs and their role within the household. This is not merely about convenience but also about securing sensitive functionalities from unnecessary access.

Moreover, many smart devices offer guest modes or limited access settings. If you're hosting guests or renting out your place, enabling these modes can provide temporary access to essential features without exposing your private data or giving control over critical systems. This ensures that while your guests enjoy the convenience of a smart home, your privacy and security remain intact.

For those deeply concerned about security, employing multi-factor authentication (MFA) adds another protective layer. MFA requires users to present two or more separate proofs of identity before gaining access. This could be something you know (a password), something you have (a smartphone), or something you are (a fingerprint).

Implementing MFA on devices and hubs that support it can drastically reduce the risk of unauthorized access.

Transparency and accountability are two more pillars in managing permissions effectively. Opt for devices from manufacturers that provide clear and transparent data policies, explaining what data is collected, how it is stored, and with whom it is shared. Use products from reputable companies known for regular security updates and a strong stance on user privacy. A manufacturer's commitment to transparency not only builds trust but also provides better peace of mind.

One of the often-overlooked aspects of managing permissions is the disposal or resale of smart devices. When devices are no longer needed, be sure to perform a factory reset to erase all personal data and settings. This step ensures that subsequent users can't access your information or misuse permissions. Proper disposal isn't just about data security; it's also about responsibly closing the loop on each device's life cycle.

Some users may prefer employing privacy-focused solutions like Virtual Private Networks (VPNs) or encrypted connections through smart home hubs. These technologies can add an additional layer of security by encrypting data transmissions, making it much harder for unauthorized entities to intercept and misuse your information. When permissions are managed through an encrypted gateway, there is less risk of data breaches or unauthorized access, providing an added sense of security.

Automated permission management tools are becoming increasingly popular in the landscape of smart home technology. These tools intelligently manage and adjust permissions based on pre-set parameters and usage patterns. For example, permissions for certain devices might be restricted when you're not at home, or certain features could be disabled when not in use. Automation in permissions management creates a dynamic security environment that adapts and responds to the household's needs in real-time.

The principle of least privilege should guide your approach to managing permissions. This principle states that any device or user should only have the minimum level of access necessary to perform its function. Start with the most restrictive settings and gradually grant additional permissions as required, rather than granting full access and trying to dial back. This method minimizes exposure to potential vulnerabilities.

Finally, staying informed and educated on best practices for managing permissions is crucial. Keeping up with the latest recommendations from cybersecurity experts and industry standards ensures that your knowledge base remains current and actionable. This can be achieved by subscribing to dedicated newsletters, following trusted tech blogs, or participating in online forums focused on smart home security. Knowledge is power, and staying updated equips you to make informed decisions about managing permissions in your smart home effectively.

In conclusion, managing permissions in a smart home ecosystem is a dynamic and ongoing process. It requires vigilance, informed decision-making, and the willingness to adapt to evolving security landscapes. By carefully reviewing permissions, setting up user-based and guest access, leveraging multi-factor authentication, and staying educated, you can create a secure and resilient smart home environment. Remember, the ultimate goal is to enjoy the convenience and efficiency of a smart home without compromising on privacy and security.

CONCLUSION

The journey through the realms of artificial intelligence intertwined with our living spaces has been nothing short of transformative. As we've navigated the intricacies of smart home technology, the picture that emerges is one of endless potential. AI brings with it a promise: a promise of convenience, safety, and a harmony previously unimaginable in the humdrum of daily life. Yet, perhaps the most profound realization is that we are just at the cusp of this transformation.

Integration of AI into our homes represents more than just the adoption of new technology; it's a fundamental shift in how we interact with our living spaces. No longer are we passive inhabitants of our homes. Instead, we are now active participants in a dynamic dialogue, facilitated by intelligent systems that learn, adapt, and cater to our needs. This synergy redefines what it means to live in a home, where every component is finely tuned to create an environment that is not only efficient but also deeply personal.

Looking back at the different facets we've explored, from smart lighting solutions to advanced home security systems, each chapter has illustrated the myriad ways AI can enhance our homes. However, the true magic lies in the seamless integration of these technologies. It's the convergence of voice assistants optimizing our daily schedules, smart thermostats ensuring perfect climate control, and predictive maintenance preventing unforeseen issues that underscores the real power of an AI-enhanced home. The holistic experience created by this integration surpasses the sum of its parts.

The practical steps and expert insights offered in this book were designed to equip you with the knowledge necessary to embark on your own journey towards a smarter home. By systematically addressing key areas like energy management, health and wellness, and even home office productivity, you've now got a solid foundation to build upon. The step-by-step guides not only demystify the process but also empower you to experiment and innovate, tailoring your smart home to fit your unique lifestyle.

Security and privacy have been recurring themes throughout our discussion, reflecting their paramount importance in the digital age. As our homes become more connected, taking steps to protect personal data and secure our networks has never been more critical. The measures and best practices shared here emphasize that security is not a one-time setup but an ongoing commitment. By staying vigilant and informed, you can enjoy the benefits of a connected home while safeguarding against potential risks.

Moreover, the chapters on DIY smart home projects and troubleshooting common issues highlight that creating a smart home isn't reserved for tech enthusiasts alone. These sections aim to democratize the process, making it accessible to anyone willing to learn and experiment. They underscore a simple truth: the future is in our hands, and the ability to shape it lies within each of us. With the right tools and knowledge, even the most complex systems can be understood and customized to fit individual needs.

AI's role in enhancing our quality of life goes beyond convenience and efficiency. It holds the potential to contribute to broader societal goals, such as sustainability and resource conservation. The chapters on sustainable smart homes and energy management reflect a growing awareness and responsibility towards our planet. By embracing energy-efficient devices, optimizing water usage, and integrating sustainable materials, smart homes not only serve us but also contribute positively to the environment.

As we project into the future, the scope of AI in homes is set to expand even further. Emerging technologies and predictive trends suggest that we are on the brink of even more sophisticated and intuitive systems. The ethical considerations and privacy concerns discussed offer a balanced perspective, reminding us to tread thoughtfully as we innovate. Balancing technological advances with ethical mindfulness will be crucial in ensuring that AI continues to be a force for good.

In closing, this book is more than just a guide; it's an invitation to envision and create a new way of living. The integration of AI into our homes is not a destination but a continuous journey. It's about embracing change, staying curious, and constantly evolving. As we step into this future, may you find excitement in every innovation and comfort in every enhancement. Every smart device, every automated system, and every piece of intelligent technology you integrate into your home is a step towards a more connected, efficient, and secure way of living. May your home truly become the sanctuary of the future.

Thank you for embarking on this journey. Here's to a smarter, brighter, and more inspired future, one home at a time.

APPENDIX A:
APPENDIX

The comprehensive journey of integrating artificial intelligence into our homes demands a compilation of additional resources, references, data, and insights that amplify the knowledge shared throughout this book. This appendix serves as a dedicated section to house critical supplementary information, offering a deeper dive into the subjects discussed and facilitating a more robust understanding and implementation of smart home technologies.

Resource List

Gaining an understanding of AI integration requires a vast array of resources. Here are some invaluable materials:

- Books on AI and Smart Home Technologies
- Research Papers and Journals
- Online Courses and Tutorials
- Webinars and Workshops
- Articles and Whitepapers
- Product Manuals and Guides
- Forums and Community Groups

Important Contacts

Sometimes direct assistance is necessary. Below is a list of contacts that might be useful:

- Customer Service for Popular Smart Home Brands
- Professional Smart Home Installers
- AI and Smart Home Technology Consultants

Common Abbreviations

Throughout the book, several technical terms and abbreviations have been used. Here's a quick reference:

- AI - Artificial Intelligence
- IoT - Internet of Things
- Wi-Fi - Wireless Fidelity
- Z-Wave - Z-Wave Protocol
- Zigbee - Zigbee Protocol
- API - Application Programming Interface

External Links

The following are links to various external websites and resources that provide further insights and tools:

- How-To Geek: Smart Home
- CNET Smart Home
- Smart Home Technologies

Frequently Asked Questions (FAQs)

In this section, we address some of the most frequently asked questions from readers:

- **What is the first step in setting up a smart home?**
  Choosing the right hub is crucial as it will serve as the central point for integrating and controlling all your smart devices.

- **How secure are smart home devices?**
  Security depends on the measures you take, such as setting strong passwords, regularly updating firmware, and using secure networks.

- **Can I integrate devices from different brands?**
  Yes, but ensure compatibility and consider using a versatile hub that supports multiple protocols like Zigbee and Z-Wave.

Usage Guidelines

Implementing AI in the home requires mindful understanding and respect towards privacy and security. Follow these guidelines:

- Regularly update device software to patch vulnerabilities.

- Read and understand privacy policies before using smart devices.

- Maintain awareness of the data being collected and its use.

This appendix is meant to support your journey towards creating an efficient, interconnected, and secure smart home environment. Use it as a go-to resource for detailed information and guidance that complements the core content of this book. Armed with this knowledge, you are well-equipped to embrace the exciting possibilities that artificial intelligence brings to everyday living.

GLOSSARY OF TERMS

This glossary provides explanations for terms related to the integration of artificial intelligence into smart homes. Understanding these terms will help you navigate the complexities of making your home more connected, efficient, and secure.

Artificial Intelligence (AI)

The simulation of human intelligence in machines that are programmed to think and learn. In a smart home context, AI powers devices to operate intelligently and autonomously.

Automation

The use of technology to perform tasks without human intervention. Home automation can include setting schedules for lighting, climate control, and security systems.

Hub

A central device that connects and controls various smart devices in your home. Popular types include Amazon Echo, Google Home, and Apple HomePod.

Mesh Network

A network system that uses multiple access points to extend Wi-Fi coverage throughout a home, ensuring a more stable and extensive connection.

Zigbee

A wireless communication protocol used for connecting smart home devices. Known for its energy efficiency and ability to support a large number of devices.

Z-Wave

Another wireless communication protocol designed for home automation. It operates at a low radio frequency to avoid Wi-Fi interference.

Voice Assistant

A digital assistant that uses voice recognition and natural language processing to interact with users and control smart home devices. Common examples are Amazon Alexa, Google Assistant, and Apple Siri.

Smart Bulb

An internet-connected LED light bulb that can be controlled through a mobile app, voice assistant, or automation system. They offer features like dimming, color changes, and scheduling.

Smart Thermostat

A thermostat that learns your preferences and schedule to automatically adjust the temperature in your home, often integrated with mobile apps and voice assistants.

Smart Camera

A security camera with advanced features such as motion detection, facial recognition, and cloud storage. Can be monitored and controlled remotely via a mobile app.

Motion Sensor

A device that detects movement within an area, used as part of security systems or for automated lighting.

Smart Lock

An electronic lock that can be controlled remotely to lock or unlock doors, often integrated with mobile apps and voice assistants for added convenience and security.

AI-Powered Television

A TV that uses AI to enhance picture and sound quality, provide personalized recommendations, and integrate with other smart home devices.

Smart Speaker

A speaker with built-in voice assistant capabilities that can play music, control smart home devices, set reminders, and more.

Streaming Device

An electronic device that connects a non-smart TV to the internet, allowing users to stream video and audio content. Examples include Roku, Amazon Fire Stick, and Google Chromecast.

Smart Appliance

A home appliance equipped with advanced features and internet connectivity, enabling remote control and automation. Common examples include smart refrigerators, ovens, and dishwashers.

Robotic Vacuum

A vacuum cleaner that uses sensors and AI to clean floors autonomously, often with scheduling and remote control features.

Predictive Maintenance

The use of sensors and AI to predict when home systems and appliances will require maintenance, preventing unexpected failures and optimizing performance.

User Profile

A personalized account that stores individual preferences and settings across various smart home devices, enabling customized experiences for different household members.

Smart Art Frame

A digital frame connected to the internet, allowing users to showcase various artworks and photos. Often features scheduling and remote control options.

Smart Feeder

A device that automates the feeding of pets, controlling portions and feeding times through an app, sometimes with integrated cameras for monitoring.

Energy-Efficient Device

Devices designed to use less energy while maintaining performance, often integrated with smart systems to monitor and reduce energy consumption.

Data Protection

Measures and protocols to ensure that personal and sensitive data collected by smart home devices are kept secure and private, preventing unauthorized access.

Secure Network

A home network with enhanced security features to protect connected devices from cyber threats, including strong passwords, encryption, and firewalls.

Useful Resources

Harnessing artificial intelligence to create a connected, efficient, and secure home is an exhilarating endeavor, one that necessitates a reliable foundation of knowledge and tools. In this section, various resources at your disposal will be outlined to support you through every stage of your smart home journey. From online communities to authoritative books, the sources provided here aim to enrich your understanding and practical skills, ensuring that you can navigate the intricacies of AI-driven home automation with confidence.

Websites and forums dedicated to smart home technologies are abundant and invaluable. Platforms like Reddit's r/smarthome and Smart Home Solver, provide insightful user experiences and troubleshooting advice. These online communities are excellent for connecting with other enthusiasts who can offer first-hand recommendations and insights on the latest in smart home devices and AI integrations. Regularly visiting these sites can keep you abreast of new developments and common issues faced by users, enabling you to anticipate and resolve problems more effectively.

Authoritative books can also serve as a cornerstone for your knowledge base. Titles such as "Artificial Intelligence: A Guide for Thinking Humans" by Melanie Mitchell and "The Fourth Industrial Revolution" by Klaus Schwab are not solely focused on smart homes but delve deeply into the principles and future of AI. For a more concentrated look at smart home technologies specifically, "Smart Homes For Dummies" by Danny Briere and Pat Hurley offers a comprehensive overview that spans the basics to more advanced topics.

Moreover, several online courses are designed to provide structured learning opportunities in AI and smart home technology. Websites like Coursera and edX offer courses from esteemed universities and institutions, focusing on various aspects of AI and its applications in everyday life. For example, Andrew Ng's "AI For Everyone" on Coursera offers an accessible introduction to AI, laying a strong foundation for anyone interested in integrating these technologies into their home.

Industry blogs and news websites also play a crucial role in keeping you updated with the fast-paced advancements in smart home technology and AI. Websites such as TechCrunch, Wired, and Ars Technica regularly feature articles on the latest breakthroughs, product launches, and industry trends. Subscribing to newsletters from these sites can ensure that you receive timely updates and in-depth articles straight to your inbox, keeping you ahead of the curve.

Podcasts have emerged as an engaging medium for learning and staying informed. Shows like "The AI Alignment Podcast" and "The IoT Podcast" provide rich narratives, expert interviews, and discussions that explore the broader AI landscape and its particular applications in smart technology. Listening to these podcasts allows you to absorb information while multitasking, making the most of your time.

Beyond these general resources, product-specific forums and official websites from major smart home tech manufacturers such as Google Home, Amazon Alexa, and Apple HomeKit, offer extensive documentation, FAQs, and support communities. Engaging with these resources can provide you with detailed instructions and updates tailored to the devices and systems you use in your home.

For those who prefer visual learning, YouTube channels specializing in tech and smart home setups can be incredibly effective. Channels like Linus Tech Tips, Smart Home Solver, and The Hook Up offer detailed reviews, tutorials, and how-to videos that demystify the process of integrating AI and smart devices into your home environment. Watching these videos can give you a clear visual representation of the setup process and potential issues to watch out for.

Social media platforms such as Twitter, LinkedIn, and Facebook also serve as dynamic spaces for ongoing learning and networking. By following AI experts, smart home influencers, and tech companies, you can receive real-time updates, participate in discussions, and gain diverse insights from across the sector. LinkedIn groups focused on AI and smart home technology further offer a space for networking and professional growth, providing opportunities to connect with like-minded individuals and experts in the field.

To ensure robustness in your smart home setup, it's beneficial to delve into technical standards and protocols such as Zigbee, Z-Wave, and Wi-Fi 6. Organizations like the Zigbee Alliance and the Z-Wave Alliance provide comprehensive resources, including white papers, technical documentation, and forums for developers and users alike. Understanding these standards can enhance your ability to choose compatible devices and troubleshoot connectivity issues effectively.

Libraries and online databases such as JSTOR and IEEE Xplore offer access to scholarly articles, research papers, and conference proceedings that explore advanced topics in AI and smart technology. These resources are particularly useful for those interested in the theoretical and research aspects of AI, offering deep dives into the principles, challenges, and future directions of artificial intelligence.

Local workshops and tech meetups can also be invaluable. Websites like Meetup.com list numerous local events where enthusiasts and professionals gather to share knowledge, demonstrate new technologies, and collaborate on projects. Attending these events provides hands-on experience, opportunities for networking, and direct interaction with experts.

Online troubleshooting resources and service manuals from manufacturers can assist greatly when issues arise. Websites like iFixit, which offer detailed teardown guides and repair manuals, can be incredibly useful when you need to fix or tweak your smart devices. Access to schematics and detailed repair procedures empowers you to handle technical issues independently, saving time and resources.

Error logs and diagnostic tools provided by various smart home platforms can also be helpful. Many smart home hubs and devices come with built-in diagnostic tools that record error logs and offer troubleshooting steps. Understanding how to access and interpret these logs can significantly streamline the problem-solving process.

Finally, professional consultancy services are available for those requiring more personalized guidance or complex installations. Companies like Control4 and Crestron offer expert consultation and support for designing and implementing sophisticated smart home systems. These services are particularly beneficial for extensive projects or when integrating advanced AI functionalities across multiple platforms.

Leveraging a wide range of resources can transform the daunting task of setting up a smart home into an exciting, manageable endeavor. Whether you prefer reading, listening, watching, or hands-on learning, the tools and communities available can provide the support needed to turn your vision of a connected, efficient, and secure home into a reality.

www.ingramcontent.com/pod-product-compliance
Lightning Source LLC
Chambersburg PA
CBHW051225050326
40689CB00007B/805